FAITH GONE ASTRAY

UNVEILING THE KIRTLAND CULT MURDERS

BY RON LUFF

FAITH GONE ASTRAY, Unveiling the Kirtland Cult Murders
Copyright © 1993, 2008 by Ron Luff

Published by Refiner's Fire Ministries, Independence, Missouri

Additional information and resources are available on the Refiner's Fire Ministries website at www.help4rlds.com.

All Biblical references are from the King James Version (KJV), unless otherwise noted.

Scripture quotations marked NIV are from the Holy Bible, New International Version. Copyright © 1973, 1978, 1984 by International Bible Society.

Book of Mormon (BOM) references are from the RLDS 1908 Authorized Edition and Doctrine and Covenants (D&C) references are taken from the RLDS 1978 edition.

August 2008

ISBN 978-0-9707160-6-4

Library of Congress Control Number: 2008932125

All rights reserved. No part of this publication may be reproduced, stored in a retrieval system, or transmitted in any form or by any means—electronic, mechanical, photocopy, recording, or otherwise—except for brief quotations in printed reviews, without prior express written permission of the author.

Publisher's Cataloging-in-Publication

Luff, Ron.
    Faith gone astray : unveiling the Kirtland cult murders / by Ron Luff.
    p. cm.
    ISBN-13: 978-0-9707160-6-4
    ISBN-10: 0-9707160-6-0

    1. Luff, Ron. 2. Murder--Ohio--Kirtland--Biography. 3. Cults--Ohio--Kirtland--Biography. 4. Prisoners--United States--Biography. 5. Christian converts--Biography. 6. Reorganized Church of Jesus Christ of Latter Day Saints--Ohio--Kirtland--Biography.
    I. Title.

    HV6533.O5L84 2008   364.152'3'092
                                      QBI08-600175

Printed in the United States by Morris Publishing
3212 East Highway 30
Kearney, NE 68847
1-800-650-7888

To my son Matthew and my daughter Amy,
I dedicate this book.

May the paths of your lives not follow the footsteps
your parents have walked.

TABLE OF CONTENTS

ACKNOWLEDGEMENTS	i
FOREWORD	iii
INTRODUCTION	v
1 – BACKGROUND	1
2 – HOME LIFE: MISSOURI	3
3 – FIRST TRIP TO OHIO	9
4 – A SECOND LOOK	15
5 – OFF TO "THE OHIO"	23
6 – POSTPONED	33
7 – NEW IDENTITY	37
8 – PREPARATIONS FOR WAR	45
9 – THE COVENANT	65
10 – A NIGHTMARE	77
11 – IN HASTE AND FLIGHT	91
12 – SETTING UP CAMP	101
13 – CONFINED WITHOUT WALLS	111
14 – BREAKING CAMP TO BROKEN HEARTS	117
15 – "MY LORD DELAYETH HIS COMING"	121
16 – HIS KINGDOM BEGINS TO TOPPLE	135
17 – ALMOST HOME	149
18 – WHY?	167
Appendix – PARALLELS TO WACO	175

ACKNOWLEDGEMENTS

This book has endured a couple of false starts. I wish to thank Darrell and Kathy Armbrust for their encouragement and friendship over the years. And I specifically appreciate Kathy's labor in keying the book originally into the computer. Unfortunately, the file later became lost due to a computer malfunction—but a hard-copy survived and was later scanned by Keith Lassiter, placing the book once again in digital form.

I deeply appreciate the editing labor of Georgia Milliren and later Frank Grey and Paul Trask, in cutting away some of the book's redundancy. In telling the story I was forced to relive some of its emotion, and this produced repeated apology, often leading to excess explanation.

Carol Hansen and many others took an interest in the book from the very beginning and it was eventually posted on her website (www.lifeline2rlds.org) and that of Paul Trask (www.help4rlds.com). There appeared to be enough interest in the book to have it printed and Paul spearheaded the process of reformatting it for a printed edition and getting the book copyrighted. I also want to thank Frank Grey for designing the cover.

Many people have read the story on the internet, under its original title of *Why?*. The appreciation for the book that has been expressed to me through this availability has warmed my heart and I thank all involved for making the account accessible.

FOREWORD

Once in a great while you come across a story that not only horrifies you but makes you stop and seriously consider God's grace in having kept you from a similar situation. Ron Luff, the author of *Faith Gone Astray*, helped the leader of a little religious cult murder a family of five to "purify" their group of believers. At the time, Ron was convinced that he was following the will and command of God. On hearing a story like this, we outsiders shake our heads and ask ourselves, "How could anyone do something like this to a mother, father and three innocent young girls?" The answer is spelled out step by frightening step in *Faith Gone Astray*.

As a teenager, Ron Luff became devoted to the vision of building a heavenly city on earth called Zion. He was one of about 240,000 members in the second largest Mormon denomination, The Reorganized Church of Jesus Christ of Latter Day Saints (RLDS). Since 1831, virtually all Mormons have believed that they will build Zion in Independence, Missouri, the location of the RLDS headquarters. Ron's story takes place in the 1980s when the RLDS church leadership promoted changes in practice and theology. RLDS fundamentalists began separating themselves from the main body of the church to form independent congregations. Because of this spiritual crisis, a few men set themselves up to be considered the future RLDS prophet/leader, or "choice seer," who would build the hoped-for Zion. One of these men was a guide at an RLDS historical site, the 1836 Kirtland Temple, located near Cleveland, Ohio. His name was Jeffrey Lundgren.

Lundgren was described by most who knew him as a charismatic, devoted priesthood member in the RLDS version of Mormonism. He became enamored of the Hebrew poetic structure called chiasmus, or reverse parallelism, that is evident in the Old Testament. He also was convinced that Mormonism had gotten it all wrong and that Zion would be centered at Kirtland Temple instead of Independence, Missouri. Lundgren thought chiasmus was the only genuine language of God, and therefore any revelation purporting to come from God, such as the Book of Mormon and parts of the RLDS Doctrine and Covenants, would be written in that style. The only true interpreter of chiasmus would be the "choice seer," or someone taught by him. By setting himself up as the only true interpreter of God's word, Lundgren held a god-like power over his small group of followers. They felt special and God-selected to bring about building Zion and the second coming of Jesus. This faith belief led to murder and later to other perversions to satisfy the commands of their "choice seer."

By any standard, this is a story of disaster. Dennis and Cheryl Avery and their three daughters, 15-year old Trina, 13-year old Becky, and seven-year old Karen, were all murdered. Twelve other members of the cult received prison sentences varying from 18 months probation to five 20-years-to-life consecutive terms for their participation in the Avery murders. Jeffrey Lundgren, the "choice seer," was sentenced to death and, after 15 years of appeals, was executed by the State of Ohio in the fall of 2006. Most of the families were separated by prison terms, and several young children were given to relatives to be raised.

But God's grace, which is not far from any of us, did not abandon Ron Luff and a few others of the group in prison. Away from Lundgren's influence and forced to think and reason for themselves, they heard the Biblical Gospel of Jesus Christ, believed, and were saved. Ron, who will never be paroled, works with Christian prison ministry and testifies to inmates that they cannot be separated from the love of Jesus Christ. Self-taught in biblical Greek, he has earned a Bachelor of Arts and a Master's degree in Pastoral Studies from Patriot Bible University in Del Norte, Colorado. Ron is currently pursuing his Doctor of Ministry degree in Pastoral Studies.

Refiner's Fire Ministries has agreed to publish this story, in part, because the focus of our Christian ministry is towards members of the RLDS church. It is a concern of ours that there are many thousands of fundamentalist RLDS in Restoration branches who still eagerly look forward to a "choice seer" to lead them. Many of these same fundamentalists also believe that chiasmus is God's divine language. Having separated themselves from the main body of the RLDS church (which renamed itself "Community of Christ" in 2001), they faithfully hold on to the belief they will still build Zion for God. Ron's story is presented in the hope that none of them, already blinded by their belief in Joseph Smith, will fall under the spell of yet another deceiver.

Ron Luff's story also applies more broadly to anyone that has ever followed a religious leader who is considered directly in contact with God, and whose interpretation of scripture allows his followers to see the "hidden" things that God supposedly keeps away from ordinary people. By definition, those followers are members of a cult. There are millions of Americans actively involved in cults today who are considered, by those who know them, to be good neighbors, good friends, good workers, and even good Christians. But their faith is not based on a personal relationship with Jesus as their Lord and Savior; their faith is based on a human leader whose "divine" direction is hoped to get them to the heavenly goal they seek. They fail to hear the Good Shepherd's voice and instead follow the voice of a shepherd who ultimately leads them astray.

In Christ's love,

Frank Grey
Refiner's Fire Ministries

For Barbara and Dick Luff

Introduction

Fanaticism consists in redoubling your effort
when you have forgotten your aim.
— George Santayana

On the evening of April 17, 1989, all five members of the Dennis Avery family were, one by one, escorted to a barn in Kirtland, Ohio, where they were shot to death and buried in a common grave. They'd been members of a cult. And the farm where they were killed was the home of the *Choice Seer*—a man they, and the others of the group, believed to embody the promises of the Book of Mormon in end-times prophecy. As a member of the group I was involved in their deaths and now serve multiple life sentences for the horrific crimes committed that night. I played the role of the *Judas Goat* leading them from the house to the barn, and to their deaths.

This book attempts to present an account, in my own words, of how this tragedy came to occur. Other books have been written by people unfamiliar with the weightier matters of the group—how it came to be formed, the influences and doctrines that shaped its dynamic, and how this all produced the ugly fruit that is now public record.

I have now been incarcerated for nearly seventeen years. But this book was actually written quite early in my prison experience. I started the book upon entering the Correctional Reception Center, in Columbus, Ohio, but quickly lost momentum after arriving at my parent institution and began adjusting to prison life. Nevertheless, after the deadly 1993 riot at the Southern Ohio Correctional Facility, where I was residing, I acquired a renewed fervor to chronicle this tragic story. The manuscript was completed in the summer of 1994.

* * *

THE GROUP HAD ESSENTIALLY DISBANDED about a month before the arrests. The period was filled with confusion, disenchantment, and a heavy sense of impending doom. But once I entered the County Jail this all began to change—as did my relationship with Jesus Christ.

All my life I thought I had truly loved the Lord. Yet there I sat, unable to understand what had gone wrong and how my desire to serve God had taken me so far astray. For a time it was too painful to even read from the scriptures. My mind kept seeing the aberrant teachings of the cult and reflecting back through all the horror they'd produced.

The Law of Moses had been redefined within the group. Everything we'd done and endured had been performed in obedience to this *law*. When I felt ready to study again I was still unable to use my own books due to the markings and notes compiled through thousands of hours of class-time in the group. The jail chaplain brought me a paperback Good News Bible, which gave me the feeling of a clean slate—a new beginning.

Like a distant memory in the back of my mind, I recalled the simple truth that the law is fulfilled in Christ Jesus. A new desire began to grow in my heart, in the form of a question, *What* is *that law, which Christ fulfilled?* I took everything I ever thought I had known about God and placed it off to the side. Using only the Bible—with no influence of the Book of Mormon or other doctrines—I sought the answer to this question.

* * *

DURING THE FOLLOWING MONTHS THAT I REMAINED IN THAT CELL I read through the Bible—twice. My little world had come to an end, yet the refreshing waters of God's Word restored my soul. I began to see distinct differences between the Book of Mormon and the genuine Bible message. It was a message I hadn't really known before. The Lord touched the confusion of my mind, healed me and opened my eyes to see what He'd intended for me all along. I finally saw the fulfilling beauty of His Grace. At last, I saw not a "great and marvelous work" *yet* to be performed; but rather what has *already* been accomplished in our risen Lord.

That's not to say that His precious Truth hasn't been challenged—it has. At the beginning of my incarceration I entered a course in Theology and taught myself a basic level of New Testament Greek. My world was enlarged as I took in the diversity that has existed in the church since its inception: the early and latter heresies and various ways people have viewed the Bible message.

As my reading began to expose the intellectual isolation I'd subjected myself to throughout my life, I found a desire to expand my horizons. Though not at all a scholarly man, incarceration has afforded me the time and incentive to pursue a grasp of history and philosophy, of mythological tales and the fundamentals of the world's religions. At times I waned into agnosticism and even immersed myself into questions and discussions of sheer atheism. My path seemed, at times, to reflect the words of Francis Bacon. "If a man will begin with certainties, he shall end in doubts, but if he will be content to begin with doubts, he shall end in certainties." It had been in the most erroneous moments of my life that I had been unwaveringly *certain*; and this uncritical certainty had produced shameful history that sought to darken my soul with a finality of *doubt*.

In his book *Further Along the Road Less Traveled* Dr. M. Scott Peck captures these certainties in my life quite profoundly. "Virtually all of the evil in the world is committed by people who are absolutely certain they know what they're doing." A little doubt seemed a necessary ingredient in my pursuit of truth. After all, as Descartes said, "For one who is a real seeker after truth, it is necessary that at least once in your life you doubt, as far as possible, all things."

In a sense, I had done this long before when I placed all my doctrinal perceptions off to the side and began anew. But, like the opening of Pandora's Box, I found myself grappling with doubts I had never dealt with before—doubts that challenged and tried my faith into refined and renewed certainties about Jesus that I never before could have fathomed. I can now truly say that Jesus is my Friend, my Companion and Comrade in the struggles and joys of a life that, though void of so much, is so genuinely full of the blessings Grace alone can provide.

* * *

IN THE YEARS THAT HAVE PASSED since the Lord renewed my mind, my wife has left me and my relationship with my children has been severed. Oddly enough, my imprisonment wasn't the cause of these painful losses—but rather my rejection of Mormon doctrine. I've endured times when hope and purpose in life seemed nowhere to be found—times when God felt very distant and the ache in my heart was overwhelming. Yet that precious Truth I came to know in the County Jail still abides with me today.

It is my hope that in the writing of this book, the lessons of failure it records will help us avoid its reoccurrence in the future. This is my hope, my prayer and my duty to the Avery family, who paid the ultimate price for a faith gone astray.

Ron Luff
Ross Correctional Institution
Chillicothe, Ohio
July 2006

Chapter 1

BACKGROUND

My incarceration began on January 4, 1990, but the bondage tightening around me began long before. Mysticism can be an all-encompassing obsession. When misused and misunderstood, there is no greater gate to the deluding power of that mysticism than through a passionate belief in God. I now find great pleasure in reading His word and the description of His grace to me, a sinner. The height, depth, width, and breadth of God are more than the scholastic mind can comprehend. I suppose this is why patience, as a virtuous fruit of His spirit is so essential for those of us who seek to understand Him. Isaiah 45:7 speaks of the endless capacities of God as He is in complete dominion over all. "I form the light, and create darkness: I make peace and create evil: I the Lord do all these things."

He brightly illuminates our path by His saving grace, yet allows a way for us to fall by way of the agency he gives us. We must look forward with confidence in what our Lord has done for us, that we might not stumble while in search of distractions that do not lead us to His kingdom. Christ's words to the Pharisees are very fitting for the times in our lives when we feel so far from His kingdom and seek some visible sign of its coming. "And when he was demanded of the Pharisees, when the kingdom of God should come, he answered them and said, "The kingdom of God cometh not with observation: Neither shall they say, Lo here! or lo there! for, behold, the kingdom of God is within you" (Luke 17:20–21). His kingdom is the house He builds within you, eternal in the heavens (2 Corinthians 5:1).

* * *

BORN INTO AN ARDENTLY RELIGIOUS FAMILY, I lived the first 18 years of my life in Independence, Missouri. Ritually baptized at the age of eight within the Reorganized Church of Jesus Christ of Latter Day Saints (RLDS), I took membership very seriously at my young age. Youth activities placed me in an atmosphere with a purpose. That purpose was the building of God's kingdom on earth, Zion, a place prepared for the second coming of Christ. The city of Independence, Missouri (headquarters of the RLDS church) has traditionally been believed by its members to be the "center place" of Zion, and the location for Christ's return.

Along with the missionary accomplishments of my great-great grandfather, he established a sort of family heritage within the church; he did not, however, establish Zion. By age 14, with love and devotion I had participated in at least a dozen missionary ventures, called "witnessing weekends." I traveled with young members of other nearby congregations to Texas, Oklahoma, Kansas, and Colorado for the purpose of witnessing to inactive members of the RLDS church. Our common love for Jesus Christ guaranteed that these would be mountaintop experiences for me.

With zealous desires at an early age, I became frustrated at the ever-distant prospect of the principle the church called Zion. The church had managed to continue functioning since its founding in 1830, but never seemed to be any closer to accomplishing the goals set in writing within its doctrines. In my young mind, it was simple: belief makes it happen. Yet it wasn't happening. As I watched members get older, I noticed that even my parents began to lose their zeal and accept the fact that Zion may not transpire in their lifetime.

Adolescence is a commonly frustrating stage and mine was in no way different. In fact, it was a particularly lonely time I've often tried to eliminate from memory. However, the ramifications of that time seem to have followed me, as weakness, ever since. Everyone feels the need to belong: the urge to be a part of something, but the only way to actually be part of anything worthwhile is to first be a whole, healthy person, not a dependent one, with feelings of deficiency.

I finished high school having made little preparation for college. Desiring to do something constructive with my life, I joined the U.S. Navy for the training it would provide. I was denied my training of choice because of extremely low entrance exam scores. Knowing I had the capacity to learn, I took a field of training in which I was qualified, and enlisted. I completed six years in the Navy, eventually cross-training into a new field that I not only enjoyed but which would also prove useful to me as a civilian.

During this time I married Susie, a very precious lady. She was a distant cousin, so we had not only the same religious upbringing, but also the same family tree and strong church heritage from my great-great grandfather. We became active with the local congregation where I was stationed. Later I would be called and ordained to the priesthood. The priesthood within the RLDS church is mostly a layman structure, with no theological training required. Priesthood members believe they are called into the ministry at specific levels by the prompting of the Lord through the local pastors and church officials.

My specific office of RLDS priesthood was that of Teacher, which is defined as a congregational level of ministry. With service demands of both my church and the Navy, I found it increasingly difficult to be away from my family for long periods of time. Discontinuing church service was not an option, so I began to feel that finding a career outside the Navy was what I should do.

Chapter 2

HOME LIFE: MISSOURI

Having already bore us a son, Susie was three months pregnant with our daughter. We believed our Lord always provides, though neither of us was employed when I left the Navy. We moved into the vacant home of Susie's grandmother, who was living in a nursing home in Branson, Missouri. It was a large two-bedroom mobile home with a two-car garage on five acres, just outside of town. Branson is a tourist town, bursting with country music shows, motels, and many other forms of recreation. Being nestled in the hills of southern Missouri with my wife and two small children, I felt we were in a virtual paradise with a hopeful future. Neighbors included family members; my wife's uncle and his family on one side of us, and Susie's parents, brother and sister, on the other.

While in the Navy and living in Florida, we had been on our own. But with no employment, our savings began to dwindle. Susie's family was willing to help, sometimes seemingly beyond necessity. We became as close by heart as by locality. In Florida, we had taken the responsibility of cleaning the church building when I was in port and Susie taught summer Bible school for the children. Now, in Branson, we resumed similar responsibilities additionally serving as leaders of Zion's League, the church program for teenage youth. As often as the doors were open, we were in church.

Soon I found employment in Branson at a building supply store and was later hired by a utility company in nearby Springfield. My training in the Navy with gas turbines, generators, and associated systems and powerhouse work was what I'd hoped to do upon discharge. Working at the powerhouse gave me the opportunity both in operations and maintenance. With the job I had hoped and prayed for, two precious children and a loving wife, and membership in the local congregation, life was pretty much as it now sounds: too good to be true.

* * *

RLDS CHURCH LEADERS in 1984 legislated steps that many "Restorationists"[1] thought would throw the church into apostasy. While in Florida and just prior to my discharge from the Navy, Susie and I noticed the struggles these changes seemed to be causing. Perhaps not so strangely, similar struggles

---

[1] "Restorationist" is a term commonly used among fundamentalist RLDS members. It is derived from an early phrase "restored gospel." Today, many of the independent fundamentalist RLDS congregations call themselves Restoration Branches. *–Editor*

were also resident among the members of the Branson congregation. As idyllic as life in Branson was, such changes were devastating to us: our church and our devotion to Christ through the church *was* our life. I found myself digging into our scriptures (Joseph Smith's "New Translation" of the Bible, commonly known to RLDS members as the *Inspired Version,* the *Book of Mormon,* and the *Doctrine and Covenants*) to try and understand what was happening.

I also began reading RLDS church history to see why the early church had failed to build Zion in preparation for Christ's coming. Not realizing it, I began worshipping the church structure rather than the true author of our faith, Jesus Christ. I had become very much a Pharisee, ever frustrated over the operation of the church organization, yet all the while losing sight of the basic beauty of Christ's precepts. Church history, along with other books containing prophecies and experiences (dreams, visions, etc.) of people within the church since its inception in 1830, seemed to indicate a falling away of the church would occur.

The doctrines of the RLDS church are extremely complicated and even bizarre when compared to those of traditional or evangelical Christian denominations. There are teachings that speak of angelically delivered gold plates translated by Joseph Smith and known as the *Book of Mormon.* Within the plates was contained a "sealed portion," so called because it was sealed shut by God until the RLDS people would reach a particularly high state of obedience and righteousness. Not even Joseph Smith was allowed to see inside these pages. Although by Smith's account, the entire set of gold plates was taken back to heaven, much hope has been pinned on the promise that the sealed portion would someday be returned to be translated. Also prevalent within the RLDS culture were the *Book of Mormon* apostles known as the three Nephites. In the *Book of Mormon,* these three were supposedly so righteous that Christ spared them the death process, and therefore they have been alive and walking the earth doing good deeds since 30 AD. Yet even their divine influence has not been sufficient to bring back the sealed portion. Though many RLDS claim to have seen these three Nephites at various times of need or inspiration, the church was not then nor now, any closer to fulfilling its "cause"—Zion.

The RLDS *Inspired Version* is replete with changes not found in the King James translation. Even Smith's book of Revelation has significant differences. Changes to the wording, sometimes entire chapters, were made after Smith's introduction of the *Book of Mormon* and *Doctrine and Covenants,* and therefore, upholds his progressively shifting doctrines. The Christian Bible points to Christ, whether through the fulfillment of the law that Moses gave, or the words of the prophets and apostles. Conversely, the *Book of Mormon* defines the fulfillment of its prophecies will come through a "choice seer" (not the Messiah), who is to accomplish these things in the last days. For *Book of Mormon* believers, the miraculous works and writings of this seer are anticipated in the coming forth of the sealed portion and the building of a New

Jerusalem (Zion) on this continent for Christ's return. The reader should note that this "choice seer" doctrine came to play heavily in the circumstances precipitating the writing of this book.

Smith's *Doctrine and Covenants* (D&C) is comprised of revelations from the prophets of the church. After Smith's 1844 death, elected delegates at the RLDS world conference, held every two years, would vote on revelations for inclusion in the *Doctrine and Covenants*. According to church doctrine and tradition, no one but the church prophet receives authentic revelation concerning the direction or governing of the church.

For over 150 years, members have placed their confidence in the prophet for divine guidance. I have discovered, however, the necessity to continually re-evaluate our confidences. Whatever we honor as "authority" will always have influence, if not completely dominate, our reception of information as well as our perception of it.

* * *

WITH FRUSTRATIONS INCREASING IN THE 1980S, many congregations across the United States were simply shut down because of their failure to comply with new doctrines being promoted by the RLDS world church.[2] This repositioning by church leaders increased the growing dissatisfaction of the grassroots members. Those who had been lifelong members of local congregations were finding themselves unable to worship in the buildings they, their parents, or their grandparents had built through monetary donations, and for many, their own labor. Since church headquarters had the deed to these properties, buildings were often sold once the majority of local members opposed the RLDS world church. The outcome of this vying for authority was that the grassroots members did not perceive the church as being equipped to tell them how to conduct services, and because those members would not accept the many doctrinal changes, the church did not perceive them as equipped to conduct services.

I searched my scriptures with prayer and fasting in an attempt to understand what was happening. Along with these studies, I began to write poems that expressed my heart's desire. I had never written poetry before, nor even had an interest in reading it, but at these times and many to follow, poetry would become an unparalleled vehicle for expressing my feelings.

According to the *Book of Mormon,* if Zion were not accomplished, those who had received its teachings would be under condemnation. Although more voluminous, the extant *Book of Mormon* is considered from a spiritually enlightened standpoint to be the "lesser part," while the smaller, sealed portion (which no one has seen) is referred to as the "greater part." Therefore, those who accept it as inspired, yet fail to live righteously enough to "merit" the

---

[2] "World church" was a phrase adopted by the RLDS church in the 1970's to reflect its growth in Africa, Asia, Latin America and Haiti. The term took on a double meaning to fundamentalists as the church became more liberal and "worldly." *–Editor*

sealed portion's return to earth are under condemnation. I didn't know what this meant for those who had lived and died in the church with unfulfilled dreams, but it became very burdensome to me that Zion *must* be fulfilled. As ridiculous as these things now sound, at the time they were as real to me as seeing an automobile racing toward a street full of playing children. My attitude was one of serious urgency. I thought it necessary to accomplish the task set before us lest we be condemned. And to those who were not of like faith, we needed to take the truth of the gospel. It was as though the church had all the answers to the world's problems, but by failing to provide them, the problems were only growing worse: and this, to the peril of everyone. I began to panic. The task seemed so simple, yet why wasn't it being acted upon?

The sermons I preached as a lay member expressed that urgency and were received as powerful by those who heard them. I was unwaveringly sincere. I spoke on issues commonly ignored yet necessary, in my thinking. Quite often these issues seemed new to members and this, too, became frustrating. Why did these issues appear fresh? Why was there no Zion, when we of the "true" church had the message and mission for its accomplishment? And why was there such a lack of world peace?

Susie's passions and mine toward serving God were identical, thus we seemed to mirror the same panic and frustrations. By my ministry of preaching she, as well as I, began to believe that I would, in some way, be "chosen" to work with the seer referred to within the *Book of Mormon.* The poems I was writing, the sermons I was preaching, and acceptance by those whom they reached, confirmed the idea that the last days spoken of so often in Mormon texts were actually close at hand.

In light of what I've learned through years of reflection and what has become my life, it's become clear that those passions of dedication were not what I thought them to be. Indeed, many topics are worthy of sincere and fervent passion. However, we must carefully monitor our passions, making certain our desire to remedy the problem is the motivation, supported by our capacity to do so.

During this impassioned period, Susie became bombarded with stories of personal experiences that included visions, voices, and the unusual timing of a number of unique coincidences. Her experiences confirmed to her that I was not only to work with this choice seer, but that I, indeed, *was* this seer. While I had no doubts about my dedication of service to God, I had no personal indication from Him that He was calling me to such an important task. Susie's recounting of her visions frustrated me since God was not speaking directly to me. I didn't know if her visions were true or false. Yet, I was experiencing tremendous guilt in the event that they actually were true. I had no comprehension of how to discern the good or evil of such an encounter.

Eventually I found myself frantically looking for answers, not due to the passions and questions for sincere service, which were my previous motivation, but to prove one way or the other Susie's experiences about me. Susie, at the same time, became ever so persistent that they were true. My desire for a

Chapter 2 HOME LIFE: MISSOURI

better world along with the need for all mankind to prepare for Christ's return seemed to weigh heavily upon me as *my personal* responsibility. The pressure became overwhelming and I'm sure this had an effect on Susie as well. Our perception of reality was an extremely isolated view but one which seemed quite normal to us. Everything I believed in was built upon the foundation of Smith's "first vision," a very isolated religious belief that dictated we were to "join thou none of them," as "them" (the rest of Christendom) were an abomination in God's sight.

To consider the history and struggles of traditional, denominational Christianity by Smith's small view of God is complete rebellion as expressed by the words of Isaiah 52:11, "Touch not the unclean thing." This chapter of Isaiah is disjunctively quoted in *Book of Mormon* 3 Nephi 9:79, where it refers to the restoration movement of 1830 and the building of Zion in preparation for Christ's return. Differences between the RLDS view of the world, and that of non-Mormon believers, were viewed with pride—as a degree of holiness. We, of the Restoration movement, perceived ourselves as being more keenly aware of God's great and blossoming plan, more "inspired," and more "chosen." I've always had a strong desire for peace. I wanted to see no more Ethiopian famine, no more homelessness in our country, none of the poverty and sickness I had witnessed in other countries while in the Navy. Many people in the world are not as fortunate as in this nation, and the doctrines I had believed my whole life offered promise of a cure to all this.

* * *

IT WAS AT THIS POINT that we began to consider a trip to Ohio, in order to see the Kirtland Temple. It is owned and operated by the RLDS church and esteemed as much more than merely an historic landmark, having been built in 1836 through much sacrifice by early church members. To RLDS members, a trip there would be not altogether unlike a pilgrimage to Israel's Holy Land undertaken by committed Christians. In addition to Kirtland's local area offering a rich history of the early church, even more so, as a shrine, the Temple is considered to offer spiritual insight to those who travel there seeking guidance concerning God's will in their lives. I'd heard and read many testimonies concerning supernatural experiences of church members while visiting Kirtland. Many of these experiences included powerful manifestations stemming from activities in the Temple. By now I was no longer that child with youthful dreams. I truly believed the words and the eventual possibility of the utopia. Unwittingly, I was becoming a fanatic.

Chapter 3

FIRST TRIP TO OHIO

Driving to church one Sunday in May of 1987, Susie and I were discussing the possibilities of either a trip to Kirtland the following week, or of taking the children to Chicago's Museum of Science and Industry. After some discussion, we decided we would, in fact, go to Chicago.

Arriving at church, a man who had been friends of my in-laws for years was the guest speaker. About halfway through the sermon, he switched to a different topic altogether, saying he felt impressed to share a personal testimony. He then detailed his earlier desire to see the temple in Kirtland and how, for reasons not much different than my own, decided not to. But a peaceful assurance convinced him to proceed with his original plans, a trip in which he related being very blessed. He met a tour guide at the Temple Visitor's Center who seemed sincere in his recognition of our friend's desire. The tour guide played host in his very own home next door to the Center as they spent hours discussing the concerns they both had for the church. He also told us how they discussed the significance of the Temple as holy ground for the Lord's purpose.

Many things our speaker said that day precisely defined my struggles. As he finished his testimony, he recommended a visit to the Temple for anyone who had not yet done so. I felt as though he was speaking directly to me. I don't know why he said what he said on that particular day, but I do know that he had no intention of that testimony being a persuasive instrument that would result in the events that would later transpire. After the service, I mentioned to him our decision and concerns. Recommending we make the trip, he suggested we call and plan to have a tour given by the guide who had hosted him, Jeffrey Lundgren.

Upon leaving the church services that day we felt that the Lord had truly answered our prayers. Perhaps there really was something special about the Temple in Kirtland and that we should go and "seek the Lord's instruction" for His will in our lives. Susie's parents would watch our children. We were looking for answers to questions—questions about church doctrines, the *Book of Mormon,* and its role in bringing Christianity to the American Indian as well as to the Jews. We had questions about various revelations which were in the *Doctrine and Covenants*; which ones were truly inspired by God and which ones might have been only fervent desire, or even "cover up" (increasingly accepted by Restorationists) by past "apostatized" church prophets; why the church seemed to fail at the tasks outlined in these doctrines, and what was the direction that it was now going? We believed there was to be a "great and marvelous" work to be done, yet the description of it in the *Book of Mormon* and *Doctrine and Covenants* showed that it was, at best, incomplete. Perhaps the Great and Marvelous Work had not even begun.

* * *

WHEN WE ARRIVED IN KIRTLAND, OHIO, our first stop was at the Temple Visitor's Center. It was already late afternoon as we introduced ourselves to Jeffrey Lundgren. He suggested that we return the following morning so that we could catch the first tour. He indicated that there would probably be few, if any, people on the morning tour, which would give us more individual time for meditation and discussion.

True to what we had been told by the guest speaker in church, Jeff had indeed acquired an insight to the Temple, but whether or not it was based on fact, I don't know. He claimed to have invited some rabbis from the Jewish community to tour the Temple. They were able to declare it "the house of God" by explaining the Hebrew meanings behind the many symbols throughout its architectural details, both inside and outside. Supposedly, these symbols declared an open message as to Whose house it was. My ignorance of what temples in the Bible really looked like was quite evident. Jeff explained that there was a "pattern" in the Temple called chiasmus, a Greek term meaning, "to mark with an X." Basically, it is symmetry. Just as the letter X is symmetrical top to bottom, so it is from left to right. The Temple architecture reflected this symmetry left to right and front to back. Jeff determined it to be a standing example of this pattern, for much the same reason Moses' tabernacle had been built (Hebrews 8:5 and Exodus 25:40). The temple in Kirtland is clearly an architecturally symmetrical building. But I now know this is more characteristic of the architectural period of which it was built, than a revelatory characteristic of God. And there is no resemblance of pattern between the Kirtland Temple and temples built in Old Testament times.

Explaining the concept of chiasmus as "mirror imagery" Jeff continued to "teach" us that it was a more correct way to read God's inspired word. Prior to this visit, I had read an article about chiasmus in an RLDS church publication. It was apparent that at least some scholars concurred there was proof of this pattern of writing in the *Book of Mormon*, justifying evidence to them that the book is of Hebrew origin, as it claims to be. Although I now see chiasmus as an imaginative semantic manipulation process, any explanation of it will not only be difficult, but inadequate in presenting the influence hundreds of hours of class time (indoctrination) bore in our lives and thoughts.

Following is an example of how a chiasm would be written:

> A – Old King Cole
> B – was a merry old soul
> B – and a merry old soul
> A – was he

The similarities identified as A or B in this nursery rhyme, present a mirror image. When looking for the "pattern" one does not start from the top, rather, one would find the middle, known as the center point and work outward. Writings of poetic structure seem to be the most applicable to this type of rhetorical manipulation as well as a great deal of the Old Testament, also in poetic form. These writings, along with their symbolism (which often needs interpretation anyway), are the most easily divided. However, with enough imagination, almost anything can be read (divided) in this manner.

Quite foolishly, I was amazed at these things. I had prayed that we could receive some insight to the purpose of the church and answers to the questions I have mentioned. Could we be getting answers? In listening to Jeff explain that there was a divine purpose in the Temple, he told us our body's physical symmetry was like that of the Temple. Further he spoke, that the Bible says if He dwells in us, we are to be the temples of God. All the while, Jeff spoke of experiences he'd had, and we discussed topics of church history, and meanings of passages from the *Book of Mormon* and *Doctrine and Covenants*. Jeff took us next door to his house, provided by the church in return for his tour guide duties. We met Jeff's wife, Alice, who had studied church history to a noticeable degree and appeared as though she knew her "purpose" in life, confident of where she was.

* * *

GENERATIONS OF RLDS MEMBERS have anxiously awaited the building of a temple in Independence as prophesied in the *Doctrine and Covenants*. Their inability to do so lay in the belief that a specific, divinely appointed location for its construction was designated over 160 years ago. Efforts had been made for years by both the Mormon (LDS) and RLDS churches to purchase this "appointed" Independence property from another of the Joseph Smith factions called the Hedrickites, or Church of Christ-Temple Lot, who actually hold the land title. After much frustration in not being able to obtain the historically and spiritually significant land, the RLDS world church broke ground across the street from that originally designated plot in 1992, and a new RLDS temple was built, much to the objection of Restorationists over its location.

Jeff's belief was that, having "apostatized" many years before 1992, the church should never have left Kirtland in the 1830s. He used scriptural justification to instruct us that due to "sinfulness" within the early church, early members had to leave Kirtland. By this "pattern" changes in successive printings of the *Doctrine and Covenants* would show up. He cited Section 83, a major source for the identification of where Zion is to be built. It will be important for the reader to see the first verse and a portion of the second in order to grasp the point Jeff was making. I no longer believe these doctrines, and therefore, no longer believe this section to be even partially a revelation from God. It is quite clear that it is nothing more than an introduction. Jeff, however, was not alone in his belief among fundamental church members that this introduction was added at a later date by the church leadership of that period in order to justify plans for moving the church to Missouri.

> "A revelation of Jesus Christ unto his servant Joseph Smith, Jr., and six elders, as they united their hearts lifted their voices on high; yea, the word of the Lord concerning his church, established in the last days for the restoration of his people, as he has spoken by the mouth of his prophets, and for the gathering of his saints to stand upon Mount Zion, which shall be the city New Jerusalem; which city shall be built, beginning at the Temple Lot, which is appointed by the finger of the Lord, in the western boundaries of the state of Missouri, and dedicated by the hand of Joseph Smith, Jr., and others, with whom the Lord was well pleased." (D&C 83:1)

Moving on to verses 2a–b, it should be evident that the original revelation had indeed originated in Kirtland.

> "Verily, this is the word of the Lord, that the city New Jerusalem shall be built by the gathering of the Saints, beginning at this place, even the place of the Temple, *which Temple shall be reared in this generation*; for verily, this generation *shall not pass away* until an house shall be built unto the Lord." (D&C 83:2a–b)

It is hard to argue with historical facts: Within four years a Temple *was* built in Kirtland, which is still standing today. In the same sentence reference is made to the temple being built in "this generation" (anyone living in 1832), which has certainly all passed away. So, while there simply can be no other than the Kirtland interpretation, for those who believe in the inerrancy of Smith's writings, careful scrutiny of these conflicting verses regarding the designation of the "place of the Temple" would, of necessity, render this a false prophecy. This is not the only reference Jeff offered but it best illustrates the issue of location that we were confronted with that day: *to what location should the church gather to Zion?*

I was amazed at how these sections of the *Doctrine and Covenants* seemed to back up Jeff's argument. He and Alice seemed very sincere and energetic about being in service to God. They mentioned that Jeff was teaching a Sunday school class at the local congregation, but that they, as we, were not in agreement with the direction the church was presently headed. I was impressed with how confidently they proclaimed that they were where the Lord wanted them to be, doing what He wanted them to do. After more than six hours, Alice told us "You'll be back," as though she could sense our sincere search for the truth.

We'd gone to Kirtland in search of answers, but now we had many more questions. Alice had stated that she knew who the choice seer was. I felt she was perhaps referring to Jeff. Like a foolish little fish, I nibbled at the bait. Years later at my trial I would hear by Alice's own testimony that she no longer thought of Jeff as a prophet of God. But I'm sure there was a time when she (as did Susie) strongly believed it would be her husband who would be the next prophet. Susie had many experiences of her own to indicate I was this choice seer. I was one hundred percent dedicated to doing God's will, but I could not understand why He would not give direction to me. I felt guilt at being so deaf to His instruction; how could Susie be so certain about her claims of me? It was confusing and frustrating, and caused arguments between us. Her first reaction to Alice's statement about knowing who the choice seer was, was that Alice was talking about me, and that Jeff and Alice were in Kirtland in order to help with whatever it was that I was supposed to do. She seemed to believe Alice "knew who I was," and could confidently proclaim that we would return.

After sharing our hearts with the Lundgrens and studying *Doctrine and Covenants*, section 38, "Go to the Ohio and there ye shall receive my law," we were somewhat leaning toward a move to Kirtland. Jeff and Alice strongly insinuated that we could not learn the things that they were learning until we moved to Ohio. Although not prepared to make such a move, I was intrigued. I had done a great deal of praying and fasting in search of the Lord's guidance. With the visit concluded, we drove back to Missouri. You've heard that if you place a frog into boiling water, it will immediately jump out, but if you put it into cool water and slowly raise the temperature of the water, the frog will sit there until cooked to death. Similarly, Jeff's "cool water" control over us would come slowly. The result would be the death of our individuality and, eventually, even our thoughts. Our visit lasted only six hours, and although we were not yet ready to move to Ohio, it had, indeed, taken a foothold that would eventually lead to a second visit.

※ ※ ※

THE CONFUSION WE'D FELT would turn to frustration during the months to follow. Hadn't I prayed and fasted in search for the truth? With the coincidence of a sermon message speaking to my personal dilemma, hadn't we made a trip to Kirtland after initially deciding against it? What now? With lifelong background of doctrines regarding Zion, accompanied by some condemning scriptural backing for not having fulfilled it, could I possibly be turning my back to His instruction? These questions would become paramount during that summer of 1987.

Summer came and went and I was invited to preach at a few congregations around the area. We began attending church with about 30 people at my father-in-law's house, a practice becoming increasingly common, due to the church's growing practice of silencing priesthood members. During this time, I also continued writing poems as an expression of my desires toward God. Believing our doctrines to be true, I was troubled by what appeared to be the church leaders ushering members away from church doctrines. Disturbingly, to Restorationists like myself, it appeared as if they were coming more into line with Protestantism.

The chiasms received by mail that summer from Jeff reminded us of the necessity to be in Ohio in order to receive the law (truth). He said the chiasms reflected how essential it was that anyone desiring truth and understanding should move to Ohio. Exhibiting an attitude of nonchalance, it seemed not to matter to him whether we were interested in what he had to say; there were no outward appearances of his seeking a following. All this helped to relax my defenses with no obvious threat that he was trying to manipulate us. I was aware of deceitful people in the world, but I was under the misguided conception that I would be qualified to recognize such a person.

Again, I prayed to know what the Lord wanted from me, because I felt driven to be a part of what I believed in and thought it my responsibility to run for the prize.

I had been studying some chiasms for a couple of days considering the conclusions Jeff was drawing from them when some church friends returned from a trip to Alaska. They showed us a videotape of the Aurora Borealis. With Jeff's teachings in my head regarding the symmetry of nature, the narrator stated that the exact same shapes, colors and sounds that are seen and heard at the north pole are also being presented at the south pole, at the same time, but in mirror image. I was shocked and amazed. The timing of this information had more impact that the information itself. Again I had to question, "Was God trying to say something to me here?" The coincidences that surrounded this time of our lives were staggering. Looking back, I often feel as if I was "set up." My intentions were so strong and sincere; did I really have any choice, considering the timing of so much we had experienced? The answer to such a question doesn't really matter. Yet, not understanding its consequences can be a matter of life and death. Ignorance is what allowed the enticement to become my entrapment.

Chapter 4

A SECOND LOOK

According to Jewish custom, each fall commemorates the beginning of the Jewish high holidays, marked by blowing the shofar, or ram's horn, to gather the people. (Some Christian groups call this event the Feast of Trumpets.) Although by no means Jewish, RLDS identify with the custom in an illegitimate way as an occasion for their "gathering." The church had always taught of a gathering that would one day take place, culminating with the construction of the temple in Independence. The belief is that that event will bring together people from all over the world for the formation of Zion. The *Book of Mormon* speaks of the North American continent as the land upon which these things will occur, with simultaneous events occurring in the Holy Land. Susie's unshakeable convictions about me, along with our mutual anxiety about living in the last days made what we had heard in Ohio—and the coincidences associated with it—a great seduction for making a second trip. Our thinking was, perhaps we should gather to Ohio, if indeed Zion was to be built there.

In the RLDS church, the ordinance of "laying on of hands" is used in a number of different ways; for ordination to a specific priesthood office, administration for healing, a patriarchal blessing, or even as a blessing at a time of indecision. One night we called Susie's father, an elder in the church, for a blessing that I might be able to make the right decision about whether or not to pursue the issue. We didn't tell him specifically what our concern was, but merely that I needed a blessing to open my mind to hear more clearly the Lord's instruction. The things he said as he prayed seemed to indicate our need to make a second trip. He spoke of my work for the Lord as unique. Perhaps though, not so much what he said, but rather how we *heard* it, made the impact. I decided that night a second investigative trip should be undertaken.

In early September we finalized our decision to go to Ohio again. Susie was quite emphatic about what she perceived my work for the Lord to be. This time we took our tent and stayed at a nearby campground. It was still warm enough to camp, saving the expense of a motel. We also allowed ourselves more time than the previous trip. As would be expected, I called ahead before leaving Missouri to let Jeff know we would be coming. But upon arriving, his response was "So what do you want?" A bit taken aback by so gruff an attitude, especially in light of the fifteen-hour drive we had just completed, I stated that I had come to hear more of what he had to say. I was sincere, but it was apparent that Jeff was not convinced. His overall demeanor placed me in the defensive position of having to prove my sincerity, and also of having to ask the questions.

One of the things I had been searching for was a way to tell which of the revelations of the *Doctrine and Covenants* were divinely inspired and which were "man made." Jeff's letters explained that by this pattern of chiasmus we could not only tell if something were of God, but it would also open up the hidden meaning deep within the words.

Poems flowed like water out of my pen, at times so fast I could barely keep up. Out of appreciation for what I wrote, people sometimes stated the poems must be inspired of God. As any Christian would, I gave and still give God the credit. They were my way of expressing the God-given passions within my heart. But that day, thinking that if they were inspired in a supernatural sense, they should be able to be measured by this pattern or chiasmus. I gave Jeff a copy of a recently written poem and asked if it fit the pattern. What an absurd thing to do, as what is from the heart can never be measured. Jeff wouldn't use chiasmus on what I had written, but said he would look at it later. "Later" never came, but Jeff's deprecating manner eventually would convince me my poems were not of God since they had not been given to me by "an angel." By way of this interpretation, that meant they were of Satan and needed to be repented of. This set in motion feelings of foolishness and guilt about what I had written. I hope to convey here the importance of never exposing the expressions of our hearts to abuse. This can cause feelings of painful worthlessness should such intimate expressions be rejected, but also can ignite feelings of guilt about their means of origin.

* * *

SOME OF THE FOLLOWING WORDS AND PHRASES were clichés that were prevalent in RLDS scripture, therefore, terms common to us. However, Jeff redefined them and applied chiasmus to their interpretation. So, as with everything else, they too eventually took on new and different meaning.

Terms such as "renewing of the mind," "having the mind of Christ," "being transformed/translated," were presented as a result of discovery, not as a point of intent. Initially, terms seemed to speak of this pattern without requiring division. "Study to show thyself approved unto God, a workman that needeth not to be ashamed, rightly *dividing* the word of truth" (2 Tim. 2:15). Jeff taught us that God's word (truth) must be "divided" in order to correctly interpret it. "Whom shall he teach knowledge? And whom shall he make to understand doctrine? Them that are weaned from the milk and drawn from the breast. For precept must be upon precept, precept upon precept; line upon line, line upon line; here a little, and there a little" (Isaiah 28:10).

We were taught that God's word is not only twofold, but that it was made that way for the *purpose* of being divided, therefore correctly interpreted. "For God speaketh once, yea twice, yet a man perceiveth it not" (Job 33:14).

Smith's *Inspired Version*[3] says Adam was commanded to "keep a book of remembrance...in a language pure and undefiled." This language Jeff interpreted to be chiasmus, a new and yet a very ancient language which *must* be taught by a seer, or interpreter, in order for us to come to the knowledge of God. "For a book of remembrance we have written among us, according to the pattern given by the finger of God: and it is given in our own language" (Genesis 6:47, *Inspired Version*).

Nephi, a major personality of the *Book of Mormon* supposedly used this pattern of language when recording his own account. "Yea, having had a great knowledge of the goodness and the mysteries of God, therefore I make a record of my proceedings in my days: yea, I make a record in the language of my father, which consists of the learning of the Jews and the language of the Egyptians" (1 Nephi 1:1). Jeff identified the term, "learning of the Jews," from this passage as the pattern. They, as God's chosen, were knowledgeable of God's pattern. Yet, the pattern was only the style of writing; the characters used were to have been in "the language of the Egyptians." Jeff taught that Joseph Smith was not only knowledgeable of this mystery-revealing pattern, but declared it to those of the early church movement. "And again, I will give unto you a pattern in all things, that ye may not be deceived; for Satan is abroad in the land, and he goeth forth deceiving the nations" (D&C 52:4b).

It is important here to note that we would later be taught that the center point of a division could be anywhere. But in the beginning we were taught that knowing where the center point was, was a gift only the seer had. Not surprisingly, chiasmus was the vehicle that Jeff would eventually use to establish himself as the chosen seer. The one constant throughout the experience would be our growing total dependence on Jeff, as God's predestined and chosen seer. This established him as a necessary part of our lives and prepared us for the next step: that he was the only one who could explore, or had the spiritual eyes to see a division from just anywhere. In the beginning it was a matter of knowing where the center point was in order to rightly divide the word, but evolved to the point of being able to rightly divide from anywhere, once the "truth" of the words could be discerned. When the center point could be defined as anywhere, divisions were infinite: but only the seer knew the way to the truth within them. Eventually, Jeff became our only source to truth and, ultimately, our only source to love. Nothing would be possible without him.

The list of examples we studied goes on ad nauseam. We thought God was revealing clues to us about a process of reading and interpreting scripture. We believed evidences were abundant within nature and the human body. We were given examples of chiasmus in nature with roots that descend, gripping the earth for support and nourishment, while the upper leaves or branches

---

[3] *The Holy Scriptures: Inspired Version* is a revision of the King James Version Bible with extensive deletions and additions made by Joseph Smith, Jr. from 1831-34. It is the only Bible published by the RLDS church, now named Community of Christ.

reach up and out to the heavens for nourishment there, resulting in bearing fruit. Another example from nature, previously mentioned, was that sometimes a second rainbow could be seen beneath another. In the human body, we were taught chiasmus as the nose being the center point, then an eye opposite an eye, ear opposite an ear; a vertical mirror image. Horizontally, the human body has two arms opposite two legs and ten fingers opposite ten toes.

In the beginning the divisions were simple, without much variation from what one would obtain by simply reading. Initially, although such elementary divisions were not adding new concepts, the process of seeing it continually in use conferred credence to it and developed a sense of normalcy regarding its use. Classes consisted of Jeff teaching division after division so that eventually there existed no other way to study. Soon we believed there to be a great deal more evidence than not, in support of reading scriptures in this manner. This continual emphasis and method of redefining "truth" through use of scriptural study became our only reality.

Much to my dismay, there are still people using this method of thought and reading and they, too, claim it to be a tool for revealing the hidden mystery deep within scripture. However, what I've discovered is that what appeared to be the depth of revelation from God's word was in reality only something that Jeff wanted to exploit. I was blind to it because it was never resident within me to find.

*   *   *

MY SISTER AND HER HUSBAND attended the RLDS congregation of Slover Park with Dennis and Tonya Patrick in Independence Missouri. The Lundgrens, and Averys whom I had not yet met at this point, also attended the congregation prior to all three families migrating to Ohio. It was not a deciding factor, but it did help to reinforce our decision to move when my sister later expressed what good people these were, and of the spiritual blessings which flowed through them and the congregation.

The thoughts and motivations of the Patricks mirrored those expressed by Jeff. Again, here was another family who seemed so sure of God's purpose in their life, and equally sure that they were where they needed to be in order to fulfill that purpose. This impressed me. Searching for answers and seeking direction for my own life, I had no idea what that might be. And by the doctrines that I was, at that time, calling scripture, I was convinced it was very important for me to understand exactly what that purpose was.

Jeff had explained chiasmus briefly on our first visit, with a mild hint that it was able to unlock the hidden mystery of God's word. Now, on this second visit, he spoke of specific instruction that could only be found by the use of chiasmus. The claim he made in class that night was that he had applied the Pattern and received the Instruction. The class topic he was teaching was "actually feeling and seeing Christ;" not simply the amazement of such an event, but the extreme salvation-pending necessity of it. The necessity to "feel and see" would become a common term to us. Anyone who had not experienced this as Jeff taught was considered spiritually dead. It was not that he had claimed to "feel" and "see" but that he had to wait on us to do so; the first of many tools he would use for continuing abuses in instilling guilt to us. This was the essence of the class taught that night, though the conviction of it and the depth of all that it meant were still very far from us.

Jeff asked us what we thought about coming into the presence of Christ. Susie asked Jeff how he knew that it "really worked"—how he knew that this process of chiasmus would unlock what needed to be known in order for the Endowment[4] to take place and save the world. He stated that he'd found adequate proof and was certain of it. But Susie pushed a little further and asked, "But how do you *know* that it works"? With this, Jeff broke down in tears and stated that he had done it—he'd seen the Lord. In addition, he said the Lord told him that he was to lead others to do likewise. (The *Book of Mormon* character, Moroni also told Joseph Smith to bring others.)

I didn't understand what he was attempting to say that night, and it would be months before I would be able to grasp Jeff's concept of the necessity to see Christ and to feel the nail prints in His hands and feet. However, I was persuaded that Jeff had experienced something that had a tremendous impact on him. Naïvely, I wasn't aware that such emotional scenes about things of God could be nothing more than an act. Perhaps the answers I had been praying and fasting for were being taught that night. I felt the need to hear more. We weren't in Kirtland simply as tourists; we were there in a sincere and fervent desire to know the truth about Zion. When would it occur and why hadn't it been built? The "own due time of the Lord" is proclaimed several times in the *Book of Mormon*, yet, always associated with the faith and state of righteousness within the church.

That night Susie and I used the opportunity to get acquainted with Jeff's other followers who'd become convinced their spiritual destiny was to move to Ohio. We accompanied Jeff and his family back to their home that night desiring to hear more. What a pity: to have such a love and passion toward God, and yet so little vision of truth. Several other people (absent the Averys) from the class that night sat around Jeff's dining room table while he continued to declare his views. I recall how no one but Jeff and I had any input. I now know the others who were there had already become accustomed to the process of instruction being a one-way exchange from Jeff. My excitement belied how little, if anything, which I had to say was given credence. Before long I would come to know better than to *speak*, when I could *listen* to God's chosen seer.

The events that would occur long after this class and many others were not for the purpose of merely "coming into the presence of God." Rather, they

---

[4] "Endowment" was an empowering spiritual event or experience for the RLDS priesthood prophesied to happen in the Temple as a prelude to Christ's return. *–Editor*

emphasized the *necessity* of such an encounter in order for there to be any hope for mankind.

We were all fervent with desire to serve God. The assurance expressed by each as being where he truly felt he should be at that point in time was refreshing. The next day we heard testimonies of those who had moved there. The night before, I was impressed by a statement made by Greg Winship, also a tour guide at the Temple. I asked him how long he intended to stay there as a guide. I remember phrasing my question as, "How long are you planning to be here"? The look of dedication in his eyes, along with his answer, took me by surprise. "As long as it takes." While I'd addressed his plans as a tour guide, he addressed plans of service to God. This dedication and energy was unmistakable. They'd all sacrificed good jobs and homes. They'd all moved on faith in their relocation to Ohio, with that faith as their only promise of success. God had indeed provided.

* * *

JEFF TOLD US THAT TRADITIONAL PRAYER WAS OF NO REAL VALUE. He said that we could only speak through our own corrupt speech and since "no unclean thing can enter the kingdom of God," our spoken prayers could not reach God and were only darkness. "Who is this that darkeneth counsel by words without knowledge," as expressed in the book of Job. We were told it was necessary to learn to speak chiastically in order for your language, and therefore your prayers, to enter God's presence as pure and undefiled.

My ignorance allowed me to fall blindly into the snare. This perception of prayer did not mean that we had no communication with God but rather that our hearts spoke for us because our utterance was not pure. Therefore, the desires of our heart were the truest sense of prayer, and if we acted upon our desires toward God, then we would learn His perfect language and thereby learn to utter back to Him the words that He wanted us to say (by way of the pattern). This became, in time, a fundamental aspect of all we believed. Another topic we all too quickly embraced was that of the "mountain."

Jeff stated that a man would one day walk into the Temple and converse with God by way and use of the pattern, and that the result would be a great earthquake which would thrust the Temple up into the heavens. Though this is bizarre concept, it was that outrageousness that made it so believable. Hadn't every holy prophet had a high place or a mountaintop? The second chapter of Isaiah opens with a vision of "the mountain of the Lord's House." Having believed from earliest childhood that the Kirtland Temple was the Lord's House, it was only a small step to quite literally believe Isaiah's mountain as the vehicle that could lift the Kirtland Temple above all surrounding mountains and hills. Would anyone be so completely brazen as to propose such a thing, unless perhaps it were true? Known as the "Big Lie" theory, Nazi propagandist Joseph Goebbels found that the bigger the lie, the more believable it becomes. I guess there's deceptive power in audacity. It will be

Chapter 4 A SECOND LOOK

difficult for anyone with a less mystical background to comprehend its acceptability but I believed this ridiculous prospect. Unfortunately, there's more.

Along with the actual raising of this mountain, there was also to be an entryway opened up to a supernatural library. Section 101 of the *Doctrine and Covenants* speaks of a library and its keeper. This was the basis of thinking that at one time there was actually a library of ancient records. This was not a new concept to accepted church teachings. In fact, an elderly RLDS priesthood man made the claim of having gone into the library himself. His experience, in keeping with the more traditional belief, occurred in a region of Central America. Due to his respectability, many people within the church embraced his claims for years. He claimed he'd been shown the library by the three Nephites. But when Jeff made the claim of the library being in Ohio rather than in the Central American region, we believed him in the same context that we did of Kirtland being the authentic location of Zion, rather than Independence. In other words, Jeff didn't come up with these ideas; they were long-accepted (though bizarre) concepts that had been conceived, embellished, and embraced by church leaders, teachers and members for decades.

According to Jeff, the location of the "library" was at the area rock quarry where the stones were cut that had been used to build the Temple. The quarry is preserved by the local MetroParks and is also considered a historical site for people who embrace the Mormon belief system. Susie and I went there on this second visit and as I stood mentally savoring the activity that must have taken place in the 1830s on the very ground, it seemed as though I could feel the passions of the people who labored to construct the Temple—it was as though someone passed by me, but as I looked, no one was there. When we shared the effects of this pleasant emotion with Jeff later that day, he suggested it was much more than that. Turning to Section 101 he said that it was possibly not really the stir of emotion from a historic event, but rather the actual presence of the library keeper. He introduced to me the thought that it could have been the keeper of the library that I felt walk past me. It seemed to place us in touch with our religious roots.

The "sealed portion" was a major curiosity to me in those days and the prospect of actually finding, or rather, being given access to the library, would be a major step in receiving the sealed portion. Again, supernaturally, I was receiving answers to issues I had long prayed about. Zion had been a dream and passion within me since I began going on witnessing ventures. The topic of the library, along with many others, became an intrinsic part of everything else that Jeff would later teach. During this trip however, Jeff finally suggested that he could really say nothing else until we either made the move or decided against learning more.

Here we met confident people; confident because they had moved on faith and it had worked. There really was nothing more that could be said. It simply became a matter of would I move or not? I'd been searching for direction and this seemed to be it. Bible history is full of people who risked life-altering moves and the sacrifice that goes along with it. Mormon history is full of faith in action as the Latter-Day Saints often relocated hundreds of miles from their home territories with nearly always an element of sacrifice involved. During our short time together, many areas of doctrine had been touched upon. It all seemed to return to one thing—to move felt right.

* * *

I REMEMBER MY HANDS TREMBLING as I wrote my letter of resignation in Branson. Six years in the Navy had prepared the way for getting that job. Yet, it appeared I needed to re-establish priorities and shed my worldly desires in order to allow God to work in my life. I never liked being in debt, so our debts were few and small. We managed to sell one of our two cars, leaving us the one that was paid for. Other adjustments were made in order to leave for Ohio as debt free as possible, although finding a job quickly would be essential. The unknown was frightening, but our families, without any opposition, embraced the circumstances of our move.

My dad had been very concerned which sections of the *Doctrine and Covenants* were true and which were merely creations of men to meet needs of the times. We brought back some of Jeff's divisions which we believed exposed the lie of changes within certain sections, thereby giving credence to Jeff's idea that the pattern can reveal fallacy. As dad looked at what I showed him, his voice broke as he said, "This is beautiful!" The doubts he would later have about it were not resident in what I observed in his eyes that night. By my own misinterpretations and many to follow, I sensed approval from him. What was "of God" and what was "of man" in the *Doctrine and Covenants?* The pattern gave the appearance of being that method of definition. Within two weeks, our journey began. A U-Haul truck, with our car hitched behind, moved our young family of four to Ohio.

Chapter 5

OFF TO "THE OHIO"

The mind can do strange things. It can be difficult knowing whether dreams or feelings are simply the product of the moment and anxieties of the mind, or if they're some type of visceral warning system against the unknown. In a dream I had while moving to Kirtland, Jeff seemed to be in charge of the group of people we had just met. At the time, I was not aware that those who studied with him in Kirtland were a "group" in the conventional sense. But in my dream, they were organized and quite militant; like nomads with no fixed residence. They seemed to be in an active state of combat with authorities in some small town. Guns were being fired from the sides of buildings and it was as though I was, and yet was not, a part of it. Though nothing in the dream seemed to display it, I felt as though the women might be prostitutes.

I don't claim to know why dreams like that happen, but upon waking that winter morning in a motel somewhere between our past home and our home-to-be, I dismissed it as anxiety or perhaps even an evil influence trying to discourage our trip. While I forgot the dream almost instantly, the memory of it would come back years later in the Lake County Jail. The dilemma we face is whether, in failing to listen to a warning like that, one loses the opportunity to prepare, or by investigating every passing thought and dream, one ends up losing his mind in the resulting chaos.

In September, an event occurred that would have far-reaching effects. Jeff's approach to his unorthodox teachings had so incensed the church officials that they promptly revoked his ministerial credentials. Angered, Jeff retaliated by withdrawing his membership. Of course, he could no longer live in the church housing, so he had to start looking for a new residence. We stopped in Kirtland and saw Jeff, who was, at that time, on his way to his new residence, a large farmhouse on acreage at the outskirts of town. He asked if we needed anything and wished us the best at finding a place to live.

We needed a map so we might more easily find our way around the new surroundings. In any experience with relocating, I'd found that real estate agencies usually had the best maps; most gasoline stops don't give that kind of service anymore. As we drove back through Kirtland, Susie noticed a real estate office. Ron, the agent, was a very friendly, helpful individual. He wanted to know why I was seeking a map and where I worked. I'd seen the East Lake power plant exhaust stacks in the distance and knowing what they were, told him I hoped to find work over there. I told him I had no job and that we needed a map in order to help us find our way around as well as a place to stay. I'd left a good job and a nice home near family to relocate to an area of strangers; no job and no place for my family to live. Yet even in such a time as this, God was merciful to us. He began taking notes of my naval and power plant experience.

I had no idea why he was so interested in my credentials, but we were quite literally living on faith, and I sensed that a door of opportunity was opening, though I had no idea how. After leaving the office for a moment and going to his car, he came back with an application for employment for CEI (Cleveland Electric Illuminating Company). As it turned out, he was a supervisor at one of the CEI plants and he worked real estate part time. I was to fill out the application and he would see what he could do for me. Ron went on to say how lucky we had been to run into him that night, because it was his night for going to an evening class, but he'd stayed behind to meet a client who never showed. Coincidences such as this began to validate that we, along with the others, were now exactly where God wanted us to be.

Receiving a blessing is not always a reward for the path we have taken. With so much instability in our lives at the time, we interpreted anything good to mean we were doing God's will and that He therefore blessed and watched over us. I'm getting ahead of my story now, but within four months I was working for CEI at the very plant that I had pointed to on Day one. Was God meeting the desire of my heart? Whether He actually was didn't matter, because we believed that He was.

But that first day we still had to find a place to live so the hunt began. Our first night was spent in a vacant rental apartment Ron had arranged for us, saving the cost of a motel room. After that, Greg offered to let us stay with him for several weeks. On my way to a job interview one day, I noticed a school bus unload in front of an apartment complex. Even though both our children were still very small (ages 2 and 5) we wanted, but couldn't afford, a three-bedroom home. When I saw all the children getting off that bus that day, I thought that perhaps these apartments might not be so restrictive about children, so I pulled in. The application was full of background questions about employment, income and local references but I never had to fill it out. I had the amount needed for the deposit, almost to the penny, and we made plans to move in as soon as our apartment was ready.

We were excited as things seemed to open up for us. We shared our good fortune with Jeff and Alice, who confidently responded in a way that said, "See what happens when you move out in faith?" Their assurance seemed to crystallize the conviction within us that we were where God wanted us to be and that He was watching over us.

Once the apartment was available we moved in, quite excited to again be in a place of our own. Within only a day or two of moving, I found a job in the want ads for an evening supervisor at a petroleum testing laboratory. I had very brief experience with that type of work while in the Navy and felt vastly under-qualified for the position they were seeking to fill. Nevertheless, the job was offered to me and I took it. I enjoyed the work there and it gave me an

Chapter 5 OFF TO "THE OHIO"

opportunity to learn a number of test procedures and to place them into written job descriptions so that novices such as myself could be more easily trained. I worked the night shift at the laboratory for approximately four months, during which time CEI contacted me regarding a position at the power plant.

* * *

WE HADN'T MOVED TO OHIO because of any particularly strong desire to be there, geographically speaking, and it certainly didn't place us nearer our family. We moved to Ohio to assist in the building of Zion. We had already given away a great many pleasures and securities. Being the newcomers placed us in the position of needing to catch up on lessons the others in the group had been taught. It soon became common practice to go to Jeff's home and talk with him individually about the pattern and how to apply it, along with what had been learned already. Greg had extensive notes from previous classes that Jeff had taught, so I reviewed those as well. But the real learning came during one-on-one study times with Jeff. Others in the group had day jobs, so while they were at work, I could get more individual attention, which once again seemed to be the blessing and opportunity to get caught up.

As Jeff, his family, and the single people in the group settled into their new home at the farm, the energy of a common goal became visible. Everything was organized and everyone had a function. Coming from six years in the Navy, orderliness and structure was not new to me. And in reality, there was a sense of security in its rigidity. The view of the group as a "family" with much structure came slowly. In fact, not until I began work at CEI, which required a change in my working hours, did I begin to see how tightly knit this group really was.

I recall being impressed by Danny Kraft one Saturday while we worked together in the barn. With all still fairly new to me I saw the people in the group as individuals rather than as the collective subjects of Jeff they had become. Danny showed me a book containing sketches of the human brain and an area called the optic chiasma. I was intrigued to find that our own vision is produced, or relayed, by a process of mirror imagery. Evidence supporting chiasmus seemed to be an integral part of all nature. There seemed to be this essential truth, and process to the perception of it, resident throughout all nature. As I later expressed to Jeff how impressed I was with what Danny had shown me, Jeff supported the inference to chiasmus as a key element of nature, while at the same time downplaying the ability of Danny to adequately see it or convey its existence. Slowly, surely, and subtly, Jeff became the sole source of all our information gathering. Anything worth knowing came either by way of or directly from him.

I soon arrived to study with Jeff in the mornings before I went to work, my hours at the farm increasing as the weeks and months went by. Jeff took Susie and I through previous class topics, partly for receiving information, but primarily to see that we embraced the pattern. It was essential to Jeff that we have complete and unwavering confidence in the pattern as the language of God and the manner by which we cannot err. Later he would openly state that if we did not accept the pattern as the only way to communicate with God, then God could not communicate with us. It was essential to Jeff during these early days of exposure to his teachings that I not only see the pattern, but that I be able to use it with proficiency and without hint of disagreement. Jeff was very efficient; anything he taught would be of use to him down the line. I wouldn't find out exactly how extensively he'd planned his agenda until after I left the group, which, by then was far, far too late.

He brought us to the point where he allowed no other way to see words on paper but by the chiastic process. During this time my parents came to spend Christmas with us. In just the few short months we'd been gone, they noticed changes in our religious principles and became decidedly opposed to them. They could not accept Jeff's teachings on prayer, previously explained, and this created a great deal of friction. As a result of the tension that arose, they cut short their visit and returned home earlier than planned. They had no idea what was happening to effect such a change in us—but for us it meant that we had to study all the harder so that this truth we had could more clearly be imparted to our loved ones and the rest of the world. It also meant, as Jeff suggested, that we would need to reduce or completely sever any communication with outsiders. He explained how difficult he'd found it to stop writing or phoning his family in Independence, and how they, too, could not let go of their traditions and embrace the truth he had found.

It's good to question tradition, but what we find by our questioning does not necessarily guarantee truth. However, this is not about the reason behind tradition—rather it's about the loss of reason altogether, thereby creating a new means of rationalization which is quite irrational. What Jeff taught about prayer seemed to be logical and have a great deal of scriptural support as well. But that didn't make it true. While truth may seem elusive, relative to individual perspective, it is immutably consistent. It is our *perception* of truth that is forever changing, and it is in the existence of that changing perception of truth that makes us vulnerable to deceptive interpretations.

A college sociology textbook I once read defined *authority* as "the legitimate use of physical force." In other words, within the accepted guidelines of a given society, those in authority have the right to use physical force. War is perhaps the ultimate example of authority as an action within the heart and soul of a government's people. The authority of a nation both identifies the enemy and legitimizes that death.

Sometimes negative examples are necessary in order to convey a point to be made. The bombing of Hiroshima and Nagasaki at the close of World War II was accepted, legally and morally, due to the authority that dictated it. During the Gulf War, friendly fire destroyed two U.S. tanks. When the missiles were fired which destroyed those tanks, a serviceman shouted a sendoff salutation, "This Bud's for you!" But the expression used when the target was the destruction of the enemy was far different from the one exhibited when it became evident that this target was not the enemy after all. A shocked voice was heard saying, "Oh my God!" What occurred in that brief span of time was that a target identified as the enemy, later turned out not to be the enemy. The ramifications of that changing identity involved issues of moral trauma and legality.

This is the power of authority. The tanks contained human life, yet when appearing as the enemy, the impact was far less, morally and emotionally, than once that identity changed. Whatever becomes the authority in our life will dominate our moral perspective of the world around us. Society cannot exist without authority, because without it we have no order, only anarchy. The cult leader, as the spokesman for God and revelator of His will, is the complete authority in the most totalistic and encapsulating way. The shifting, or transfer, of the working authority in one's life is what cult mind control is all about. I've seen its results. It's very powerful, very dangerous and very, very real.

* * *

MY BROTHER RICK also came to visit. Employed by General Electric as a technical representative, he traveled a great deal of the time. After attending a training seminar in the state, he drove to stay with us for a couple of days. Concerned after talking with mom and dad, he hoped to understand some of the discord that our move to Ohio seemed to be causing within the family. In fact, so assured must we have appeared that he considered the possibility of moving to Ohio himself. The interest he displayed instilled passionate hope within Susie and me that one day we would be able to share this truth in full with our family members. Once he arrived back home, the influence of our convictions seemed to dissolve. Only recently, I learned that Susie expressed a desire to him to move back to Missouri on that trip. Whatever she said to him during that visit, I am certain that a schism had already developed between Susie and me. Completely overwhelmed now by the memory of her unwavering dedication, despite the numerous hardships and frustration we endured together, I am equally convinced that her convictions were as sincere as my own.

One night during that first four months we lived in Ohio, Susie and I lay down to sleep, and like two spoons in a drawer we were cuddled together. The cold winter wind was really active outside the window that night, and yet there we were, safe and warm. "God has truly provided," was my thought that night. We had moved out in faith with no place to live and no employment to support a family. We left behind loved ones who had supported us when we needed help. Just like so many others we had read about in the scriptures or in church history, we had done it!

As Susie and I lay there that night feeling safe and secure, we had no comprehension of the agenda that was hard at work isolating our thinking and destroying our happiness. We had no comprehension of how isolated our thinking had quickly become, and even less understanding of how limited it would yet become. In our minds, we had been blessed. We had become so entirely focused on preparing to come into the presence of Christ that any chronological importance regarding our activities seemed to blur into insignificance.

By the doctrines I believed, there was no reason for such good fortune not to be present with everyone. Anyone who's never known zealous involvement would find it difficult to understand such addiction. Our scriptures were everything to us—our link to God. We had experienced tremendous turmoil in our lives from new doctrines presented at the church World Conference in 1984. That conference had an impact on the lives of many people, and differing opinions split congregations, severed friendships, and ruined families. It was a very traumatic juncture in RLDS church history. As I look back now, I see where I not only made stands on issues that were not worth it, but were also very contrary to how I presently perceive them. It's shameful because of the tragedy that came from it and sad because of the distortion it created of some otherwise beautiful dreams, altruistic passions, and strong hope for the future. Unless such passions have been experienced, there's little hope of understanding the impact of their influence in the lives of those who function by them, in the belief that their hopes of ultimate truth are valid.

* * *

IN MARCH OF 1988, I began work at CEI, the East Lake Power Plant. It meant more money and daytime hours, and Jeff had plans for both. The change in hours left my evenings free, so we were able to begin attending the regular classes that Jeff had all along been teaching the others. The "raising of the mountain" was a continually evolving plan. Prior to our move, Jeff taught that the mountain concept would be performed by a supernatural occurrence of an appointed man entering the temple and communing with God in quite a literal way after which we would simply go into the Temple at night and the great revelation would occur at dawn. Shortly after our arrival it began to take a different turn, Jeff teaching that we would be required to go in with this man at night and overthrow the Temple. Christ would then return with the coming of the dawn. That scenario quickly evolved to one of it becoming an issue of sneaking into the Temple and having to hold it by force from authorities as they discovered our presence and would order us to leave. The reason for this change, and the multitude of other changes to follow—was our sin. As Jeff gained control (which we gave him relative to our conviction that he was the seer spoken of in the *Book of Mormon)*, his ability to define sin was as effective as any of his other forms of interpretation.

It's important to understand the passions of a large number of church members. The longed-for "choice seer" (also called "one like unto Moses"

Chapter 5 OFF TO "THE OHIO"

and "Prophet Number Seven"[5]), is a key figure within the doctrine, history, and general literature of the church. The times in which we live have sent a number of people in search of this person who was to build Zion and prepare the world for Christ's return. My present reality may be the future hindsight of a number of other people who, like myself, simply had a passion to serve God and became extremely misguided. There's no way I could then have comprehended my present circumstances or believed that this is what my future would be.

A few days prior to my new employment at the power plant, Jeff did a division for me at a morning class. In the *Doctrine and Covenants* Sec. 98, there is a parable about a vineyard, some servants, and the failure to build a wall with a tower for defending the vineyard. This resulted in the vineyard being overrun by the enemy. Through chiasmus, Jeff identified the vineyard as being the Kirtland Temple and the surrounding garden area upon which it sits. The servants who were scattered he identified as the church member's failure, at the time of the construction of the Temple, to build Zion then. He proceeded to further interpret our day and our mission regarding the retrieval of the Temple for God's Holy purpose. Applied liberally was Jeff's implication that we, in our day, had also failed to answer the call, or erred in our response to it. This meant that more sacrifice would be required. Within these scenarios, we all began to believe the assumption that the authorities would attempt to force us out of the Temple and we would have to withstand them.

With the beliefs and applications of Mormon doctrines blended into the existing text of the Bible, basic concepts became weakly interpreted. The precepts of grace and the full impact of the blood of Jesus' cleansing power became more opaque as interpretations of works, and our necessity to accomplish them became paramount; we would not be able to simply sneak into the Temple, we would have to hold it from authorities who would try to force us out. This wasn't in order to punish us. It was more closely related to a test or trial for purging any final dross before coming into the presence of Almighty God. After all, no one would want to enter the presence of God unworthy.

Such a stand against the world would provide the final preparation necessary for such an event. Jeff became more and more an accuser—keeping us reeling from one blow of guilt to another. Each time something detained us from our mission, more would be required. During that time, the concept of taking over the Temple evolved to the point of murder. Jeff defined murder as "to make war." He began to reveal how we would need to cleanse the vineyard, (killing the enemy that had taken it over). This meant killing people living within the immediate vicinity of the Temple, specifically members of the church—it would be a Holy War. Verses like Ezekiel 9:4–6 became much

---

[5] At the time this was written, there had been six RLDS prophets (Joseph Smith, Jr.; son Joseph III; three grandsons: Fred M., Israel A., and W. Wallace; and great-grandson Wallace B. Smith). Many RLDS fundamentalists believed that a seventh prophet would appear, greater than all the others. –*Editor*

more a part of our view of God and His purpose for us than any New Testament passages.

> "And the Lord said unto him, Go through the midst of the city, through the midst of Jerusalem, and set a mark upon the foreheads of the men that sigh and that cry for all the abominations that be done in the midst thereof. And to the others he said in mine hearing, Go ye after him through the city, and smite: let not your eye spare, neither have ye pity: slay utterly old and young, both maids, and little children, and women: but come not near any man upon whom is the mark; and begin at my sanctuary. Then they began at the ancient men which were before the house." (Ezekiel 9:4–6)

One thing that seems to be common in religious militant activity is the amplification of Old Testament law and rage, along with a misplaced value as to what the New Testament refers to as the fulfillment of these things through Christ. In other words, leaders like Jeff lead people backward from the "new" into the "old."

It's obvious I had no concept of grace. I now see precepts in the Bible differently. Inadequate interpretations to traditional passages fail to defend us from more subtle false precepts. Because of this, there are many passages that can be used to convince us of the need for works within our beliefs, even instilling guilt for things that have nothing to do with sin. Perhaps what I've come to appreciate least about the *Book of Mormon* is the way it merges Old Testament practice and ritual with New Covenant grace.

* * *

BEFORE MOVING TO KIRKLAND, I prayed almost constantly throughout the day. With the passing of time and Jeff's teachings, my prayer soon became limited to simply a phrase to God occasionally, without the method and constancy I had formerly practiced. Finally, I came to the point where I knelt and said one last prayer to the Lord, expressing that I was placing my life in His hands and trusted Him to protect my family and myself. I then ceased to pray in the traditional fashion, and I asked forgiveness if what I was doing was wrong, and for protection for us. For the first time since moving, I was apprehensive. There was so much evidence to support what Jeff was teaching and the pattern itself seemed to be validated by so many passages. Yet it was still very threatening to let go of my view of God and how I might best serve Him. While Jeff's new method of teaching held the church as a whole responsible for the failure, ultimately, it held me individually responsible for not having achieved the goal. I would have to answer to God for my life. And I believed that I would come up lacking.

This more radical plan to cleanse the vineyard was cancelled in early April, soon after I became aware of it. While the takeover plan was one that both frightened and sickened me, I had come to believe that any form of postponement of God's command would result in even more death and affliction of every kind. I had moved to Ohio to prepare people for the return of Jesus Christ and to help build Zion—not to go to war, not to kill people. With no intention of disrespect to the Avery family, or lack of sympathy toward them, one might note that they were also participants in these classes. Though in time Jeff would mark them as the enemy, as far as I knew, there was never a time that they planned or even attempted to leave the group. On the last day of their lives, they enthusiastically spoke of the wilderness experience that we had all prepared for. They were a very gentle family who were, unfortunately, assigned a different role in Jeff's game of madness.

The postponement of our mission to raise the mountain, along with the increase in my salary at CEI, created the need for new goals on which to focus our energies and money. Yet, our failures seemed to heap upon us even more condemnation. Not only upon us, but also upon all of mankind. I feared what would next become expected of us.

My free time was spent at the farm with either chores or workouts. Weight training was something I had done off and on most of my life, so Jeff developed workout schedules for the two of us that were different from the schedules of the others. I see it now as more of a ploy to create an illusion of secrecy, intimidating the other men in the group, thereby separating me from them.

At a workout one day, I asked about the "spokesman" Jeff mentioned in class the previous night. He then informed me what my position would be within the group: I was to be his spokesman, his "Aaron." He was to be like Moses and I was like Aaron. He expressed that he had been waiting a very long time for me to finally start seeking the truth and therefore work with him, in our predestined positions of service. Each person in the group had an image created for them by Jeff for his own purpose. In this respect, he was definitely a creator. This allowed him complete control in our relationships with each other and within our families, eventually interpreting even our individual spiritual servitude to God. This control formed barriers around and through us that would eventually extend to a spouse's necessity to keep secrets from the other.

Within a couple of days, he introduced the idea that he wanted his following to become a self-supporting community at the farm. He told me he had previously raised rabbits and that a living could be made with them. If I would be willing to give him $350 per month, within a year I could have a good business. His position as seer was well established within our thinking by this time and to refuse such a proposal would have meant a denial that he was the great infallible seer that had been prophesied about. There was really no decision to be made about it, so from that point on I gave Jeff the amount he specified each month. Eventually all other monies (income tax refunds, overtime pay, even some gold and silver we had purchased years before) beyond the allowance he defined for us, went to him. The difference in gifts that his children received, compared to those received by other children, should have told the story, but perhaps I was too deluded to see it—or accept it. The amount of rage that the public has expressed toward me in the outcome of all this is no greater than the self-hatred for what I have deprived my own family of, not to mention the impact on others.

The rabbit business never amounted to anything; however, it was quite useful to Jeff. Its continual failure was another of the affects attributed to our sin. We never had more than eight to ten adult rabbits at any one time because they were repetitively dying, we believed, due to our sin. Dennis Patrick had worked with Jeff at a boy's farm in Missouri several years before and he spoke of how successful Jeff had been at raising rabbits. I have to wonder now if Jeff wasn't killing them himself. Death didn't stop with rabbits. A puppy unfortunately hung itself in its leash looped over a fence rail, some kittens died, and even a deer landed in the front lawn after trying to cross the road. Looking back, I believe Jeff used these deaths to instill a deeper sense of guilt in us. He used the opportunities provided by these and many other events to make us feel responsibility toward the result of our sin. Time and energy continued to be more and more dominated by Jeff's agenda.

Chapter 6

POSTPONED

Before I knew of Jeff's temple takeover plan, he mentioned a specific date when this miraculous event of an earthquake and mountain raising was to occur. Symbols, a part of the millwork on the exterior temple doors were the basis for his conclusion. This gave us an actual date, which became not only the revealing of a mystery of God's great plan for mankind, but also meant we must be able to come into His presence on that date. To fail would mean postponement for another year. Yet, worse than postponement, would be the cost for our sin and failure. What would next be required of us if we were to fail or be unprepared at the appointed time? This was a very real and threatening question, which urged us on in an increasingly reckless manner. I am reminded of a recent prison review in which was discussed the possibility of my security level being lowered. One of the staff members asked me if drugs or alcohol were associated with my crime, to which I responded, "There were no drugs or alcohol, but I was most definitely intoxicated." Indeed we were all intoxicated; mentally, emotionally and spiritually.

It was essential for us to be prepared to enter the Temple upon the designated day; not only for ourselves, but for all of mankind. What a pity to look at it all now and see how completely ridiculous it was.

With plans to raise the mountain cancelled, we began seeking instruction for the next window of opportunity the following year. Even though we knew that more would now be required because we had failed, it seemed Jeff's urgency was also less than it had previously been. Basically, he'd managed to con us into another entire year of servitude by the cancellation of so great an event. I guess he felt he might as well use us to get things a little more comfortable around the farm. With so many willing and helpful hands, it began to look more like a park than the collection of junk that it had been before.

Jeff and Alice kept everyone pretty busy with various chores, yet we also began a number of new projects. Sharon was talented at quilting and Susie had created beautiful embroidery work since her childhood. We brought a loom with us, so the prospect of an old-fashioned crafts center began to take shape. Danny excelled at most any form of art. He could make dollhouse furniture with tiny tools, which he used under a magnifying glass. Referenced in the *Book of Mormon*, we accepted our responsibility to be "an industrious people," and each of us had a specific function. Jeff and Alice "burdened" themselves with the arduous task of antique shopping. Jeff hung some sheetrock in the barn, dividing it into rooms for various shops, although it was never completed. Much like the apple trees on the farm's thirteen acres, none of Jeff's projects ever seemed to bear fruit. But then again, they did manage to keep us quite busy and gave us purpose—and this may have been the only real intention that ever existed in them.

Regularly scheduled chores were assigned to all, but I took up the slack, working anywhere I was needed. Susie was assigned the laundry, which she took home each day to be returned at night prior to Jeff's evening class. Richard was the landscaper, planting trees and flowers throughout the yard wherever Alice designated. Debbie was the main cook whose duties also included the grocery shopping. With the *Book of Mormon* to guide us, we were to become "one heart and one mind," and to some degree we were. But not to the glorification of God, since everything we did was to the subjugation of ourselves to the agenda of Jeff.

Life developed into a robotic revolution of work and study. Susie and I would awaken at 6:00 a.m. to begin her day of laundry and my workday at the power plant. At 4:00 p.m. I would come home, pick up the laundry Susie had done to that point, eat supper, all within about 15 minutes, and leave again to do chores at the farm. Around 7:00 p.m., I would return home to pick up Susie and our children and be back at the farm for 8:30 class. The kids would be in their pajamas with sleeping bags ready so that when we arrived back at the farm, we could lay them down to sleep.

Susie's domestic labors increased. Besides laundry she was told to become more intense about keeping house. Susie was a good housekeeper, but she was told she should consider her tasks "as unto God." She had beautifully stenciled the walls, which she washed weekly. When I came home from work, supper was on the table. By the standards of today's culture, Susie was subservient to me. She was told God had a purpose for her, which was to provide on earth the most heavenly atmosphere possible for her husband and children. Even there was the ever-present threat of the price of failure. I was as a servant in Abraham's household and if Jeff said "go and do," I "went and did." Susie and I were also to be one, unified in our purpose to God. Ironically, we both became so busy with chores that we were quite subservient within the greater Lundgren household.

Class would last from 8:30 p.m. until around midnight or later. A new development was that of "sessions" held after class, for the chastisement of any who were identified as having a particularly rebellious sin issue to deal with. Again, the definition and identification of sin within the group was relative to our belief that Jeff was the choice seer. There were totally ridiculous issues held up before us as sin. One such issue was the purchase of chocolate chips. Jeff had given Richard a specific amount of money, with instructions to go to the convenience store and buy a large bag of Nestle Toll House chocolate chips. As ridiculous as this scenario will sound, I hope the reader will sympathize with the fact that these were real and threatening issues to us. When Richard arrived at the store, he was faced with a dilemma. They had Nestle chocolate chips, but not in the large size bag. There was another brand

Chapter 6 POSTPONED

in the large size and there were small bags in the Nestle brand, so he had to choose. To complicate things, he only had enough money for one large bag, but not enough for two small ones. Panic set in as he tried to make a choice based on Jeff's instructions. Should he buy a large bag of a different brand and have enough, or should he buy the designated brand in the smaller bag and not have enough? Unfortunately, Richard made the wrong choice (assuming, of course, that there was a right one), and brought back a large bag of the other brand. Such a silly little scenario resulted in Richard having to endure a session (chastisement) after class, which lasted for nearly four hours. This session involved everything from personal humiliation as a sinful failure, to the threat of Almighty God's wrath in the form of some massive devastation of lives. How did we allow such a trivial event to create such intense anxiety?

In military boot camp if one failed, all failed. If an undershirt was folded the wrong way it could bring fury from the training instructor toward the individual, but had an effect on the entire group, as well. This, of course, develops discipline and harmonizes the efforts of many into an organized and formidable force, for purposes of war. Yet with us, it was not boot camp for induction into the nation's military—we were being inducted into a service of "higher" authority and more needful purposes—purposes of saving an already dwindling number of people from the coming judgment of God. We were, therefore, under great scrutiny, not by a training instructor of our nation's military, but by God Himself. Nothing, then, was considered too trivial because it was the trivial things that were identified as the dross of our purging process.

A person who becomes subject to such a surreptitious process begins to use the very programming that is, in fact, destroying them. Like a computer virus, the more it is used, the more the virus is spread. Each movement creates more mutilation. Similarly, our minds became locked in a maze and each turn spiraled us deeper into the entrapment. All I had to do was stop and accept the freedom of what Jesus accomplished when He died upon the cross and rose on the third day. He fulfilled the mystery. He opened the way for us simply through our faith. As a child, I endured terrible nightmares. Yet there was always a point when I realized I was dreaming. In my dreams, I could escape the monsters by waking up. But I was not dreaming now. I was very much awake.

* * *

I LOST MYSELF IN PREPARATIONS for threats that were not there. Eventually, we began to panic as, feeling always off balance, we would stumble along seeking sure footing with God and our service to Him. On such occasions, Jeff would state that he'd far rather his children enter into God's kingdom "halt or maimed" than to be whole and "cast into everlasting fire." This teaching was taken from the biblical passage of Matthew 18:8, but like everything else he taught, it was subject to gross misinterpretation.

One night at class, my children were talking instead of going to sleep as they were told to do. Their little voices drifted into the living room where we sat in class. Jeff heard them and told Susie to bring them out to him. No words can adequately express the shame I now feel over watching them stand in front of him, trembling, while he showed them a huge stick that he slammed on his desk. God had become legalistic to us. He had become a God of toe-the-mark-wrath and judgment. We were so wrapped up in fear of our children's eternal souls that it seemed necessary to create this display of threat and anger.

Verse six of Matthew 18 speaks of those who "offend" his little ones. That word is translated from the same Greek word from which we get scandalize. To scandalize or seduce a child into sin is an awesomely terrible thing; it would be better to maim oneself than to exhibit such behavior. In a sense, this could be taken as a warning against false prophets such as Jeff who prey upon the naïvely innocent at heart. We are called to be as little children, faithful and trusting. But people such as Jeff are desirous of only one thing, to scandalize those with the innocence of a childlike heart. With a distorted perversion of this precept, we were instructed to watch over our children vigilantly for hints of sin in misbehavior. In my deep shame, I recall spanking my children, too hard at times. This was not due to anger toward them, but rather due to fear that I might lose them. The most precious gift of stewardship a man can receive from God is his children. That opportunity to parent is now gone from my grasp.

There are many reasons I could hate Jeff, but my purpose in writing is not to express hatred. Rather, it is to provide some way to clearly view what is otherwise a very dark and incomprehensible issue. Jeff created abuses and even the deaths of his followers. Though I could find a degree of pleasure in exercising a father's vengeful wrath upon Jeff, there is neither opportunity for, nor healthy benefit from such otherwise justifiable passions.

Chapter 7

NEW IDENTITY

During this time of becoming more unified in "one heart and one mind," Jeff began associating each of us with various Biblical identities. As an additional blessing to us, we would be able to receive chiastic divisions. Through Jeff, these divisions would reveal our "true" identities. We were all part of an end-time climax and the characteristics, failures, and future blessings were all revealed long ago for this awaited day. Our perception of this, as well as our acceptance of it, grew as Jeff continued building upon this topic in his classes.

My identity was Pergamos (Revelation 2:12–17), known as the "fortified tower." I had faults which needed to be repented of, in that God's faithful martyr had been slain in my region, a region "where Satan dwelleth." The irony here is that the Avery's were murdered at the farm where Jeff's headquarters (or "seat") was, and by this time we too had moved there. Such parallels and symbolism are easily found in Revelation. Richard was the church of Ephesus, Danny, the church of Smyrna, Damon, Jeff's oldest son was Thyatira, Dennis was Sardis, Greg was the church of Laodicea, and Jeff was Philadelphia. These identities were assigned to us prior to the drought of 1988 and helped to create in us the scenarios which best suited Jeff's purposes for us.

Applying the name Philadelphia to himself, along with what would become an ever-increasing abundance of scriptural identities, Jeff also took upon himself the name Cyrus. Cyrus was the king of Persia who defeated Babylon and thereby enabled the restoration of Jerusalem. Cyrus is the contemporary pronunciation of the name; the Aramaic pronunciation would be Kores or Koresh. Vernon Howell, the leader of the Davidian cult in Waco, Texas, changed his name to David Koresh for much the same reason as Jeff. Both claimed to be Deliverers for the restoration of Jerusalem (see Appendix A). Jeff's mission was that we had to be prepared to come into the presence of his god.

In teaching, Jeff would take a specific precept that he knew we would not be ready to receive, and plan a series of thirty to forty classes as building blocks up to that particular precept. Once the blocks were in place, he could teach the precept that was the purpose behind the preparatory classes. After that precept was taught and accepted, it became a building block in yet another structure. One thing I've learned is that I greatly underestimated the irrationally of evil. Before moving to Ohio, I could not comprehend anyone doing anything solely for the purpose of destruction. But if the lie is big enough it becomes all the more believable. Most of us look for a motive to explain anything bad that happens. I have learned to not assume it to simply be beyond us, as in "God's will," but now question such "bad things" as possibly being the work of pure evil in an effort to destroy our lives and happiness.

We thought Jeff was imparting God's interpretation of scripture, in accordance with God's timing and will. Equally important was our belief that God's revelation of these interpretations was strictly in accordance with our righteousness; or rather, purging sin from our lives. Even sin became a relative term, determined by Jeff's warped logic and his necessity to humiliate or threaten us. Mostly, I think it was due to his own inability to become that which he claimed to be. In other words, he could never be the choice seer of the *Book of Mormon* and he knew it, so he used the position as a means to elevate himself.

Jeff was building within us a structure of his own design by means of a preplanned, surreptitious process. In true Christianity, the process within us is created by the workings of the Holy Spirit to the renewing of the mind.

> "For we know that if our earthly house of this tabernacle were dissolved, we have a building of God, an house not made with hands, eternal in the heavens." (2 Corinthians 5:1)

> "And be renewed in the spirit of your mind; And that ye put on the new man which after God is created in righteousness and true holiness." (Ephesians 4:23–24).

With many ex-cult members, trust in God is so damaged by this intense deception that their faith becomes fragile, if not altogether destroyed.

The concept of destroying a person's past while forming a new identity within them is not at all new. In the book of Daniel, we read how certain vessels of the Lord were stolen from the temple in Jerusalem and taken back to Babylon in order to place them before their god. Likewise, certain choice vessels, in the form of royal children, Shadrach, Meshach and Abednigo, were also taken and placed before King Nebuchadnezzar. But prior to their entrance, they were given new identities (Daniel 1:7). These new identities were not merely for convenience, they were cunningly assigned to contradict their previous names. Quite obviously, these children were of far greater character than myself. They managed to victoriously sustain the truth they had within their hearts. I give God thanks that through their experience we have a vicarious account of success recorded to benefit us.

* * *

LATE IN THE TIME PERIOD OF OUR WILDERNESS EXPERIENCE, I had a conversation with Dennis Patrick, the recollection of which speaks more to me today than it did at the time. Dennis and Tonya had been seriously abused as a married couple, though at the time it was accepted as "loving chastisement" so

Chapter 7 NEW IDENTITY

they might be more fitting vessels for the Lord. Dennis had begun to be "acceptable" to Jeff (read: acceptable to god) and this acceptability restored to him responsibilities and privileges within the group that he had previously lost. As we talked one day about the hopeful progress of the group toward our common goal, I expressed my concern regarding Richard Brand. Richard had fallen into a heavy series of chastisements. As Dennis and I talked about these chastisements (within the guidelines of which we were allowed), he told me how he, too, had worked and studied quite closely with Jeff upon his arrival in Ohio. Dennis began to tell me how, at the arrival of Richard, he was replaced as Jeff's more immediate partner for the Lord. This same replacement process seemed to have occurred with my arrival, to Richard. In my case, the emphasis was on grounding me into a confidence toward chiasmus. Once established, I could be brought up to speed with the mysteries of God's word that the others had already been taught. It was emphasized that my family be prepared for God's purpose in our lives, as were the others in the group. I see now a quite different purpose. Any new initiate into such a group is seen in need of nurturing, yet in need of close observation. I believe Jeff took new members under his wing in order to observe them more closely. Getting to know them intimately would allow him to assemble a strategy for controlling them.

We have characteristics that make us individuals, so what works as a control agent of one person may be counter-productive for another. Jeff had good skills when it came to the management of people (as I suppose would be the case with most any cult leader). Jeff coddled each new member according to the need. Perhaps some members were seen as more useful to Jeff in his delegation of authority than others. There may have been an appearance of a second-in-command relationship, but I'm quite confident that the only real second in command, if anyone, was Alice. Any other perceptions were only a temporary facade in order for Jeff to keep people organized and busy. Eventually, I was labeled as Jeff's spokesman. I don't really know why he placed this title on me; I never did anything in fulfillment of what the spokesman was to do. However, I did see its impact on me and on others of the group. By labeling me his spokesman it offered the illusion to all that we were moving toward the goal.

We were all used in different ways at different times. Once so initiated, it was less important for the leader to exercise immediate close observation. This was what took place with Dennis prior to my involvement with the group, and with Richard when I arrived. Perhaps if the group had stayed together for a longer period of time, someone else would have replaced me. With the use of chiasmus and Jeff's imagination, I'm certain he would have had no problem justifying my replacement—and probably already has—for those who still believe in his divine appointment. My death had been prophesied, so that too, could have been an option if at any point it would have served his purposes.

KEITH JOHNSON AND HIS FAMILY ARRIVED AFTER ME, but they received the indoctrination so quickly that I believe Jeff trusted them not to retaliate against the deeper aspects of his agenda. Perhaps Jeff already had formed intentions of taking Keith's wife, Kathy, away from him. They embraced his doctrines rapidly. I'm certain Jeff saw no need to pull Keith in close, and equally saw no need to give him any position within the group. Jeff gave status within the group to whomever he decided to give status, and likewise, dished out humiliation to each in the same way. His agenda was quite opaque to us, and much like a god, he exalted and abased as he saw fit.

Our studies through the remainder of 1988 explored many areas revealing our true identities. "Spokesman" was more a title than a name. Our real names were to be revealed to us through the seer's eyes. It was considered a great blessing for the eyes of the seer to be opened for the revelation of the mysteries of God. For them to be closed would mean his people were in a state of sin. Jeff was not inclined to give blatant "thus saith the Lord" instruction to us. He seldom shared the things he had experienced (or claimed to) which related to his call as seer, yet when doing so he avoided detail. Experiences were presented as being intimately sacred, and not to be loosely spoken of. This aspect of Jeff's propaganda process is, perhaps, unique. To hold foundational experiences as supremely sacred is not at all uncommon, but Jeff used his imaginative skills through the words themselves. In fact, he even taught the necessity of this very principle by way of the chiastic process.

We already believed the scriptures we were using were God's word, therefore Jeff was merely "opening" them to us. We both saw and heard the word of God revealed to us. We were taught this was necessary. We would "see" the words before us while "hearing" the interpretation of them through God's chosen seer.

> "And behold, the heavens were opened, and they were caught up into heaven, and *saw and heard* unspeakable things. And it was forbidden them that they should utter: neither was it given unto them the power that they should utter the things which they saw and heard." (3 Nephi 13:25–26; see also 3 Nephi 8:18)

The passage quoted is an illustration from only two verses of many throughout the *Book of Mormon*, which speaks of how chosen ones saw and heard the things of God that were revealed to them. This principle was combined by Jeff through chiasmus and various class topics to be applied not only to a vision of sorts, where one would enter and experience the kingdom, as with Isaiah 6:1–3. But for us it was to be applied to the written words alone. "And blessed are they because of their exceeding faith in the words alone which thou hast spoken unto them" (Mosiah 11:123). We were to exercise exceeding faith upon "the words alone," as we "saw" them on the written page and "heard" them expounded by Jeff's voice.

Chapter 7 NEW IDENTITY

The seers spoken of within the *Book of Mormon* were greater than ordinary prophets in that they could translate various languages by a tool called "interpreters," which ability to see through them was also a gift from God. The way in which we eventually viewed Jeff is documented in the following passage.

> "For he has wherewith he can look, and translate all records that are of ancient date: and it is a gift from God. And the things are called interpreters and no man can look in them, except he be commanded, lest he should look for that he ought not, and he should perish. And whosoever is commanded to look in them, the same is called a seer. And behold, the king of the people that is in the land of Zarahemla, is the man that is commanded to do these things, and who has this high gift from God. And the king said, *that seer is greater than a prophet.* And Ammon said, that a seer is a revelator, and a prophet also; and *a gift which is greater, can no man have,* except that he should possess the power of God, which no man can; yet a man may have great power given him from God. But a seer can know of things which have past, and also of things which are to come; And by them shall all things be revealed, or rather, shall secret things be made manifest, and hidden things shall come to light, and things which are not known, shall be made known by them; And also, things shall be made known by them, which otherwise could not be known. Thus God has provided a means that man, through faith, might work mighty miracles; therefore, he becometh a great benefit to his fellow beings." (Mosiah 5:72–81)

These passages illustrate how the gift of the seer was not limited to merely translating from one language to another. According to the passages quoted, what these seers did was to reveal the deeper, or hidden interpretations of God's recorded word. The words "translate" and "interpret" become interchangeable as to the gift of the seer (Omni 1:35, 44).

Jeff was to have seen Christ, who supposedly asked him, "Where are your brethren?" Therefore, it became increasingly paramount in Jeff's belief, as well as ours, that Jeff was that seer, provided for our day and time in order to interpret these scriptures of ancient date. As the *Book of Mormon* records Jesus' teaching when He visited the inhabitants of this continent, words were no longer to be chronologically divided, or even divided by chapters and verses. By chiasmus, the division of God's word was infinite, without dimensions and limitations, therefore, all words became one. "And now it came to pass that when Jesus had expounded all the scriptures in one, which they had written, he commanded them that they should teach the things which he had expounded unto them" (3 Nephi 11:1). Jeff's purpose was to follow the command to expound all words into one, as he had been shown by Christ, and as had been recorded by others.

All scripture took on a texture of infinity to its application of finding truth. As seer, Jeff was to reveal to us the truth, by rightly dividing. This included the revelation of our true identity. As was quite often the case, if his eyes were not open, or if what he was seeing was not able to be shared with his people, it was an indication there was sin in the camp. I'm sure that even with Jeff's imagination, it became laborious to continually come up with something new. However, it became quite an effective method for creating guilt and humiliation within us, as well as feelings of failure and inadequacy. Mormonism is a works-oriented religion, with only the thinnest shred of emphasis upon the gift of grace offered to us through the sacrifice of Christ. Jeff played upon this ignorance by drawing us farther away from our already limited view of grace and into complete reliance upon him as our sole connection with salvation, not to mention the burden of salvation of others. When we were blessed with being able to receive instruction from the word, with Jeff as the seer, he would divide areas of the Book of the Revelation in the Bible. Jeff taught the literal interpretation of the seven servants (Revelation 2 and 3) who would prepare the seven churches for the return of Jesus Christ. Unfortunately, Revelation is commonly used by manipulative people due to the ambiguity of its cloaked message as well as the sheer magnificence of what it proclaims.

As the vessels spoken of in the book of Ether, our "construction" would not be complete until there was no light in us. "And he cried unto the Lord, saying, O Lord, behold, I have done even as thou hast commanded me; and I have prepared the vessels for my people, and behold, there is no light in them" (Ether 1:53). Only then did the vessels receive light. "And thus the Lord caused the stones to shine in darkness, to give light unto men, women and children, that they might not cross the great waters in darkness" (Ether 3:3). There's quite a complex story that surrounds the two passages. People encamped on the shoreline of a large body of water had a great obstacle presented to them. God told them to build eight vessels that would carry them across the waters. They were to be constructed in accordance to God's instruction and detail. But upon completion of the vessels, it was noticed that there was no light in them. Therefore, the spiritual leader of the people (the brother of Jared) carved sixteen transparent stones out of an exceeding high mountain. Being transparent should indicate that they would allow the sunlight to shine through them (Ether 1:61), yet this was clearly not the point. They needed to actually radiate light, as well. Jeff's mission, as it related to this passage, was to construct vessels completely void of any light within them. Each vessel that the ancient Jaredites fashioned would house two stones. By Jeff's interpretation of scriptures, we were those vessels. As such, we were to have our two eyes (stones) illuminated to a new identity, a new perception of reality. We were not immediately aware that this was what he was striving for, but through hours upon hours of indoctrination, that is exactly what occurred. We were to be prepared to come into the presence of his god, yet in a sewer of logic[6] sort of way, his god appeared to be the True and Living God. However, Jeff's god is not the Living God, but rather a god of destruction and death (2 Corinthians 4:4). I believe this god is the author of the majority of Mormon

---

[6] The origin of the term "sewer of logic" is explained in Chapter 8, page 59.

Chapter 7 NEW IDENTITY

doctrine. There are many interpretations and misrepresentations in these doctrines that can lead people astray. Mormon doctrines exalt a proposed seer, not the actual Messiah (2 Nephi 2:8). There is, however, an essential and foundational truth within the Bible, which does not coincide with the Mormon message. The Living God, through His Son Jesus Christ, builds a house of habitation for life and beyond. "Let not your heart be troubled: ye believe in God, believe also in me. In my Father's house are many mansions: if it were not so, I would have told you. I go to prepare a place for you" (John 14:1–2).

* * *

ONE EVENING DURING THE SPRING OF THAT YEAR, a tremendous clap of thunder aroused everyone at the farm. A number of us were performing assigned chores. Damon and I had been working in the barn, others were in the house and still others were out on the lawn. The lightening was extremely close, but that was not the greatest importance of what transpired. A short distance from the farm and within eyesight, there is a hill where Jeff claimed to go in order to commune with God. All the major *Book of Mormon* characters had an "exceeding high" mountain, a holy hill of sorts, from which they could call upon the Lord. Jeff, too, claimed such a mountain; conveniently within walking distance of the farm. This particular hill in Kirtland has a radio tower, and its summit is appropriately clear of trees. As the sound of the thunder resounded in our ears, we all gathered from our various areas to investigate whether it had caused damage.

At the very moment of audible thunder, the sun was shining brightly, yet the sky directly overhead was darkly clouded. Knowing those were ideal conditions for a rainbow to be seen, I walked around the barn to see if one was visible. Jeff had recently taught on the subject of rainbows and how they, along with nature as a whole, tell a story, reveal a praise, and glorify God as creator. "Sing, O ye heavens; for the Lord hath done it: shout, ye lower parts of the earth: break forth into singing, ye mountains, O forest, and every tree therein" (Isaiah 44:23). If one truly had spiritual ears, they would be able to hear these praises of God. Conversely, to not hear these praises in quite the literal way meant deafness, due to one's sin and, basically, death from God. At a point later than this, I was given permission to visit Niagara Falls in order to hear the Hallelujah Chorus that Jeff claimed he heard the falls sing. Upon arriving back at Kirtland the next day, I had to shamefully report that I still had the ears of a Gentile. All I heard was water falling.

But that evening, Damon and I noticed that the others were also standing around, looking in the direction of Jeff's holy hill. I've never seen a more perfect example of the natural occurrence of a double rainbow than that day. All of us were amazed at the beauty and brilliance of the display as it arched over the very location of Jeff's sacred mount. Rainbows are not fixed at a location, but merely reflections of light through a prism created by moisture present in the atmosphere. However, this rainbow was taken as a sign that we all were quite literally where we needed to be. Jeff was certain that it meant even more. From the book of Ezekiel we find an illustration of God's presence within the rainbow, the symbol of God's covenant.

> "As the appearance of the bow that is in the cloud in the day of rain, so was the appearance of the brightness round about. This was the appearance of the likeness of the glory of the Lord. And when I saw it, I fell upon my face, and I heard a voice of one that spake." (Ezekiel 1:28)

Of course, this was not to be taken as a literal rainbow, but rather, an example of what Ezekiel experienced. We, too, were to look for the hidden purpose and grow to observe nature for the message and presence of God that was revealed from it.

Those of us who were at the farm that night gathered around the kitchen table, investigating a few passages which Jeff believed to apply. Needing the necessary amount of time to fabricate a manipulation of the written word, it was the class topic the next night. Amazingly, Jeff associated the previous day's event with Revelation, chapter 6, as the actual breaking of the first seal.

> "And I saw when the lamb opened one of the seals, and I heard, as it were the noise of thunder, one of the four beasts saying, Come and see. And I saw, and behold a white horse: and he that sat on him had a bow; and a crown was given unto him: and he went forth conquering, and to conquer." (Revelation 6:1–2)

We were coming into place, the seer, his servants, and now the breaking of the first seal with all the unimaginable ramifications that would develop from it. It had begun.

That rainbow brought back remembrance of our friends' videotape of the Aurora Borealis the previous summer. But this time it was as though the Aurora Borealis and the Aurora Australis were performing in a large and global way—the chiastic reflections in vivid double rainbows. Susie and I had such passion for God's word to be fulfilled, for Zion to be begun, for people to be prepared for the coming of the Lord, and for His glorious return in a way not unlike the account recorded of the Nephites. We'd spent hours in fasting and prayer for it. We'd forsaken good employment and financial security in a day when such things were hard to come by. We'd moved far from family to an area where we knew no one, quite literally "chasing rainbows," and now, ironically, we had found one. We'd been blessed with employment and new friends. "Go to the Ohio; and there I will give unto you my law" (D&C 38:7b.). Many things seemed to indicate that we were where God wanted us to be. The reality is that God's word has already been fulfilled (Mattthew 5:17). By the merits of Jesus upon the cross, "it's done" (John 19:30; Revelation 21:6).

Chapter 8

PREPARATIONS FOR WAR

With the "breaking of the first seal," came an increased vigor of preparation; not as though anything was to occur immediately, but rather that it was imminent. We had a target date for our day of "redemption" (redemption defined for us as to "feel and see"), which was May 3rd. Jeff interpreted this date from some of the symbols on the Temple doors, but it being his date of birth was probably the greater influence toward his *eisegesis*.

The second seal would require the delivery of a great sword (Revelation 6:4) to thereby arm the conqueror that the first seal had sent forth. We were a small and insignificant number of people, but with God for us, who could stand against us? Therefore, we had to become a military discipline. God would do the vast majority of the fighting for us in miraculous and earth-shattering ways. However, we were to make the stand for Him, in complete reliance to provide what we were clearly not capable of. In essence, we were preparing for war.

War is an amazing element of human behavior. Basically, it's a struggle for dominance, yet those who do the fighting rarely receive any. Armies have sometimes been formed merely by payment for services rendered; but usually they are formed and motivated by a creed, with their actions at the time seen as authoritatively right and justified. The *Book of Mormon* is full of accounts of warfare. As we became more convinced of the destruction that lay ahead of us, both by war and by natural catastrophe, Jeff would speak of how scriptures were actually provided for that very purpose. "Feast upon the words of Christ; for behold the words of Christ will tell you all things what ye should do" (2 Nephi 14:4). He strongly emphasized that the *Book of Mormon* was truly the words of Christ and that the references concerning war tactics were provided that we might be prepared in all things. References to natural calamities were also provided to instruct the seer how such powers are to be called upon.

> "And thus, if ye shall say unto this temple, It shall be rent in twain, it shall be done. And if ye shall say unto this mountain, Be thou cast down and become smooth, it shall be done. And behold, if ye shall say, God shall smite this people, it shall come to pass. And now behold, I command you that ye shall go and declare unto this people that, Thus saith the Lord God, who is Almighty, except ye repent, ye shall be smitten, even unto destruction." (Helaman 3:121–124)

Next recorded is the manner in which Nephi accomplished these things.

> "And it came to pass that in this year, Nephi did cry unto the Lord, saying, O Lord, do not suffer that this people shall be destroyed by the sword; but O Lord, rather let there be a famine in the land, to stir them up in remembrance of the Lord their God, and perhaps they will repent and turn unto thee; And so it was done, according to the words of Nephi. And there was a great famine upon the land among all the people of Nephi. And thus, in the seventy and fourth year, the famine did continue, and the work of destruction did cease by the sword, but became sore by famine. And this work of destruction did also continue in the seventy and fifth year." (Helaman 4:4–7)

The drought of 1988 was noteworthy that year, as it caught the attention of both the media and a great number of farmers. Anyone with a Farmer's Almanac could have prophesied the unusually dry weather conditions that summer. For us, it became an undisputable sign that we were coming into place, as the servants of God, and that times of tribulation lay ahead. Armed with the introduction of our revealed identities, we were a group with purpose—a quite benevolent one, in our minds. By that time, we were taught from the Book of Revelation only infrequently, so received only trickling issues of information about our servanthood over the seven churches. Nevertheless, we became steadily and increasingly intoxicated with our calling. The drought that year held more significance to us than unusually dry weather, and much more than merely a coincidence—it was the Commencement. To us, the drought was not only a product of the power Jeff had obtained from God, it was the beginning of a drought of another kind which would continue on in following years.

An interesting point about the passages quoted above from the book of Helaman is that an interpretation is made concerning a biblical principle. Verse 120 of chapter 3 states "whatsoever ye shall seal on earth, shall be sealed in heaven; and whatsoever ye shall loose on earth shall be loosed in heaven; and thus ye shall have power among this people." The principle of binding and loosing is introduced in the New Testament book of Matthew. In chapter 16:19, we find this authoritative power bestowed upon Simon Barjona just at the time his name was changed to Peter. This was done by Jesus, whom Peter had just recognized as "the Christ, the Son of the Living God."

Clearly, issues of miraculous power, as illustrated in New Testament chapters, are not always clear why they were revealed at those specific times. These amazing exhibitions, though truly wonderful, beautifully illustrate that we, through Jesus, have an awesome heavenly Father. But nowhere in the Bible do we find a wholesale transfer of power from God to man for the purpose of dominion over particular people. Now we fight a spiritual fight, no differently than in how we now worship in spirit. In 2 Corinthians 10:3–5 we read the following.

Chapter 8 PREPARATIONS FOR WAR

> "For though we walk in the flesh, we do not war after the flesh: For the weapons of our warfare are not carnal, but mighty through God to the pulling down of strongholds; Casting down imaginations, and every high thing that exhalteth itself against the knowledge of God, and bringing into captivity every thought to the obedience of Christ."

This is the type of warfare aimed toward the saving of souls that was intended along with the power to bind and to loose. It comes by way of the Holy Spirit's revelation that Jesus is the Christ, the Son of the Living God, and we have a voice at the right hand of the Father, through prayer. Jesus healed the sick, walked on water, caused a fig tree to wither and die, and passed through angry multitudes unharmed. He calmed stormy seas and turned water into wine. Yet at the close of these demonstrations of God's will, miraculously active in a tangible, physical way, our Savior promised His disciples that they would do "greater works than these" (John 14:12). There's no doubt that miraculous events occurred not only soon after the death and resurrection of Jesus, but that such blessings have continued to occur throughout the nearly two thousand years since that time. However, is there any record of events greater than those performed by Jesus? Surely, the greatest of works, the mightiest of warfare, and the most beneficial restorations would be that of a soul victoriously cleansed of all unrighteousness. We, as the body of Christ, have through prayer and the power of the Holy Spirit that intercessory capacity for the souls of men yet held captive by sin. Our warfare and our worship is "in spirit and in truth." But this is not the perception of Christianity as offered through Mormon doctrines.

* * *

A COMMON ELEMENT OF RELIGIOUS CULT BEHAVIOR seems to be the persuasion of members away from New Testament teaching and back into Old Testament practice, all the while, under the illusion of grace through Christ. In other words, the Old Testament contains the view of belief in God through the practice of physical ordinances and ritual. This practice was good and essential and was at no time destroyed by Christ Jesus, but rather fulfilled by him (Matthew 5:17). There's a fine line between the fulfillment of God's law and the utter destruction of it. The law was done away in Christ. Through our Lord, we are now able to perform our worship of God in the intended spiritual way (1 Peter 2:5). Mormon teachings do not convey that message. In the book of Hebrews 10:18 we read: "Now where remission of these is, there is no more offering for sin." Yet the account of 2 Nephi, in the *Book of Mormon*, recounts the receiving of the Holy Ghost parallel with the instruction to build a temple and perform ordinances according to the law of Moses, all at a time period around 600 B.C.

"And we did observe to keep the judgments, and the statutes, and the commandments of the Lord, in all things, according to the law of Moses. And I, Nephi, did build a temple, and did construct it after the manner of the temple of Solomon, save it were not built of so many precious things."
(2 Nephi 4:14, 22)

"And not withstanding we believe in Christ, we keep the law of Moses, and look forward with steadfastness unto Christ, until the law shall be fulfilled; for, for this end was the law given; Wherefore, the law hath become dead unto us, and we are made alive in Christ, because of our faith."
(2 Nephi 11:45–46)

"And now, how could ye speak with the tongue of angels, save it were by the Holy Ghost? Angels speak by the power of the Holy Ghost; wherefore, they speak the words of Christ. For behold, again I say unto you, that if ye will enter in by the way and receive the Holy Ghost, it will show unto you all things what ye should do. Behold, this is the doctrine of Christ; and there will be no more doctrine given, until after he shall manifest himself unto you in the flesh." (2 Nephi 14:3, 6, 7)

Why would God bind them to a law which was dead, yet claim they were alive in Christ? The whole concept, now, seems a little "un-kosher" when compared to Jewish law (Lev. 11). What it does is provide a very works-oriented perception of grace, all under the guise of foreseeing a future grace through Jesus, the Messiah. A quote that precedes 2 Nephi 11, very subtly presents this works-oriented view of grace. "For we know that it is by grace that we are saved, *after all we can do*" (2 Nephi 11:44). This passage confuses the grace of God with the call to service. It implies that we can *earn* grace, but by failing to perform "all we can do," we have no salvation. This does not agree with what Paul wrote to the Ephesians 2:8–10 even under the premise that Nephi, in 600 B.C., was instructing a Christian people with all the spiritual gifts of Pentecost. This view is not harmonious with the prophetic view of Christ as conveyed by Old Testament prophets, who spoke of His coming quite differently. The Nephi account speaks of how the Nephites had already received the Holy Ghost as manifested by tongues at this early date, yet in the biblical account those who walked with Christ throughout His ministry did not receive this manifestation until fifty days after His ascension unto the Father. The Mormon doctrines would apparently have us believe that the *Book of Mormon* characters were righteous beyond anything in the biblical record while the New Testament characters were all wickedly slow. "Wherefore, now after I have spoken these words, if ye cannot understand them, it is because ye ask not, neither do ye knock; wherefore, ye are not brought into the light, but must perish in the dark" (2 Nephi 14:5). This chapter is a chastisement from Nephi toward his brethren. They were simply too wicked to receive the Holy Ghost and gift of tongues by sincere and faithful belief, resident within him.

Jesus said that He did not come to condemn (John 3:17) or to be our accuser (John 5:45). If any were to find themselves in the camp of Nephi prior to

Chapter 8 PREPARATIONS FOR WAR

the birth of Christ, the words He would yet utter would promise their sure destruction for not speaking in tongues. Apparently, the standards for righteousness were a bit higher on this continent than they were in Palestine. And according to the *Book of Mormon,* the vast majority of Israelites who lived from the time of the exile until Christ surely all perished due to their lack of faith. This mixture of scriptural issues distorts one's interpretation of doctrinal truth.

* * *

DESPITE JEFF'S TWISTED INTERPRETATION of 2 Timothy 2:15, it is still true that we must "rightly divide the word of truth." Doctrines such as those in the *Book of Mormon* only make the issue more complicated by integrating diverse principles. Much like the shuffling of a deck of cards, the texture of God's total plan becomes confusingly emulsified. God's word is supposed to work as a refiner's fire. It therefore stands to reason that false doctrine exists to confuse and perplex what God's word is striving to purge away and reveal. The issue of prayer within our group required a literal form of communication with God by this integration of Old Testament ritual, along with a distorted, nearly nonexistent perception of New Testament grace. In this fashion, we were taught that the words to say were recorded within the text and that the seer, by chiasmus, could reveal these words to his people. Then, whether calling upon God, or in His actual presence, the seer's people would be prepared in "all things what ye should do" (2 Nephi 14:4–6).

Despite the *Book of Mormon*'s claim that it is an abridged record compiled from several separate writers, some terms appear repeatedly. Through the use of chiasmus, where we dissected the context of a chapter into small terms and phrases and then integrated them back in again, the context created the division itself. And of course, Jeff was the seer with the vision of all things necessary to rightly divide the text, in revelation of God's hidden plan. A series of clichés was developed by the chiastic reading of various dissected phrases. "Wherefore," "behold," and "and it came to pass" fell into the categories which redundantly popped up in nearly every division, and as they did, they began to be used as markers to give credence to the division, confirmation that it had been properly done. Following is an example from 2 Nephi 1:79–80.

> A – Wherefore
>
> B – they stand in the presence of him
>
> C – to be judged of him
>
> B – according to the truth and holiness which is in him
>
> A – Wherefore

The "wherefores" mark the statements meant to be placed opposite one another. Working inward, "they stand in the presence of him" is opposite "according to the truth and holiness which is in him." The center point, and main emphasis of the division is "to be judged of him." Overuse of terms such as "wherefore" or "and it came to pass," eventually became clichés with an increasing multiplicity of definitions.

Now educated in the process for dividing, we were finally worthy to be taught the words to utter in specific situations, in accordance with our purpose and calling. Whether it was to perform a healing, level a mountain, or call upon the Lord for the purpose of redemption (to feel and see), these words had been previously recorded by our brethren and forefathers, so that by similar esoteric means we might learn them and accomplish our foreordained task. This principle, we were taught, was the interpretation to Malachi 4:6. "And he shall turn the heart of the fathers to the children, and the heart of the children to the fathers, lest I come and smite the earth with a curse."

Jeff, as another Elijah, had been designated to be the one once again declaring from the wilderness "make straight the way of the Lord."

> "Then the disciples understood that he spake unto them of John the Baptist, *and also of another which should come and restore all things, as written by the prophets.*" (Matthew 17:14, *Inspired Version*; compare this verse to all other translations of Matthew 17:13)

The mention of "another which should come," added by Joseph Smith, is quite a successful distraction in that it destroys the emphasis of how John paved the way for what Jesus restored, and turns the reader's eyes to look to the future for an Elijah yet to come. These additions to the authorized text send the reader in search of a seer, not the Messiah, with the illusion that all things have not yet been restored. Though many may disagree, I'm quite convinced that this passage, as distorted by Joseph Smith, typifies what is spoken in 1 John 4:3, denying what Christ fulfilled by His death and His resurrection in the flesh. How can we stand strong in our salvation by a belief in our heart and a confession from our mouth (Romans 10:9), if we only glance at the glory of our risen Lord, while all along gazing for yet another? It makes my heart sick as I consider the years of anxiety I've experienced by believing in this doctrine. But now I'm truly "restored" by the Lord's blessing in having finally found truth.

Our warfare was not so much spiritual as it was supernatural. These two are often difficult to distinguish. Improper interpretation of passages such as 2 Timothy 3:5 can enslave a person into feeling a desperate need for the supernatural. To Jeff, there was no other definition to the word *power* than that which is associated with tangible, supernatural activity. Yet, interestingly enough, 2 Timothy 3:1–4 spells out a very clear definition of Jeff. I must confess that I, too, was blinded to any other definition of the word *power* as it related to God.

Chapter 8 PREPARATIONS FOR WAR

"This know also, that in the last days perilous times shall come. For men shall be lovers of their own selves, covetous, boasters, proud, blasphemers, disobedient to parents, unthankful, unholy, Without natural affection, trucebreakers, false accusers, incontinent, fierce, despisers of those that are good, Traitors, heady, high-minded, lovers of pleasures more than lovers of God; Having a form of godliness, but denying the power thereof: from such turn away." (2 Timothy 3:1–4)

"Where is the power today?" was a question I asked, even before meeting Jeff. Displays of power as prophesied in the *Book of Mormon* through the choice seer seemed imminent and exceedingly necessary. But these things occur "by faith," according to "Mormon" nearly four hundred years after Christ.

"Behold I say unto you, Nay, for it is by faith that miracles are wrought; and it is by faith that angels appear and minister unto men; Wherefore if these things have ceased, woe be unto the children of man, for it is because of unbelief, and all is vain; for no man can be saved, according to the words of Christ, save they shall have faith in his name; Wherefore, if these things have ceased, then has faith ceased also; and awful is the state of man: for they are as though there had been no redemption made." (Moroni 7:41–43)

True enough is the fact that we must have faith on the name of our blessed Lord Jesus. Likewise, faith plays a major role in the working of miracles. But according to Mormon, if such signs are not happening, then we have no redemption.

Once again, we have the coercion 3 Nephi 12:1–4, in that by not having the greater things we were all under condemnation. To whom do these angels appear, mentioned in verse 41 of the chapter quoted above?

"For behold, they are subject unto him [Christ], to minister according to the word of his command [or the command revealed in his word], showing themselves unto them of a strong faith and a firm mind, in every form of godliness." (3 Nephi 12:1–4)

Every form of godliness became defined as we learned all things from feasting upon the words of Christ. By the translation, or transformation of becoming every form of godliness, we were to also become of strong faith and firm mind in the forms of godliness revealed through the seer. "Feast upon the words of Christ, for behold, the words of Christ will tell you all things what ye should do" (2 Nephi 14:4). By continual study of the words of Christ we were to learn all things we should do. This would increase our faith, due to the continual witness that the words were true.

In chiasmus, passages became so ambiguous that eventually they appeared to be saying the same thing over and over. Terms like *pattern*, *manner*, and *plainness* became synonymous with chiasmus. Therefore, the following would take on an altogether new interpretation.

> "Wherefore hearken, O my people, which are of the house of Israel, and give ear unto my words: for because the words of Isaiah are not plain unto you, nevertheless, they are plain unto all those that are filled with the spirit of prophecy. But I give unto you a prophecy, according to the spirit which is in me; wherefore I shall prophesy according to the plainness which hath been with me from the time that I came out from Jerusalem with my father. For behold, my soul delighteth in plainness unto my people, that they may learn...and I know that the Jews do understand the things of the prophets, and there is none other people that understand the things which were spoken unto the Jews, like unto them, save it be that they are taught after the manner of the things of the Jews. But behold, I proceed with mine own prophecy, according to my plainness; in that which I know that no man can err."
> (2 Nephi 11:5, 8, 11)

Both the "manner of the things of the Jews," and "the manner of plainness" became identified as chiasmus. This was a way of interpreting prophecy, which one could be taught. Once the seer's people are taught this manner, they then cannot err. "And now my brethren, I have spoken plain, that ye can not err" (2 Nephi 11:37).

A reference from the *Doctrine and Covenants* provided a clue to the synonymous nature between plainness and pattern. Notice that in this passage, the word "language" might be chiastically confused with the pattern.

> "And again, I give unto you a pattern in all things, that ye may not be deceived; for Satan is abroad in the land, and he goeth forth deceiving the nations; wherefore he that prayeth whose spirit is contrite, the same is accepted of me, if he obey mine ordinances. He that speaketh, whose spirit is contrite, whose language is meek, and edifieth, the same is of God, if he obey mine ordinances." (D&C 52:4b–d)

By way of the pattern, from which we may not be deceived, we speak in truthful meekness of His language, thereby becoming knowledgeable of His ordinances and strengthened in faith to perform all things.

We had to divide the words of Christ in order to learn all things. And without the pattern, the manner of plainness, we were certain to err and become deceived, as similarly did the early apostasy that necessitated the Restored Church in the first place. Why were all churches an abomination in God's sight? Because they did not have the manner of plainness by which to show themselves approved, spoken of in 2 Timothy 2:15. They did not have a seer to reveal all things to them, in accordance with this pattern. The pattern was identified as being the method of writing, straight from the finger of God as used in an ancient book of remembrance. "For a book of remembrance we have written among us, according to the pattern given by the finger of God; and it is given in our own language" (Genesis 6:47, *Inspired Version*). Chiasmus was identified as the pattern of writing from which God writes by his own finger, by which His word can be divided for interpretation, no matter which language it is recorded in. In other words, the pattern was a tool to be used in one's own language. And who, of course, could reveal this pattern from the finger of God?: Another Elijah who would come with a book of remembrance. "Then they that feared the Lord spake often one to another: and the Lord hearkened, and heard it, and a book of remembrance was written before him for them that feared the Lord, and that thought upon his name" (Malachi 3:16). While this passage is taken from the King James translation, with instruction received from the *Inspired Version* in Genesis 6, the book of remembrance, and an applied pattern, a mystical necessity for a seer is created. Bear in mind, that the return of Elijah as prophesied in Malachi 4 had been redefined away from fulfillment by John's preparation for Jesus and turned in search for another who should come (*Inspired Version*, Matthew 17:14). The other who should come would turn the hearts of the children to their fathers, by teaching them the pattern from the finger of God, thereby revealing to them their own name and identity as recorded in the book of remembrance. Jeff became this choice seer provided to us for the restoration of all things.

The Joseph Smith translation of the Bible confusingly redefines 2 Timothy 2:15. To "study to show thyself approved unto God," is performed not only by rightly dividing the word of truth, but by displays of supernatural power.

> "Now Melchizedek was a man of faith, who wrought righteousness; and when a child he feared God, and stopped the mouths of lions, and quenched the violence of fire. And thus, having been approved of God, he was ordained an high priest after the order of the covenant which God made with Enoch." (Genesis 14:26–27, *Inspired Version*)

Certain aspects of the blessings are also recorded in the book of Daniel, to be signs of approval rather than to teach us spiritual principles of God's saving grace. All this leaves one feeling as though the whole story about Daniel and the other three Israelites is missing—perhaps they were showing themselves approved by what happened to them and that we are to do likewise.

What does any of this have to do with our preparation for warfare? Warfare would be proof of our faith; without faith, it is "as though there had been no redemption made" (Moroni 7:43). In order for redemption to be complete we had to feel and see as defined by the account of the Nephites.

> "And it came to pass that the Lord spake unto them, saying, Arise and come forth unto me, that ye may thrust your hands into my side, and also that ye may feel the prints of the nails in my hands, and in my feet, that you nay know that I am the God of Israel, and the God of the whole earth, and have been slain for the sins of the world. And it came to pass that the multitude went forth, and thrust their hands into his side, and did feel the prints of the

nails in his hands and in his feet; And this they did do, going forth one by one, until they had all gone forth, and did see with their eyes, and did feel with their hands, and did know of a surety, and did bear record, that it was he, of whom it was written by the prophets, should come."
(3 Nephi 5:14–16)

This account turns Thomas' doubt into an issue of necessity (John 20:25). Frankly, I am not comfortable criticizing Thomas. Perhaps it was indeed necessary for him, as one who was required to bear an express witness to the resurrection that we might have a testimony of which to look to in faith. Consider Luke 24:39. Someone had to be assured that He was flesh and bone and not a ghost. How else but through their testimony would we today be able to exercise faith in His immortal flesh? 1 John 1:1 was written from one who was able to give first hand testimony, that we, through faith, might please God (Hebrews 11:6). Either way the account is perceived, we should be thankful that by the way of the testimonies of those who were there, we have opportunity, by faith, to please God with the assurance of our hearts that our Salvation lives.

I've introduced a considerable amount of terms, definitions, and scripture passages. These precepts were not taught us in so swift a manner as I've presented them here. I'm certain the interpretations to which we slowly became accustomed may appear openly ludicrous to the reader. In fact, the manner in which I've just related them would be "boiling water" principles, causing even an unsuspecting frog to leap. Our speech became saturated with clichés. Each cliché kindled expansive analogies, reflected through hour upon hour of class indoctrination. This discourse has not been presented as an excuse for my actions in this group. My intention is to provoke thought and recognition of a devastating issue that is generally incomprehensible by way of rational expectations in behavior. These are more than misinterpretations and word games; they are influences that cause death. It is as old as society itself. Chiasmus became our reality and there was no reality without it. We were strangers in a strange land. With no basis or footing to compare, these interpretations and daily routines of study and chores became accepted as normal to us. Using the interpretation of the watchman parable in *Doctrine and Covenants* 96, we were to be God's servants with the mission of retaking the lost vineyard.

* * *

I HAVE NEVER BEEN A GUN ENTHUSIAST, but it became essential that I familiarize myself with some of the basics. Even our wives were held responsible to be familiar with the type of ammunition used in Jeff's weapons. We would separate ammunition by bullet type and load clips accordingly, all this while blindfolded. I recall struggling with guilt. Guns were not of great interest to me, yet they were critical to our mission. Sorting bullets and loading clips was the extent of what the women were trained to do. However, the discipline of following orders was paramount. As *Book of Mormon* Israelites wandered,

Chapter 8 PREPARATIONS FOR WAR

they fought battles with their wives and children nearby. The book teaches that we men would literally be the only barrier between our families and the world. We were not actually to have much interaction with the world. The men, as heads-of-households, were to be the buffer between their families and outside influence.

I recall recently asking one of the former members of the group why she'd left. Shar had been a member shortly before Susie and I moved to Ohio, but left about six months after our arrival. After we were extradited to the Lake County, Ohio, jail she visited those of us who were there. I didn't know her well because I worked nights during most of the time she was there. But in my need to try to sort out all that had happened, I wanted to ask why she had left. Her discussion led me to believe she saw too much too fast. Jeff was not the buffer between her and the world, which he claimed himself to be. He was taking her paychecks with the promise that he would pay off some debts she had before coming to Ohio. Within time, the bill collectors avoided the smokescreen Jeff was providing and pursued Shar directly at work. This exposed Jeff's lies about having taken her money to pay her bills. More importantly, it exposed his failure to be the barrier between her and the world. The final straw would be his expression of sexual intentions toward her, which woke her up to the fact that Jeff was not at all what he claimed to be. I can't help but envy Shar's experience of rapid exposure. Perhaps such rapidity of the process could have awakened me. However, the past cannot be changed.

* * *

SOME FORM OF MILITARY CHAIN OF COMMAND WAS ESTABLISHED, though not very consistently. Jeff assigned weapons in accordance with how he wanted us armed. I recall on several occasions that Jeff would divvy out an assortment of weapons with an organized chain of command, only to change it later. Little has been said about the Avery family's participation in these drills. Although peace-loving, they too, were trained in preparation for the task at hand and provided with a weapon. The media exposed that Dennis Avery had probably purchased the very gun that killed he and his family. It may have been the day I drove Jeff and Dennis to a gun shop. Jeff instructed Dennis what he was to buy. Trina Avery, at 15 years of age, was old enough to be in attendance at Jeff's classes on weaponry. Younger Karen and Becky were not. I mention this only to present a complete picture of what all of us were subjected to. I doubt we'll ever know why, aside from the fact that Satan seeks only to steal, to kill, and to destroy. My fervent hope would be that by studying the manner in which unacceptable activities evolve, their pursuit will be avoided in the future.

The summer days of 1988 flowed into one continuous and indistinguishable haze. I don't believe our military training was ever as important to Jeff as he made it out to be. It never took priority over other projects, even though other projects, too, seemed to fall by the side. I've concluded that his projects, including the military façade, were merely ways to keep us busy, subdued, and off balance. From project to project we developed new dreams of businesses for pulling each of us out of the world's workforce and into full time employment toward God's purposes. Jeff had been quite immune from any need to work. But then he found the scripture that spoke to him. "And I will give unto him a commandment, that he shall do none other work save the work which I shall command him" (2 Nephi 2:13). Jeff's interpretation of this new finding meant that he would actually be in a state of sin to pursue any means of employment within the world. However, for the rest of us, it was expected that we do both. Looking back now, the sad fact is that we were more than willing to perform such labor. In fact, for me it was considered my "reasonable service," and I felt as though I was fulfilling God's purpose in my life. I was fervently willing to sacrifice time away from my wife and children. But now I'm faced with the memory of the foolish little robotic slave—me.

Dennis and Cheryl Avery had a dreadful time with employment. Dennis was never able to find employment of the type that he left in Missouri, which Jeff used against him. Apparently Jeff had drained them of whatever funds they had brought with them. When we moved to Ohio, the Averys were living in a very nice duplex only a few miles from the Temple. They appreciated it as a blessing that they were able to find such a place to begin with. The apartment complex where I lived had become somewhat run down and was in the process of new ownership. Where we lived was also a factor utilized by Jeff to his own convenience so when Dennis Avery ran into financial trouble and came to Jeff for help, the source of his trouble was identified as sin.

Identified as the servant over the church of Pergamos, one of the descriptive details (as earlier noted) was that the place where I dwelt was "where Satan's seat is" (Revelation 2:13). The poor condition of my neighborhood became identified as "Satan's seat." So, when the Averys were forced to move to a different location this, too, became an occurrence for scrutiny by Jeff. The three-bedroom house they moved into was nice enough, but it was a considerable distance from Jeff and the Temple. I remember how, at the time of our second visit, Jeff said that the command was to go to "the Ohio" (*D&C* 38:7b), meaning that close proximity to Kirtland was not essential. However, this changed in time, and even location of residence became an issue to be used at Jeff's discretion.

With the Avery's move labeled as an indication of sin, though unaware of it, they became outsiders. Jeff began to slander them on a regular basis. His expressions, while less than favorable towards them, even from the first time we met, were growing worse. I didn't understand these petty criticisms, since it was clear they were sincere and zealous about their service to God. I had no comprehension of the underlying agenda at work within Jeff's mind. It should have been perceived as an indication of Jeff's character, in that he seemed to have such an unnecessary and irrational dislike for them. But at the time I noticed it, I was not yet looking at Jeff as the seer. By the time he had taken

Chapter 8 PREPARATIONS FOR WAR

control over our thinking, I saw equally the burden that we all, in some way or another, brought with us.

Not wanting to be a burden, I began to scrutinize myself and my family for any such indications. The area of employment and income was obvious. One of the issues I find most troubling today, as an incarcerated person, is the reality of myself as a burden to the taxpayer. I'd been an asset throughout my life, both to my employer and to my country, but that is not now my situation. Pulling your own weight is a principle that I believed in then, and still do today. However, despite what Jeff promoted as a burden, by way of the Avery's financial struggle, I didn't view as an indication of sin. I had no idea Jeff had already drained thousands of dollars from them.

With Jeff's encouragement of a negative view of Dennis and Cheryl, he and Alice one day told Susie and me that they suspected Dennis of sodomizing his daughter Becky. Their story was that they had been watching the children after school, while both Dennis and Cheryl were working at minimum wage jobs that barely supported them. The only reason Jeff and Alice were available to watch the girls was that they had nothing else to do. They claimed that Becky was anorexic and also claimed to suspect sexual assault was the reason for this. Not introduced as mere suspicion, they said they noticed physical indications of this when Becky took a bath one day. They went on to say that they were trying to get Dennis and Cheryl to take their daughter to a counselor about the anorexia, in hopes that it would lead to expose what had been happening.

While I know that my own activities are beyond the comprehension of many people, there are many things in this world I naïvely have no comprehension of. The scenario introduced by Jeff and Alice that day, that a man could sexually violate his own daughter, is clearly beyond my ability to grasp. I now understand how the mind can justify and even precipitate some unnecessary and unjustified acts of war. I have myself become involved in that which I once could not have imagined possible for me. Therefore, I know that God is mighty to heal even the most horrendous of follies. I'm an extremely monogamous man, and have never been intimate with anyone other than my wife. We consummated our relationship on our wedding night. So such an accusation of sexual misconduct did not work so much to enrage me as it completely confused me by the incomprehensibility of it. Until it could be proven, it meant little to me. But the seed was planted and the sought-after effect was realized. The seed for speculation of blame had been planted. It could have been "someone else," yet the purpose behind the accusation was accomplished, in that it sought to separate the Averys from the rest of us. Suspicion is always a good tool for promoting an "us and them" mentality, and for this purpose, it was quite successful.

In an attempt to recall why the murders occurred, it dawned on me that just "perhaps" Jeff was the person responsible for the abuse, and by being the first to accuse, diverted attention away from himself. If this were true, it would also show motive for the annihilation of the Averys. However, by the time the bodies of the Avery family were discovered, there was no way to tell whether or not any of the girls had been abused.

* * *

THE PROCESS OF PRAYER, as we perceived it, was the desire in our hearts that spoke to God in ways that no tongue could ever utter.

> "And it came to pass, that when Jesus had thus prayed unto the Father, he came unto his disciples, and behold, they did still continue, without ceasing, to pray unto him; and they did not multiply many words, for it was given unto them what they should pray, and they were filled with desire."
> (3 Nephi 9:24)

The emphasis was that desire was the real source of communication, and that the words they used were few. Jeff became bold, eventually to say, "I will give you two words to think about and ponder upon. When I think you are ready, then I'll give you three words." The words were to be continually thought upon chiastically, and thereby spoken in prayer without adding to them. Chiasmus was provided that we might have a way to speak at all—any other speech being unclean—prayer included.

Therefore, it became our desire that if sexual mistreatment by the father were true, it would come to light and be repented of so healing could occur. Nonetheless, the Averys became less active in our purpose of restoring Zion. The most significant reason for this was that they weren't told when the majority of classes were held. This was a gradual occurrence, as in other situations, but eventually to the point that they were being notified of only about a class per week. By the sheer appearance of lack of participation, along with the other rumors, slander, and accusations, it looked as though they might not make it to the Temple by the appointed day. Media speculation, fed by the legal system, has it that the Averys were planning to leave the group and that this was the reason for their deaths. Considering the decreased amount of exposure they eventually came to have to Jeff's teachings, it is an understandable conclusion, yet I know that this was not the case.

Once Jeff assigned the responsibility to each of the men in the group to prepare a class of their own—to divide a certain area of scripture and walk the rest of the class through the chiasm. The end result was that it provided Jeff with a means to ridicule our efforts and illustrate his finesse as seer. I was impressed, however, with Dennis Avery's division and was somewhat surprised with how well he did considering his rejection by Jeff. Jeff, too, expressed a degree of appreciation toward Dennis' class, then turned it around in such a way as to make it sound as though Dennis knew better, but willingly sinned.

After having escaped the controlled setting I've conveyed here, I found similar forces at work after my arrest. First held in the Jackson County Jail in Missouri, the first article I read in the newspaper contained the promise that

Chapter 8 PREPARATIONS FOR WAR

we were all going to fry in the electric chair. After that, I pretty well stayed clear of news sources. Later, a member of the Lake County community stated, "They should take them all out and hang them—they shouldn't even get a trial." From the sound of that statement, I gathered the very strong presumption that there had already been a trial—trial by media. These personal statements should not discredit the intentions of the media, nor our necessity for it. While I was in the Lake County Jail, a series of interviews aired after Jeff's trial and conviction. Watching this first night's disgusting display of Jeff's ego I didn't tune in for the complete series of reports. He had caused death and tragedy in so many lives. After the first segment, the news anchor asked the reporter who had interviewed Jeff what it was like to talk to him. What the reporter said really caught my attention, "It was a good thing that I didn't have to work the day following the interview, because I would have had to call in sick." He went on to say that he felt completely drained and that it was as though he had been bathed in a sewer of logic. The interview had a definite impact on him. Consider that he did not meet Jeff Lundgren, the priesthood member, church sponsored tour guide, and sister's friend; he met Jeff Lundgren the cult leader, the mass murderer. He did not meet the "cool water" schemer, but rather, the "boiling water" prisoner.

Involvement in the senseless deaths of an entire family should evoke a sincere rage. What I was witnessing, was not unlike the heavy doses of mind control that I had just been exposed to, and therefore, appeared amazingly familiar to me. It became so very important to me then, and since, that we truly hate the crimes which occur, but that rage should never blind us from trying to understand how senseless crimes happen. Without an attempt at understanding, they're prone to be repeated.

Many people we'd never met openly expressed their passionate opinion about us. I don't fault strong opinions, but it was frustrating. Prior to my trial, prospective jurors were asked to place their personal opinions aside. Had it not been for the heavy saturation of prejudiced media to which they had been subjected, they might have been able to do just that. The result of this saturation was a jury that could not be seated. "Divers weights are an abomination unto the Lord; and a false balance is not good" (Proverbs 20:23). No matter the final outcome of our judgments, we should never lose sight of the very essential necessity for a balanced view. I had no anger nor dislike toward the Averys, yet shamefully must confess that given the highly strong indoctrination in and out of classes by Jeff, I perceived their deaths as being justified and necessary. What a terrible opinion to be wrong about.

* * *

PROVERBS 18:17 SHOULD BE APPLIED TO OUR PREPARATION FOR WAR, not so much that we were preparing to actually fight battles (either physically or spiritually), but, not unlike the Waco Davidians, the perception was being formed within us that war raged about us at every turn. In time, this perception would be narrowed to the view that the Averys would be casualties of that warfare, warfare being an extremely prevalent theme within the *Book of Mormon*. Our brethren and forefathers had valiantly fought to preserve the record and we were called to do likewise at all costs. The mighty men of the *Book of Mormon* are not only the main prophetic characters within the text, but also the chief captains of the righteous armies.

> "Now it was the custom among all the Nephites, to appoint for their chief captains, save it were in their times of wickedness, someone that had the spirit of revelation, and also prophecy; therefore this Gidgiddoni was a great prophet among them, and also was the chief judge." (3 Nephi 2:24)

Even as the book begins, it is being recorded by a man named Nephi who, though young at the time, fits an image that remains consistent throughout each account. "And it came to pass that I, Nephi, being exceeding young, nevertheless being large in stature, and also having great desires to know of the mysteries of God" (1 Nephi 1:47). Chiastically, the statement of his being large in stature would quite immediately fall opposite his great desires to know the mysteries of God. Therefore, the interpretation provided would define men of God as being physically capable of warfare, along with hearts full of desire to know God. What a shame, the beauty of Jeremiah 31:34 was so incredibly opaque to us. Provided for in the Bible is a historical purpose which prepared the way for a new and better covenant (Hebrews 8:6). The *Book of Mormon* claims this covenant all along. Its primary message is to preserve the record since the wicked Lamanites were out to destroy it. I have to restrain myself from going into detail on this issue, because it is an exhaustive principle throughout the entire text, which even the most inept of students should be able to recognize. Yet this is not a principle that is in harmony with Christianity, despite the *Book of Mormon's* claim to be the words of Christ throughout its message.

The beauty of the Bible message is that it provides a means for each of us, individually, to establish a relationship with God and to communicate with Him through our Mediator, Christ Jesus. But the "plainness" boasted about in *Book of Mormon* writings seeks to elaborate and to provide explanations for issues which require individual revelation, thereby stealing away our opportunity for a personal relationship with our personal Savior, while subjecting us to the interpretations provided. Forming the perceptions of the devotee, these interpretations prohibit him from establishing his own view of God through the workings of the Holy Spirit. Within the Bible are a number of vague areas that give little detail. What does it mean that Enoch was taken away by God (Genesis 5:24), or that he was translated (Hebrews 11:5)? Why did Moses' face shine, and what does that mean to us today (Exodus 34:35 and 2 Corinthians 3:13)? What is the book of Jashar mentioned in Joshua 10:13, and what does it contain? These are questions a true believer might ask—and questions which crafty, surreptitious people provide answers to.

Doctrine and Covenants 36 (and *Inspired Version*, Genesis 7:1–78) is an account by Joseph Smith to explain the unwritten history of this man named Enoch. The *Book of Mormon* elaborates upon the miracle of one's face shining, as Moses' did, and gives hint that it is to be expected of us as well.

> "And it came to pass that he turned him about, and behold, he saw through the cloud of darkness the faces of Nephi and Lehi; and behold, they did shine exceedingly, even as the faces of angels." (Helaman 2:100)

> "And it came to pass that Jesus beheld them, as they did pray unto him, and his countenance did smile upon them, and behold they were as white as the countenance, and also the garments of Jesus; And behold the whiteness thereof did exceed all the whiteness, yea, even there could be nothing upon earth so white as the whiteness thereof." (3 Nephi 9:25–26)

If these passages are believed as scripture, then they aid in interpreting the Biblical passages that are similar, yet not so detailed (i.e., Numbers 6:22–27). Compare the passage previously quoted from Helaman with following verse from Acts. "And all that sat in the counsel, looking steadfastly on him, saw his face as if it had been the face of an angel" (Acts 6:15). Perhaps the angelic face of Steven that day was as the account the *Book of Mormon* portrays as the two men in Helaman, or perhaps there's no correlation between the two. Driving forces that form our view of God often interpret His word for us in subtle ways which we sometimes fail to recognize. But such elaborate explanations develop not only a questionable and distorted view of God, but progressively build a dependency within the disciple for doctrines that provide an interpretation of God's scripture. *Doctrine and Covenants* section 22, much like section 36, provides additional detail about Moses' relationship with God. This allows the point of view that those who perceive themselves as righteous have access to privileged information the rest of the world does not have. Soon it becomes a small wonder that one would see all other churches as an "abomination in His sight."

The book of Jashar is one of several books either mentioned or quoted from in the Bible, but that are not a part of it. To my knowledge, Joseph Smith never built upon this particular mystery of the Bible. However, I've come to know instances where this book of poetry has been used, despite the evidence from researchers indicating that it no longer exists.[7] I mention it only as an example of what false prophets use as an open door for deception. With Joseph Smith's fascination and association with the occult, I'm surprised he did not make use of more fabrications. Isolation and separation are important in creating untrue perceptions of God, and thereby reality as well. By way of this perception, with war raging about us at every turn, it was the eventual culmination of these teachings which demanded the deaths of the Averys.

---

[7] New Bible Dictionary, 2nd Edition, Tyndale, p.552

A precept Jeff had taught and embellished upon from time to time was the issue of "delighting" in warfare. The Nephites were said to not delight in it, while the Lamanites were recorded as those who did delight in war. In this scenario, the term was interpreted to literally mean delight. But before Jeff introduced this to us, a series of classes had to be taught on the process of redemption, to feel and see, and becoming a fair people. Apparently Joseph Smith intended to exploit the racial distinctions to accommodate his agenda for this great and marvelous work. The *Book of Mormon* Nephites, considered righteous people, were of fair skin color. The Lamanites were cursed with apparently unnatural darker skin.

Whatever racial views Jeff had, he did not expound on them in what he taught. In fact, he would comment on how ridiculous it was for anyone to consider themselves as white in light of what he had claimed to have seen, by viewing Christ and others of His angels. In other words, the variations of pigment that we see as racial divisions were basically nonexistent when compared to the "glory which shall be revealed in us" (Romans 8:18). He considered this a great burden; he had seen what he was to be, yet could not acquire it due to us (his brethren), who were not ready to be redeemed. While in West Virginia, Alice mentioned in class one night how she had seen Jeff's face shine when they were, appropriately, away from us. This was told to us as yet another substantiation that all was well with Jeff—it was we who kept him from dwelling with God. It was never stated that a redeemed person be always aglow, but that our spiritual eyes would be equally transformed to enable a degree of perception.

> "Now, for this cause, I know that man is nothing, which thing I never had supposed; but now mine eyes have beheld God; but not mine natural but my spiritual eyes, for mine natural eyes could not have beheld, for I should have withered and died in his presence; but his glory was upon me, and I beheld his face, for I was transfigured before him." (D&C 22:7b&c)

The fair ones were primarily considered to be the righteous Nephites. When the Lamanites were converted from the wicked traditions of their fathers, they too, were a "fair and delightsome" people. Mormon laments the depravity of his people near the close of the book as they become steeped in wickedness, after having known such righteousness.

> "And my soul was rent with anguish, because of the slain of my people, and I cried, O ye fair ones, how could ye have departed from the ways of the Lord! O ye fair ones, how could ye have rejected that Jesus, who stood with open arms to receive you! Behold, if ye had not done this, ye would not have fallen. But behold, ye are fallen, and I mourn your loss. O ye fair sons and daughters, ye fathers and mothers, ye husbands and wives, ye fair ones, how is it that ye could have fallen." (Mormon 3:18–20)

Chapter 8 PREPARATIONS FOR WAR

This was not to have been unlike the fallen countenance of Cain, as mentioned in Genesis. "But unto Cain and to his offering he had not respect. And Cain was very wroth, and his countenance fell" (Gen. 4:5; 5:8, *Inspired Version*). We were to be God's fair ones, having been redeemed from our fallen state. It's clearly a ridiculous play on words, but we were to hold fast to the light which we, as dark vessels, would receive. We were not to allow that light to be lost in warfare (to de-light).

> "Now they were sorry to take up arms against the Lamanites, because they did not delight in the shedding of blood; yea, and this was not all; they were sorry to be the means of sending so many of their brethren out of this world into an eternal world unprepared to meet their God." (Alma 21:146)

The task would not be an enjoyable one, but rather an affliction that must be endured. To delight in warfare would mean that our desire would no longer be toward God and His will, but that we would be filled with desire for our own will instead. The same would hold true for love. Even during battle, love was strongly resident within God's mighty men. The epitome of such love is expressed in the 15th chapter of Alma, verses 32–34, where a faction of newly converted Lamanites were no longer able to go to war, due to their extreme compassion and willingness to die rather than cause the death of their enemy (how fortunate that was an option for them).

Even so, this area speaks quite differently when interpreted through the use of chiasmus. War raged about us at every turn. The enemy was out there seeking every opportunity to destroy us and thereby to destroy the holy record as well. Whether or not it is perceived as such, this is the same passion at work in most Mormons today as they tenaciously hold fast to their "rod of iron" against all persecution and all evidence. The seer was able to bring forth the sealed portion, which was the essential purpose behind all God's word. Without revealing this, there was no hope for mankind and all would perish at the glorious return of Jesus. We were His chosen, but not because we were so righteous. We were daily humiliated by Jeff's exposure of our sin, thereby clearly expressing that we were not chosen due to our extreme worthiness, but possibly the complete opposite.

When we were later presented to the world as monstrous demons, with promises that we would fry in the electric chair, it only helped enhance the identity and shame Jeff had so meticulously created regarding us. We had fallen the farthest, and therefore would be lifted up to the heights of His Holy Mountain as an example of His undaunted ability to cleanse away all sin. But in this warfare there would be casualties. Eventually, the division came where it was taught: "And it came to pass that there were ten more who did fall by the sword."

Chapter 9

THE COVENANT

The summer passed, along with the fall of 1988. We did not put up Christmas trees, because there was the extreme necessity to shed all "traditions of our fathers." Nevertheless, expected to be a fun time for the children, Christmas presents were bought without a great deal of emphasis on the reason. Most Christians today will probably agree that the whole holiday season is overly commercialized. However, despite all the hustle and bustle, despite the throng of the merchants to direct the flow of our attention toward the items they wished us to buy, and despite the fervent fear, or even hatred, that in some small way a courthouse or schoolyard might audaciously display a hint of the religious theme of this celebration, there was still a magic about the season. This magic seemed to touch the most depraved of hearts—even my own.

Susie and I had been giving Jeff by far the bulk of any money we had beyond what we needed for rent and utilities. This left very little for the presents I so much wanted to purchase for Matthew and Amy. But we were giving them a far more valuable gift, right? We were preparing not only for them, but also for all children, a way to have true happiness.

> "Thus saith the Lord; I am returned unto Zion, and will dwell in the midst of Jerusalem: and Jerusalem shall be called a city of truth; and the mountain of the Lord of Hosts the holy mountain. Thus saith the Lord of Hosts; there shall yet old men and old women dwell in the streets of Jerusalem, and every man with his staff in his hand for very age. And the streets of the city shall be full of boys and girls playing in the streets thereof." (Zechariah 8:3–5)

Since Mormon doctrines teach of a New Jerusalem that is to be built on the North American continent, these passages spoke to us. We were to come into the presence of the Lord, become redeemed, and thereby receive the endowment of power from on high.

> "Wherefore, for this cause I gave unto you the commandment, that you should go to the Ohio; and there I will give unto you my law; and there you shall be endowed with power from on high, and from thence, whosoever I will, shall go forth among all nations, and it shall be told them what they shall do." (D&C 38:7b–c)

The power from on high would first be received by going on high. As Zechariah described it, a "holy mountain" would be raised up, thrusting God's house (the Kirtland Temple) into the heavens. We were to sacrifice our own wants and desires in order to perform the will of God. It bothered me as I saw the quality of gifts that Jeff and Alice gave their own children, no doubt purchased with the same money with which I could have purchased better gifts for my children. Yet I repented of these sinful frustrations and my mind reflected on the frequently reinforced issue of how Jeff's family suffered many afflictions, strictly due to who he was, and the hardships it caused. I can't include Damon as a beneficiary of such blessings I saw bestowed upon the three younger Lundgren children. Damon was treated somewhat as an outcast by his father, yet ever so diligently and fearfully sought to please him.

With the restoring of Zion, a place of plenty and a place of safety for children, it would be a place where the streets would be "full of boys and girls playing," with no more starvation and no more war. Why is it that war always appears to be the only viable method for establishing peace? Could it be that the same fervency that strives for peace and tranquility creates the opposite when attempting to achieve the same things for others? One thing I've learned is that, while I can do nothing to offer peace to others, if it is resident within my life, I can bestow to those around me, by example. It's a distortion of God's plan to allow ourselves to be coerced into peaceful intentions, because these coercions, however mild, will add anxiety to our efforts of peace. We had a mission to perform and it required our all. It became a small thing that we would not be able to buy nicer presents for our two children that year. The sacrifice of these desires would place us closer to our goal, or so we thought. In actuality, it only placed us closer to more sacrifice, of ourselves and of others.

I slowly, yet clearly, became a monster during this quest to establish peace. During my court trial, a neighbor who'd lived in the apartment next to us testified of a particular conversation we had. I still recall the conversation, along with the energy that was raging within me at the time. As I spoke to her briefly about the bringing forth of sacred records and a sword which would soon be brought forth, she said she'd seen my eyes turn black and the sight scared her. She and her husband were kind to us upon our arrival in Ohio. They also offered friendship to my wife at times, as Susie would often be homesick to return to Missouri. She did well at concealing the fact from me as I can recall no indication to which she expressed this once we became settled. But establishing barriers that hinder communication is what makes settings we were experiencing so effective. Apparently, there was far less communication between us than I was aware of. As we became more involved with classes, chores, and projects, we lost touch with the friendship these kind neighbors offered. I was seldom home. I was dedicated to the cause. I became a "soldier in God's army."

Jeff would go into detail at times about the carnage that would be a part of my warfare. This created nightmares that would awaken me. Full of anxiety from the dreams, yet also shame for having so sinfully been disturbed by them I repented of these inhibitions (de-lighting). I knew that I could never come to enjoy such horror, but it was essential that I learn not to balk from it. Most of us were gradually exposed to a more violent perspective of our future, both through teachings and also entertainment. Movies that I would never have watched became "necessary" for the shock value. One movie that Jeff quite literally worshipped was *Highlander*. Jeff watched it at least fifty times, by his own estimation, and personally identified with the main character, Nash. Jeff wanted to lead me into it rather than have me watch it without proper indoctrination, possibly rejecting it as nonsense. Apparently suitably deluded at some point, we were invited to watch it. We didn't have a VCR, so we went to the farm. Represented as quite an occasion, he and Alice felt the specific need to guide us personally through the parallels between the movie and their lives. Alice became very emotional at various points, especially when Nash had to battle the wicked Kergin. I know now however, that Alice didn't then believe Jeff was the seer, let alone the character in this movie, as a portrayal of the task Jeff was to face. The movie took on the appearance of some kind of message to the world and that the main character was real—Jeff *was* Nash.

Jeff is more than just a liar and a deceptive con man. He is those things too, but he's also quite deluded. He expended too much effort in things with no real deceptive value if you think that he really didn't believe it himself, at least a little. In my naïve mentality, I could see no reason why anyone would lie about such an issue with no apparent benefit. Yet it would prove to be a benefit to him at a later date on our journey into the wilderness. Perhaps by now he has to know that he's only a liar with a gifted imagination. I'm certain even this knowledge is densely shrouded within his own blackened soul.

* * *

AS JEFF'S ASSIGNED WORKOUT PARTNER, I had a more continuous exposure to him. He began introducing heavy metal music at our workouts, under the premise that "they were the enemy" and we should "know our enemy." Music does not have the same effect on all people, but it has always had a profound effect on me. Susie and I had a collection of contemporary gospel tapes and they gave our hearts a lift. These were taken away and needed to be repented of. He didn't just walk into the house and take them away. Persons such as he find far more pleasure, and success, in subtly getting the follower to do such things on their own. These tapes were supposedly particularly evil because they professed to speak of God, wherein the other music blatantly defied Him. Therefore, Jeff's sewer logic expressed that the blatantly ungodly could be used as a source of education, whereas the more latent evil was something which we were to be protected from. My poems had been placed in this same category about a year and a half earlier.

I was to look for any discarded metal at work that could be fastened to a chain or club, thereby forming a mace. The savagery became terrible, creating images within my own mind about the necessity to get it right. My mind had become locked into the cause of Zion, and I desperately feared the loss of my own family and friends. In the *Book of Mormon*, there is an account about Jared asking his brother, the holy man (no name is ever given to him, always referred to simply as "the brother of Jared") to go before the Lord and plead that they be able to take family members with them into the wilderness. Mormon doctrines are full of scenarios of people uprooted from their homeland as they go into the wilderness to fulfill God's will for them. These repetitious scenarios add interpretations of necessity to Smith's followers today to do the same thing (Matthew 24:26). This story is to have taken place during the confounding of the tongues at the Tower of Babel. Jared was pleading that his brother ask God not to confound the tongues of their family members and friends.

> "And the Brother of Jared being a large and might man, and being a man highly favored of the Lord, for Jared his brother said unto him, Cry unto the Lord, that he will not confound us that we may not understand our words. And it came to pass that the Brother of Jared did cry unto the Lord, and the Lord had compassion of Jared; therefore he did not confound the language of Jared; and Jared and his brother were not confounded. Then Jared said unto his brother, Cry again unto the Lord, and it may be that he will turn away his anger from them who are our friends, that he confound not their language. And it came to pass that the Brother of Jared did cry unto the Lord, and the Lord had compassion upon their friends, and their families also, that they were not confounded." (Ether 1:8–11)

You'll notice this as one more example of how prophetic leadership is through a man who is clearly described as large in stature, a mighty man, consistent throughout the book. We were about to embark upon our own wilderness venture, and I did not want anyone to be lost. Such was not to be the case.

Jeff taught an issue which culminated one night with the Jaredites. The friends Jared requested of God to bring along with them, would later be made responsible for the fall of the people. Jeff had already determined I was to be his spokesman, a reflection of the Jaredite story. The next day while working out, Jeff stopped and told me "Don't request to bring along any friends." He went on to explain that since these were the last times, indeed, end of time, it would not be as it was with the Jaredites. We were to be wiser then they, and therefore, were to avoid the mistakes they made. This was why Jeff was the choice seer. He would avoid all the mistakes of our fathers before us. Jeff knew of my concerns for family members and friends. His instruction would be enforced not long afterward, toward members of our own immediate family and friends in Kirtland. About this same time a class was taught on the loss of ten people as endured by Mormon.

> "And when they had gone through and hewn all my people save it were twenty and four of us, …it came to pass that there were ten more who did

fall by the sword, with their ten thousand each; yea, even all my people, save it were those twenty and four who were with me." (Mormon 3:13, 16)

With the capacity for semantic manipulation through chiasmus, along with Jeff's finesse at using it, these already fictitious words were taught to indicate a loss which we too, would possibly have to undergo.

There's no way to avoid confusion on this; the author of the entire topic was "confusion" to begin with. As we became more intoxicated with such thought processes, Jeff increasingly gained power over us, which led to an even greater degree of intoxication. Counting the Averys, and our children, there were twenty-nine people among us. Numbers held great significance to us. First identified was the loss of ten people. Later revealed was that our remaining number would be twenty-four. When encamped in the wilderness area of West Virginia, Jeff would validate this reduction from ten to five, as further revelation from Isaiah. "One thousand shall flee at the rebuke of one; at the rebuke of five shall ye flee: till ye be left as a beacon upon the top of a mountain, and as an ensign on an hill" (Isaiah 30:17).

I have described how Jeff used a pre-planned process in systematically teaching these things. I hope a method of progressive prophecy is visible here, along with our foundation in previously taught RLDS issues as well. The ten who were lost to Mormon also meant the loss of ten thousand each. Yet by the loss which Jeff would endure of his own people, a thousand per each loss would be freed.

It also seemed to explain our necessity and Jeff's good judgment in fleeing Kirtland as we fulfilled God's will toward the raising of His holy mountain. By the fulfillment of His will, and the denial of our own, we would be established as an ensign to all nations as a means of peace and refuge. Surely the reader will find it difficult, if not impossible, to see how such illusionary control could ever be established. But reflect upon a movie which at one time brought a tear to your eye or a fictitious character who toys with our emotions, ultimately developing into a loyal friend as he points toward the sky in a need to "phone home." Dormant passions of the past somehow come to life by memories from reflections on the screen. But the characters in movies are not real.

The greeting card company whose commercial grips our heart by triggering memories of our own life experiences, if it were not effective, would not have paid the enormous amounts of money spent to air its 30-second commercial during the Super Bowl to an estimated billion viewers. These powers of suggestion, which make movie writers famous, are quite similar to the type of stimulation used by Jeff. Movies and the power of suggestion were used in a literal way, to desensitize us from our previous moral codes. But in a far more effective and less literal way, he used the same suggestive powers to create a new perception of reality by way of what we already believed to be true—Mormon doctrines. Instead of seeing the tearful tragedy of lives lost in a movie which we knew to be not real, therefore having a short-term effect, we would be exposed to revelations about ourselves through God's word, which we believed was not only real, but told was the Essence Of All Truth. Jeff utilized the same principal as entertainment does in the way and degree to which it plays with our emotions—except his principles were not fictitiously applied for entertainment.

His teachings, each one paramount within the sphere of its separate purposes, finally culminated once again to a pinnacle precept called the "Blood Covenant." This covenant basically covered all other teachings and took on the identity of the Law of Moses. The covenant was the law. Under this guise, it was a reparative ordinance. We were to be the servants called to reclaim the vineyard which had been lost, according to the parable of *D&C* section 98:6–8. Even so, the covenant was not entirely isolated to that specific purpose. It was not a ritual as illustrated by human sacrifice of the Aztecs and other cultures, yet was equally a very necessary performance. War itself would probably be the most clear definition as to what the covenant was all about, in that it entailed the authoritative shedding of blood in order to prune the vineyard. It was a cleansing. What we were taught generally came from the *Book of Mormon*, thereby creating imagery more closely associated with that story than with the Bible, yet biblical passages were also used. Eventually everything was interpreted by the vineyard principle.

Some biblical accounts that point to similar purposes are the Israelites who were twice led to the Jordan River. Due to their failure to cross over the river and enter into the Promised Land they were destined to forty years of wandering in the wilderness, and the subsequent death of that generation. The command had been given; they were shown the land promised to them. They were to take it and this meant war—it meant shedding blood. When the next generation was brought back to the river they crossed over, the following, from the book of Joshua, is what occurred at the first encounter in the Israelite's new homeland. "And they utterly destroyed all that was in the city, both man and woman, young and old, and ox, and sheep, and ass, with the edge of the sword" (Joshua 6:21). This wasn't merely the act of moving into a city and taking up residence, it was the utter replacement of a nation and culture. Such an act of complete annihilation followed by restoration of a new people is also spoken of in the account of Noah. Notice God's response.

> "The Lord smelled the pleasing aroma and said in his heart: Never again will I curse the ground because of man, even though every inclination of his heart is evil from childhood. And never again will I destroy all living creatures as I have done." (Genesis 8:21, NIV)

I had no correct view of the Biblical message, having always been interpreted through the false lens of Mormonism. "But as the days of Noe were, so shall also the coming of the Son of man be" (Matthew 24:37). We were unable to see this passage from Matthew by the principle taught in the Biblical message. We saw it and others through the destruction prophesied through Mormon teachings. Once again, interpretation came through the perceptions provided

Chapter 9 THE COVENANT

by a false belief. I have discovered that the Bible gives us much to work with when it comes to the false prophet's agenda and his distortions of God's truth.

Samuel the prophet was another example of a holy man within this context of cleansing. "Now go and smite Amalek, and utterly destroy all that they have, and spare them not: but slay both man and woman, infant and suckling, ox and sheep, camel and ass" (1 Samuel 15:3). Saul was more than seriously chastised for not carrying out the command to annihilate the Amalekite nation. Then Samuel carried out his duty by following the given command as applied to Agag. "And Samuel said, as the sword has made women childless, so shall thy mother be childless among women. And Samuel hewed Agag in pieces before the Lord in Gilgal" (1 Samuel 15:33). Once again, these teachings provide examples toward a spiritual warfare. However, integration of Old and New Testament teachings made this type of warfare not only applicable, but demanded of us. Obviously, such teachings as provided in the 10th chapters of both First and Second Corinthians were stealthily avoided by Jeff. "These things happened to them as examples and were written down as warnings for us, on whom the fulfillment of the ages has come" (1 Corinthians 10:11 NIV). "For though we walk in the flesh we do not war after the flesh" (2 Corinthians 10:3).

Aside from Jeff's scrutiny of various satellite passages applied to add witness to the existence of his covenant, there was the covenant itself. This covenant came from the book of Genesis in Joseph Smith's *Inspired Version* of the Bible. In this translation, there were many additions to what is recorded in the authorized King James Version. The King James translation is the *Inspired Version*'s main body of writing, yet Joseph Smith felt inspired to make no small amount of changes and additions. The book of Genesis houses a large quantity of these modifications such as the account of Enoch, previously mentioned (Genesis 7:1–78) and Adam's redemption, complete with water baptism (Genesis 6:67). The ninth chapter of Genesis in either translation speaks of God's covenant with earth and/or with man, but Smith, through the *Inspired Version* provides more detail. The common elements of either version, however, would have worked appropriately for Jeff's intentions.

The divisions applied to this chapter portray a covenant that requires the blood of man. There is a principle that man is a twofold creature, spiritual man and carnal man. A passage in the book of Ecclesiastes identifies what we are without spiritual man.

> "I said in mine heart concerning the estate of the sons of men, that God might manifest them, and that they might see that they themselves are beasts. For that which befalleth the sons of men befalleth beasts; even one thing befalleth them: as the one dieth, so dieth the other; yea, they have all one breath; so that a man hath no preeminence above a beast: for all is vanity." (Ecclesiastes 3:18–19)

There are two breaths spoken of in the Bible, one within us and one received through the nostrils. We are to avoid those whose sole breath is in their nostrils. "Cease ye from man, whose breath is in his nostrils: for wherein is he to be accounted of" (Isaiah 2:22).

Though I feel very blessed in that the Holy Spirit so beautifully reveals God's word to me, it is not the view of God I once had. Unfortunately, there is a degree of truth to the principles Jeff taught. The wicked were identified as beasts, and beasts were to be slain for meat. Meat took on a different definition in this application. Jeff referred to it as wood for the fire rather than as an item for food. Mankind had been previously identified as trees wherein this message from Jeremiah took on supporting imagery. "Wherefore thus saith the Lord God of hosts, because ye speak this word, behold, I will make my words in thy mouth fire, and this people wood, and it shall devour them" (Jeremiah 5:14). Passages like Deuteronomy 20:19–20 were bypassed during this segment of Jeff's instruction. War was a means of cleansing away iniquity while simultaneously establishing righteous dominance. Much like the Israelites at the river Jordan, we were not desirous of the task that lay ahead, but harbored beyond a shadow of a doubt, convictions of the ramifications of denying God's command. There was no turning back for me. I had already endured tremendous guilt in that my sin had caused millions of men, women and children to perish.

Jeff would later set aside his oldest son Damon, Greg, and me as his "three witnesses" as mirrored in Ether 2:3, (*Book of Mormon*). But at this time, Greg and I had been identified as his two witnesses, or anointed ones as in Revelation 11:3 and Zechariah 4:14. The reference in Zechariah would later be fulfilled by Jeff's chiastic translation identifying Jeff as the God of this earth—not of all things, but of this earth, for dominion. By interpretation of 2 Corinthians 4:4, I would have to agree, "In whom the god of this world hath blinded the minds of them which believe not...."

I was named Jeshurun at one point, yet this name also identified me to be Israel by name, as used in Isaiah 43.

> "But now thus saith the Lord that created thee, O Jacob, and he that formed thee, O Israel, Fear not: for I have redeemed thee, I have called thee by thy name; thou art mine...For I am the Lord thy God, the Holy One of Israel, thy Saviour: I gave Egypt for thy ransom, Ethiopia and Seba for thee." (Isaiah 43:1,3)

Because of the names Jeff assigned us, he taught that all the destruction that had occurred in those regions was our fault (Greg's and mine). Even the ten plagues that Egypt endured by their rejection of Moses' plea for his people were deemed our fault; it was due to our sin that God hardened Pharaoh's heart as a means to vent His (God's) wrath. This had a profound effect on me. From an early age I'd had a fervent desire to serve God and now it appeared that my failures along the way had created catastrophic ramifications throughout history. Everything being present to God, therefore, issues of centuries ago were being dealt with by our sinfulness now, broaching all time. All that those

Chapter 9 THE COVENANT

people suffered paid the price as a ransom for me. God had to vent His wrath toward them rather than consume me, since He had chosen me to serve Him at this final hour. I had been a peaceful man with no desire to dominate nor harm, yet this apparently had infuriated God. Peace was not what I had been called to, at least not yet. As stated in Matthew 10:34, I had been called to be a warrior. These words of Jesus, as recorded in Matthew, speak a purposeful message concerning our convictions to serve God, but the god Jeff taught had a warring and destructive agenda, to be enacted in the most physical way. I did not affectionately embrace this god, but Jeff had reconstructed our perception of God to be able to see his god in this distorted manner.

Much later, when others and myself left the group, we still had an issue of denying God (the unpardonable sin) as an apostate action of not being able to go on. I was beginning to have doubts, but was still a long way from any degree of certainty that Jeff was not who he claimed to be. I just couldn't continue. It got to the point where the desire to serve had been drained away and the repugnance of continuing on had come to outweigh the fear of leaving. In this frame of mind, abstaining from suicide can be a battle.

The covenant was to end massive, widespread destructions, both past and those yet to come, and establish God's judgment on earth. The seer would be able to judge the people, thereby enacting a peculiar sense of mercy.

> "Now this is the state of the souls of the wicked; yea, in darkness, and a state of awful, fearful, looking for, of the fiery indignation of the wrath of God upon them; thus they remain in this state, as well as the righteous in paradise, until the time of their resurrection." (Alma 19:47)

I've stated my opinion of Mormon doctrines, but equally, I hope, have conveyed that the process of chiasmus grossly misinterpreted the words therein. Such is the case with the passage just quoted. However, the result of the teachings from Jeff's divisions of that chapter created the view that the souls of the wicked were in an actual state of misery as they anticipated their coming destruction.

Sometimes the anticipation of an event, whether pleasant or unpleasant, can far exceed whatever pain or pleasure is experienced by the actual occurrence. The divisions Jeff used to teach this principle conveyed it to be an act of mercy to end the anticipation of fear and anguish and allow the person to become extinct (Job 17:1).

> "Thus saith the Lord, which maketh a way in the sea, and a path in the mighty waters; Which bringeth forth the chariot and the horse, the army and the power; they shall lie down together, they shall not rise: they are extinct, they are quenched as tow. Remember ye not the former things, neither consider the things of old." (Isaiah 43:16–18)

This was not only an act of war, it was a simile of the pulling down of great powers.

* * *

THE BARN IN WHICH THE AVERYS WERE KILLED IS RED, and the area within it where they were killed was usually under water. Passages like "digging a pit for one's neighbor" (Proverbs 26:27) to be assured, was taught in order to box us in on every side so that we had no escape from fulfilling God's command. This is now so clearly ridiculous, yet also illustrates how irrational and intoxicated we had become. The barn and flooded area became known as the Red Sea. Pharaoh's army, representative of the powers that were to be subdued by this "strange act," was to be led into the Red Sea—which restoration of God's dominion upon earth would be established, through Jeff.

> "And your covenant with death shall be disannulled, and your agreement with hell shall not stand; when the overflowing scourge shall pass through, then ye shall be trodden down by it...For the Lord shall rise up as in mount Perazim, he shall be wroth as in the valley of Gibeon, that he may do his work, his strange work; and bring to pass his act, his strange act."
> (Isaiah 28:18, 21)

By the performance of the covenant, the wicked would be placed before the judgment seat of God, thereby increasing the rage of His fury, no differently than Nebuchadnezzar's furnace was increased in temperature seven times hotter, due to his anger (Daniel 3:19). This act was to be done for two reasons; first, to cleanse the earth from unrighteousness, and second to test or try God's chosen servants. Passages like Isaiah 43:2, "when thou walkest through the fire, thou shall not be burned; neither shall the flame kindle upon thee" and Hebrews 11:34 "[they] quenched the violence of fire, escaped the edge of the sword, out of weakness were made strong..." were interpreted not as examples of God's salvation through various chosen vessels throughout history, but as required acts of faith done in order to be approved of God.

Consider these verses from Genesis, chapter 14 of Joseph Smith's *Inspired Version*.

> "Now Melchizedek was a man of faith, who wrought righteousness; and when a child he feared God, and stopped the mouths of lions, quenched the violence of fire. And thus, having been approved of God, he was ordained an high priest after the covenant which God made with Enoch."
> (Genesis 14:26–27, *Inspired Version*)

From this version, these things were not done to glorify God, merely by our faith toward Him at times of extreme opposition; they were required by God in order to be approved of Him, which again negates the true beauty of His grace, while reaffirming the already dominating belief of a works oriented salvation. We had to show ourselves approved by "rightly dividing the word of truth" (chiastically) therefore, revealing God's esoteric covenant. We had to endure the wrath of His fire, by way of the concise instruction given to us through His Choice Seer. It was not really a ritual as much as it was an act of war that had to begin in Jeff's own household.

> "And to the others he said in mine hearing, Go ye after him through the city, and smite: let not your eye spare, neither have ye pity [i.e., don't 'de-light']: Slay utterly old and young, both maids, and little children, and women: but come not upon any man whom is the mark; and begin at my sanctuary. Then they began at the ancient men which were before the house. And he said unto them, Defile the house, and fill the courts with the slain: go ye forth. And they went forth, and slew in the city." (Ezekiel 9:5–7)

The Kirtland Temple was to have been the standing example of chiasmus as the pattern of God standing in our midst. Jeff thought, as the choice seer, he had the express mission of revealing this pattern. We, as his servants, were his children or members of his household. Therefore, we were children of the pattern, or reared up by way of the pattern. When we look up the word pattern recorded in Exodus and used in the passages to describe the tabernacle Moses built, we find that God showed Moses a pattern on the mount by which to build. The New Testament author of Hebrews speaks of this as well. "Who serve unto the example and shadow of heavenly things, as Moses was admonished of God when he was about to make the tabernacle: for, See, saith he, that thou make all things according to the pattern shown to thee in the mount" (Hebrews 8:5). By Hebrew definition in the Old Testament, "pattern" can mean "to build a structure" or "to obtain children."[8] We were taught that the pattern or chiasmus is the manner *through which* a structure is built and *through which* children are obtained. In a tragic sense this is true, in that we became Jeff's children by way of the subjugating structure of belief with which we were encapsulated. The war was to begin at the house (or temple, Ezekiel 9:6) which was defined as Jeff's household by way of the pattern, of which we were family members. Mormon lost ten who were a part of his people from his household. Jeff was to restore all things as another Elijah, and he would have to do so by way of the covenant. The covenant was war and the war had to begin with the seer's own household. "And a man's foes shall be they of his own household" (Matthew 10:36, Jesus quoting from Micah 7:6). What defined a man was also heavily taught, which added to whose household this would be referring. Jesus had Judas. Therefore, Jeff was to have had a Judas, of sorts, to deal with as well. To my utter shame, I must confess that the only person within the group who even remotely resembles that character was me. I was the Judas Goat, to betray the trust of innocence and lead stray sheep to the slaughter.

---

[8] James Strong, *New Strong's Exhaustive Concordance of the Bible*, (Nashville: Thomas Nelson, 1984), Hebrew/Chaldee Dictionary p.22, definition 1129, and p.122, definition 8403.

Chapter 10

A NIGHTMARE

Our ignorance of the law of Moses, as well as the tabernacle he built, was shamefully apparent. There are many references to commands and the law, yet little on what that law and those commands actually were. After my arrest and when I was able to begin studying again, I had a very strong desire to know what this Law was that Christ fulfilled. Luke 24:44–45 became a precious passage to me, as I began to see for the first time what the Biblical message really is.

Keith and Kathy Johnson were the last to move to Ohio. They responded quickly to so very much, but there was quite a powerful dynamic at work within the group by then. Keith was actually contacted by Jeff and invited to visit, even providing his airfare. Keith was at the farm only hours on the visit, yet the persuasive influence of Jeff and his use of chiasmus, along with our sure conviction, convinced Keith to move. Our convictions were surely an influence that affected him, yet his speedy acceptance of the things he was told at that time worked as a further confirmation within us as well. It was taken by us as first-hand evidence that people could be taught, and repent, and that perhaps there was yet hope against the coming destruction we all saw hanging over us. Keith was not merely sold on the issue of chiasmus as the pattern of God that day. He had been taught, through division, what Jeff had only recently taught us concerning the covenant. Keith's immediate embrace of such "strong meat" doctrine was amazing to me. Though sad and unfortunate, it's very clear to me now how the delusion was reciprocal between us, as we affected one another. As Keith returned home, leaving the influence present at the farm, the challenge was upon him to maintain the momentum of those convictions while in Missouri preparing to move.

My recollection of being confronted with the possibility of moving to Ohio was that each mile away from Kirtland seemed to be an awakening from a dream. By the time we returned to Missouri, I was drained of any feeling about the matter and could hold only to the memory of the conviction I felt while there. I assume that similar thoughts and confusion were associated with Keith's experience. Jeff became impatient for the Johnsons to complete their move to Ohio. Perhaps this was due to how freely he had shared his doctrine with Keith at his visit. It was a bit of a testing time for Jeff too, as he had given Keith much to deal with and now it was time to see if he would respond or reject it. It must have appeared to Jeff that the Johnsons were dragging their feet a little about moving, as they were trying to sell off livestock and other items in order to pay off debts from their Missouri farm. Jeff didn't care about their debts and saw this as early signs of "rebellion." He sent Greg and me (his two anointed ones) to Missouri on our first "gathering" mission. He equipped us with a few divisions to show them and instructions to expedite their arrival to Ohio. We were rehearsed so as not to waver in our presentation to Keith and Kathy. As with any interactions we found ourselves involved in at this point, we had explicit instruction what we were and were not to discuss. The covenant was an area we were to cover, somewhat more for Kathy's benefit, since she had not come to Ohio on Keith's first visit.

In that timeframe, Susie and I also made a trip back to Missouri. Jeff had taught some classes on being able to see the enemy a long way off (Jeremiah 5:15) and interpreted this to mean the necessity of a long-range rifle. After all, "the words of Christ will tell you all things." And with that thought ever firmly implanted in our thinking, such instruction became the norm for us. An ATV and two horses were purchased. Susie comes from a family of very talented craftsmen and artists. One of her brothers made a fifty-caliber rifle before our move to Ohio. I'd only seen the gun briefly, but remembered it when Jeff began his quest to find one. In mentioning it to him, he instructed me to contact Susie's brother for information about the gun and the possibility of buying it. Eventually, he and Jeff talked. With an agreement made, Jeff allowed Susie and me to get it. Jeff wanted me to go alone, yet realized how peculiar this would seem to Susie's family. It was also clear that we could not go such a distance as that and not at least visit with her parents who lived on the way. Therefore, Jeff decided that Susie would go with me, but that we would not take our children. The explanation we were to give as to why we didn't bring the kids was that we should take Greg's car, a small two-passenger Honda for reasons of needing to save money on gas. Obviously, it was threatening to Jeff that we might take our children with us on the trip and perhaps not return. We hadn't seen Susie's family for at least eighteen months. Her mother was a very strong supporter of our purpose in Ohio, but it was clearly Susie's father who kept them from moving at the time we did. Such a move on faith by RLDS members was not at all considered as abnormal, even before our move to Ohio. An essential aspect of Mormon doctrine entails the eventual necessity for all the saints to gather to Zion anyway. We simply believed that Zion would be built in Ohio rather than in Independence, Missouri.

Back at the Johnson home, we found very little time to cover the areas Jeff had sent us to emphasize. They were so busy trying to get things in order for moving that we found only a brief time to talk.

Shortly after the Johnson's arrival in Ohio they were informed of how Dennis and Tonya Patrick were slated to die. This was particularly difficult for them as they lived with the Patricks until the time we left for the wilderness. Divide and conquer is a common strategy for destruction, and this was the basic platform Jeff maintained as well. This principle was essential to all his dealings with us in that he best kept us controlled by keeping us separate. Most of the adult members of the group understood that the Avery family were slated to die, yet I must emphasize again that it was impossible for anyone to "know" they would, and a sin even to suppose that anyone *could* know. Dennis and Tonya were taught that death was imminent, but were given little indication as to who would be the victims. They, along with Richard and Sharon, were told that the Averys would possibly die, yet nothing concerning the potential for their own deaths. The Averys made up five and the three Patricks, along with Richard and Sharon, made up the other five—the ten prophesied to be lost—and everyone else in the group was taught who those ten were to be.

This was beneficial to Jeff in that everyone was taught concerning the death which we all believed to be present in our future, yet had varying perceptions as to what that meant, and to whom it applied. The Averys were kept isolated from what was taught to the rest. They were limited as to how much class time they received yet the other five were isolated while attending all classes. After a while, Richard became concerned that he and Sharon might be slated to die. The first response was, of course, that he had sinned by supposing such a thing. But the interesting thing about it as I look at it now is how he did what he was trained to do. He "inquired" of Jeff (1 Samuel 9:9). Sharon had been given to Richard as his wife, just as Debbie had been given to Greg, and Shar had been given to Danny (prior to Shar leaving the group).

As the seer, Jeff "knew" who belonged to who in marriage ("flesh of my flesh: bone of my bone," Genesis 2:23–24) and thereby only he could properly match us up. Otherwise, we would be living an adulterous marriage, which was the explanation he would use later for taking Keith's wife, Kathy, away from him. Because Richard and Sharon were one, the judgment against them was one of unity. Even though Richard properly inquired about the matter, receiving a session for having done so, he obtained no direct answer about whether or not he was slated to die yet he and Sharon still remained at the farm. They would not know whether they would die until the night that the Averys were killed—even then, not until afterwards. But was that really the issue? Why didn't they just leave? Who could ask, let alone understand? No one had been told outright that they would die, yet not only we were all willing to accept death if it were to occur, no one did anything to prevent it. After all, by understanding the position and power of the seer and to accept that Jeff was that seer, also meant to understand that there was no place to hide where the judgment of God would not find you. There were only two of us whose deaths had been 'prophesied,' myself and Greg. Yet even in that, no specific plans were outlined of which I was ever made aware.

* * *

PREPARATIONS NEEDED TO BE MADE in order to go to the wilderness. Jeff had divided passages indicating that we were to purchase an ATV and two horses. By this time, the Johnsons had arrived and were living in the Patrick's home. Kathy, who was quite knowledgeable about horses, was assigned the task of purchasing them. Jeff found the ATV that he wanted, but Richard and I were the ones who bought it. Actually, we only obtained it on credit in the way of a loan that we never made payments on. At this point we were the Israelites preparing to leave Egypt and this required us to "spoil" Egypt on our way out to the wilderness and our communion with God. "And the Lord gave the people favour in the sight of the Egyptians, so that they lent unto them such things as they required. And they spoiled the Egyptians" (Exodus 12:36). Passages such as Psalms 37:21, "the wicked borroweth, and payeth not again..." somehow failed to come to mind. We managed to obtain a generator on credit. Slowly, we began to compile all things that were considered essential, however, this was also a time for letting go of things that were considered not to be essential. We were to depart from the world, and by way of the seer, we had God's prudent servant to prepare us in all things. Therefore, our departure would not be in "haste nor by flight," but by way of God's omniscient foresight and predestination toward us.

> "And then shall a cry go forth, Depart ye, depart ye, go ye out from thence, touch not that which is unclean; go ye out of the midst of her; be ye clean, that bear the vessels of the Lord. For ye shall not go out with haste, nor go by flight: for the Lord will go before you; and the God of Israel shall be your rearward. Behold, my servant shall deal prudently, he shall be exalted and extolled, and be very high." (3 Nephi 9:79–81, also Isaiah 52:11–13)

However, despite our preparations and 'god' as our forward, we seemed continually to be in haste and in flight from this moment on.

This was not only a departure from society, it was also a final blow to our individuality as well. Aside from the few allowable necessities assigned to us, we had nothing left to remind us of the life we once knew. Photo albums, school yearbooks, and things like my military records and discharge were all discarded. We had a full set of encyclopedias that were considered useless and had to be either sold or trashed. But this was only the beginning. Susie had a beautiful set of china that was hand painted and gold trimmed. She had antique tables that had been in her family since her grandmother's wedding two generations before, along with furniture that her father made for us as a wedding gift. I had a handmade rocking chair adorned with carved designs and brass and copper inlay that I brought home from Pakistan while in the navy. I had a number of souvenirs from those days of family separation while traveling in the navy, along with either coins or currency from each country I had visited. The list could go on and on. We had to separate ourselves from all the mementos that reminded us of where we'd been and what we'd done in life—who we were. Susie's college degree, my various diplomas of naval training, much was lost; yet the two items lost which now cause the most pain as I look back were our wedding rings. Jeff and Alice, of course, were to hang on to theirs because, as our "mediators" to the world, they would have to interact at times with the world. It would be best that they kept their rings so they would

Chapter 10 A Nightmare

look as they should in the dealings. All we had, we gave for a dream. But the dream slowly and steadily became a nightmare from which none would escape unharmed: and some would not escape alive.

* * *

THE AVERYS HAD BEEN SEVERELY WARNED MANY TIMES about what lay in their future. Jeff taught several classes where he pointed out the failures of the wicked, then correlated them to their own failures. He would state what happened to the wicked, then state what presently hung over their heads. They understood that they were being labeled and they understood that they were under threat, yet they did nothing in order to avoid it, such as staying away, or going to authorities. But, where would they go? Whose authority could they turn to for protection? These are valid questions. Dennis Avery would often inquire about matters in his home life. Effort was being made to repent, yet by Jeff's judgment they were not successful—and never would be. In our democratic society, where each person is expected to have enough information for a decision on personal matters, this may seem impossible to comprehend. But I'm acutely certain that if we don't understand these dynamics better, that we'll see "death" continue.

With a mission to perform, around the end of March or early April 1989, I quit my job at CEI. We had been called and chosen to restore Zion, the New Jerusalem. Many failures accrued between us. Millions had suffered and died because of the sinfulness and procrastination of which we were now being accused. Vivid, tangible examples were provided to illustrate our failure—the continually failing rabbitry, dying kittens, the puppy who hung itself on its leash and the deer struck by a car landing on the front lawn of the farm. Death surrounded us in every way as if to remind us of the death and suffering we had caused to millions by our sin and procrastination. The rabbitry was to provide an income for me the day I left the world's work force and began working full time at the farm. However, it never grew into anything; the rabbits continually died and the money I provided to Jeff for them was steadily spent elsewhere. But this no longer mattered. We now had to go before the Lord. I quit my only source of income, without looking back. It was time to go into the wilderness, as all our forefathers had done.

We stayed in our apartment until April 15th, then moved to the farm. What had been the utility room of the farmhouse became the Luff's new residence, our belongings by this time reduced to a mattress on the floor, our "scriptural" books, my assigned weapons, and whatever clothes we had left as appropriate for wilderness living. Fine apparel was interpreted to be sin, and identified as anything nice we had. Such would not stand up well in the nomadic lifestyle. Due to the late night hours we kept at the farm in class, and in time spent doing chores and preparations, it seemed as if we had been living there for quite some time. In actuality, Susie and I had moved there only a day or two before the deaths of the Averys.

The Avery family likewise completely emptied their house about two days prior to the night they were killed. Each family was given an area in the main room of the barn, where their belongings were gone through and organized to ensure nothing excessive was taken. I had ribbons and medals from my military service that Jeff suggested I bring along for future use, yet later humiliation over them would cause me to throw them away. Jeff and Alice had done likewise; either selling or throwing away nearly all they had. The antiques they had bought for the farmhouse (with our money) had been sold as we liquidated all our assets into cash. Credit cards were overdrawn, loans were defaulted. "Egypt" was spoiled.

The nightmare began to take form as Jeff gave instructions to some of us to dig a pit in the barn. With several scenarios of death outlined by Jeff, violence as a whole, had become paramount to the doctrine he taught. As it was narrowed down to members of his own "household," vivid imagery was again provided for the very purposes it met. This stimulus would elicit different responses in each person, ranging from fear to repugnance, or any mixture thereof. Then, of course, there was love and mercy, in that such acts were eventually identified and perceived to be acts of love and mercy toward the soul. For anyone to know what would transpire was not really possible, but I know of no one who participated in the digging of the pit that failed to understand its purpose. Even so, as Richard helped in the preparations, he understood that it could very literally be him who would fall therein. "Whoso diggeth a pit shall fall therein; and he that rolleth a stone, it will return upon him" (Proverbs 26:27). However, passages like Psalms 94 were much more picturesquely dominant within our thinking.

> "The Lord knoweth the thought of man, that they are vanity. Blessed is the man whom thou chastenest, O Lord, and teachest him out of thy law; That thou mayest give him rest from the days of adversity, until the pit be digged for the wicked." (Psalm 94:11–13)

We had moved to "the Ohio" and gone through much chastisement, now it was time to execute the Law.

Along with having few belongings left, the Averys also had no car. Arrangements had been made for them to stay at a motel for the remaining few days before our departure. Dennis Patrick also quit his job, perhaps Greg and Richard had quit theirs. The 17th of April came with no particular emphasis. We had no awareness that it would be a unique day in Jeff's agenda. I had driven the Averys from their apartment to their room in a motel, then I returned to the farm. At some later point, Richard brought the Averys to the farm where we were to eat and then have class. Because the furniture had been sold in preparation for a wilderness experience, the farmhouse was bare and we sat wherever feasible in order to eat. The meal that night was no different from countless others, prepared by one of "Jeff's children," as we were called. The setting was to be one of supper and then class. Class in the eve-

Chapter 10 A Nightmare

ning hours after the small children were laid down to sleep was a customary part of the lifestyle by that time.

During the previous few days Jeff had told me and others that the number lost would be reduced from 10 to 5 and I "hoped" (which was the closest form of prayer we had) for the number to be reduced again. There we were, twenty-nine people in all, sitting in an empty farmhouse with plans to leave the world for the wilderness. Our "rebellion" had caused many to die, so now it was time to follow god's will. In doing so, we might save souls in the long run—such extreme captivity and depravity of thought. I was asked once by a prison guard at Lucasville (Southern Ohio Correctional Facility: Ohio's maximum security prison), what it was like to be under mind control. Without hesitation, I responded by saying that it was a greater form of captivity than being in prison.

Jeff summoned Damon and other male followers, Danny, Greg, Richard and me into the downstairs bedroom and upon entering the room himself, closed the door. He was armed with a .45 caliber handgun. His possession of the gun did not seem that abnormal. Paramount in my consciousness was what he was saying. To his followers, words that Jeff spoke were taken as instruction directly from God himself. To do anything but embrace those words would have been, to Jeff, direct denial of God's will. Looking at each of us he said, "Are you in or are you out?" The response that was given by each was that we were "in." He was armed, but that was not the deciding factor to me. Aspects of coercion and duress saturated my own life. We were to be unwavering in our convictions and completely altruistic about our own will. God's will was the only will we knew and it was revealed to us piece-by-piece, line-by-line, through god's chosen seer. The full revelation of his plan was still not conveyed to us, though someone's death appeared to be imminent. I am not attempting to be deceptive as I write this, but only very mindful to convey the extremely convoluted state of affairs around us, though a great many circumstances and observations should have been clearly obvious of that night's eventual outcome. He handed me a stun gun that had been purchased previously by Greg, and told me to follow him to the barn.

Once in the barn, Jeff instructed me what he wanted done and told me to explain it to the others. I was his spokesman; his mediator for what he wanted done that night. He told me what he wanted and how we were to do it. Use of the stun gun, taping the hands and feet, each detail was to be relayed from him to me, then to the others. The stun gun was to paralyze each of the Averys and it was also intended to make them numb so they would not feel pain. No one was to experience pain or fear. This was to be an act of "mercy"—an act of "extinction." However, the effort greatly failed in that respect.

After the others were instructed as to what was expected, Jeff told me to get Dennis. I was to bring him out to the barn on the premise of assisting with sorting through the remainder of his belongings. There were two main areas to the ground level of the barn. One had a concrete floor and the other was dirt. The room with the dirt floor was where the hole had been dug. There were three windows and a large double opening door in this room, all of which had been padded with chair cushions and mattresses to silence the sound of the gun. A chainsaw was also run outside the barn by Greg, for the purpose of overriding the sound of the gunshots. The room looked hideous, completely closed in and dark with the exception of the single incandescent bulb that hung on the wall over the hole which had been dug in the corner of the room. A junk car, a washer and dryer, and other various furnishings were present, half buried amidst the trash that covered nearly the entire room several feet deep. A single passage had been cut through, leading from the interior entrance up over the heap of trash and dirt, and to the pit. This was the only entrance between this room and the area with the concrete floor. The mere sight of the room was both terrifying and sickening. Yet, as a manifestation of death and hell, it was to be expected, and we were the executioners of Judgment. The odors of the room also added to its repulsiveness. Among the distinguishable odors of the barn were the truckload of hay purchased for livestock we never obtained (another incomplete project), the smell of books that had been discarded, old clothing, and containers of perfume and talcum powder. Before the night's duties would be finished, the smell of gunpowder and blood would be introduced to these aromas to create a sickening odor which would linger in my nostrils for a long time afterward.

I have since learned how powerful conscience can be in reviving memory involving the senses. I have also learned how the grace of God, through our Savior Jesus Christ, can free us from the captivity of such sensations and trauma. As I walked with Dennis out to the barn, my mind replayed the instructions Jeff had given. When we entered the main area of the barn, I pulled the stun gun from my pocket and touched it to Dennis in the area where I was told it would be most effective, then turned it on. He jumped away and started to ask what I had done, but by this time the others were already holding him. While trying to fight as they taped his hands and feet, he cursed us and told us this "wasn't necessary." I recall how hearing those words seemed to reconfirm the conviction I already had concerning Jeff's judgment. "Surely this was a man of sin, that he would deem the instruction of god's seer as being 'unnecessary.' " It was not a malicious thought on my part, but more like an amazement that he could respond contrary to the will of god. Perhaps it would be like a prison guard, while shacking down a prisoner's cell, to wonder how the inmate could be so audacious as to complain at the throwing about of personal items. Judgment had been made, orders given, and we had a job to do.

To me, Dennis was stating that we didn't have to do that; he and his family would simply stay behind as we left for the wilderness and the mountain. Yet sometimes I've wondered if he was willing to die and that I simply didn't need to keep painfully applying that stun gun. I strongly doubt that that was the case, yet such willingness to die by Jeff's dictates had already been accepted by other members of the group, myself included. I caused Dennis a great deal of pain as I applied that stun gun over and over, foolishly hoping to paralyze him and make him numb. The only effect it had was to cause more

Chapter 10 A Nightmare

pain. His mouth was covered, but his eyes were not. It had been explained that Dennis was to be able to see Jeff. I did not carry him into the other room, as I would the remaining four. Shots were fired while Greg ran a chainsaw outside. Then it was over.

Jeff called us all into the room where the hole was. There lay Dennis. There was such an eeriness about what was happening, yet I could not allow myself to "de-light" in it. The surge of adrenaline seemed to balance out the remorse and stress. This was the work of death and there would be more of it in our future in the establishment of "righteousness." Jeff realized that he needed Dennis' keys to dispose of the Avery's bags from the motel room where they were staying. Jeff told Damon to climb into the pit and search Dennis for them, but Damon could not move. Seeing his hesitation, Jeff told me to do it and I did. I had never been that close to death before, aside from an open casket at a funeral. This was far different, and the keys were not found. Jeff went into the house and asked for them from Cheryl, who handed them over to Jeff with no questions. He then returned to the barn to see how each of us was holding up. Damon was very upset, so Jeff sent him out of the barn for a while.

I had to focus my thoughts on what we were to do and how. I recall holding back tears of my own as I told Jeff that the stun gun didn't work and that it only caused pain. I also recall how cautiously I stated this, not wanting to be guilty of the sin of "supposing of myself" especially at such an essential time of following god's command. I remember telling Richard, who'd endured many sessions with Jeff, "There's no turning back now." Previously identified as doubt, I saw that doubt was not an issue with us that night. Jeff now told me to go with him, and we walked around the barn and lawn area of the farm. I suppose he did this to ensure nothing had alarmed nearby neighbors. I also see it now as another of Jeff's attempts to provide the necessary imagery to introduce suspicions of secrecy within others of the group. Each night, leading up to this one, Jeff had told me to follow him out to the barn to check on the rabbits. I'm certain it created the suspicion in others that Jeff was planning things that only I, or whoever else he would invite, were privy to. However, much like this walk around the farm, little was ever discussed that was secret and usually we were silent with nothing being said at all. It did, however, create curiosity within the minds of the others, which had an effective purpose aside from it being a way to "try" us. The best way to know the thoughts of others is to be the source and inspiration of their thinking. Jeff mastered this principle, as our thoughts became solely a reflection of what he had given us to think.

It was now time to bring Cheryl to the barn. Jeff did not identify them as "people" on this night. He had instructed me in all things, telling me the sequence in which he wanted each person brought to the barn. This instruction having been given, he would only say, "Bring out the next one." There was no difficulty in getting any of the Avery family members to follow me; a command from Jeff was all that was needed. Cheryl walked with me across the lawn area and into the barn. I did not use the stun gun, yet somehow, she seemed to understand what was happening as the others in the barn moved toward her with the tape. She stood paralyzed and trembling as they wrapped duct tape around her ankles and wrists. It sounds so pitifully ridiculous now, but I was concerned that she might fall down and hurt herself as they taped her ankles, so I put my hand on her shoulder to steady her. She was trembling, very frightened. As gently as I could, I told her, "Just let it go." And she did. Many versions of this have erupted throughout the media coverage and judicial process, but I carefully and tearfully record here things exactly as they happened. Richard and I picked her up, carried her into the other room, and placed her in the hole. Turning and walking away, we heard the shots fired. At a later date, I repented to Jeff about this, thinking that I shouldn't have been bothered by not wanting to see it. I'm thankful now that I have so little visual memory about what happened that night. My eyes never focused on the bodies within the hole, yet my memory of searching Dennis for the keys is quite vivid.

Another walk around the farm was made, and Jeff said again. "Bring out the next one." Trina was the oldest of the Avery children; the one I was to bring. Even the sequence of this act was incredibly evil. Unless we identify ourselves with Cain (Genesis 4:7), we should feel a responsibility for our fellow man. The death of Dennis was a violation of that responsibility. Once Dennis had been killed, we became responsible for a widow among us: Not only accountable for the *way* in which she became a widow, but by our failure toward her in her own death. Thus, when Cheryl was killed, we became responsible for three "orphans." Yet we failed them too, from the oldest to the youngest. The sequence of these deaths reveals who the author of its planning really was. Trina had no idea what was happening. We had told her it was a game and she had no fear. In carrying her to the hole, the light fixture fell and the bulb broke. I knelt down next to her until it was repaired, to keep her calm and to prevent her from discovering where she was. This clearly sounds ridiculous, and it was. I'm not attempting to sugarcoat the horrible tale. I want to portray, in some clear fashion, the contradictions between the actions that were taken, and the intentions which motivated them. This was not a crime of hatred, yet intense evil was very present. We were not angry nor hateful toward the Averys, in fact, we mourned the loss of them. This was an act of "justice." Judgment had been made and we were not to question it. In the same way an executioner pulls the switch to the electric chair, his heart may tug and he may shed a tear at the loss of another human being, but justice has been served and judgment rendered. This was Jericho and we were not to waver from the task we had been commanded to perform. I heard the shot, and Trina say, "Ouch!" and start to cry, then Jeff shot again. Somehow, I felt that that sound of pain would live long in my memory—and it does.

One more walk around the farm, then once again, "Bring out the next one." Jeff was never present in the entry room to the barn. He stayed in the back room, next to the hole. I brought young Becky in, and like Trina, she was

Chapter 10 A Nightmare

at ease and happy, thinking it was a game we were playing. At first, she was able to see the horses as I had told her she would, then she stood still while the others taped her. During my trial, it would be pointed out how I failed to remember little Becky's name when making the videotaped confession to the U.S. Bureau of Alcohol, Tobacco and Firearms (ATF). It's unfortunate that such scrutiny did not also reveal that I failed to remember Danny Kraft's name, as well, whom I had just spent many months with in our day-by-day endurance of the "wilderness experience."

The last to be brought out was little Karen. If memory serves me, Karen was 7, Becky was 13 and Trina was 15. As we stepped out the back door of the farmhouse and across the yard, I reached down and picked Karen up from behind, bringing her over my head and onto my shoulders. She shrieked in laughter, then giggled. For some reason, I just wanted her to laugh. It would most likely be the last time for her to experience joy so I treated her as I would my own child. This, too, would later become twisted. The jury might have thought it more in character for me to have dragged her along kicking and screaming, but nothing about our actions that night were in "character" of what would be any form of normal or rational behavior. Perhaps in my own very pitiful way I'm simply asking that I not be hated for wanting to hear a little girl laugh one last time: There are so many other reasons to hate me I hope not to be hated for that. Karen never knew what happened to her. Once she had been taped (which was not done to bind them, but as commanded for god's purpose), I picked her up again, as I had many times done with my own children, and placed her on my shoulders. It all happened in a playful way and she was not afraid. I'm a fool, that's quite clear. But let's learn how these children came to die so that we might be better prepared to recognize the dangers.

With the exception of Dennis, the eyes of each had been covered with tape so that they could not see the hole and the bodies of the others. To my knowledge, none of them ever knew that they were in a hole, nor that others were present. But since I did not stand by and watch, I have no way of being certain.

As Jeff and I walked the perimeter the last time, he mentioned a coming storm that we would endure. I said I hoped it would come quickly, and he said that it would definitely happen quite soon. I don't give Jeff any credit as having foreseen that the very next morning, the FBI would "storm" the farm. But that night, the task was finished: we had performed god's will. Instructions were again given on how we were to fill in the hole. Their bodies were first to be covered with lime, then with rocks that we had gathered a couple days before. Then we were to fill back in the dirt that had come from the hole. Even the issue of what Jesus said about letting the "dead bury their dead" (Matthew 8:22), was explained by Jeff that we were not the dead, by way of this burial.

Where the hole had once been, we moved a pile of discarded belongings. This made a huge pile in that corner of the room. Jeff called the Patricks and Johnsons at their common residence and told them to come to the farm for class. It was after midnight by this time, which illustrates how completely "on call" we each were. We assembled for class and Jeff explained what had occurred and why. It was at this class that Dennis Patrick first heard Jeff say that he and his family had also been slated to die. Dennis was speechless at first, then apologized for having been a burden to Jeff and also for not being called upon to assist with the Averys. The Patricks and the Johnsons lived in Kirtland, almost directly across the street from the police station. Dennis had just been told that he and his family were to have been killed as the Avery family had been that evening, yet Dennis responded with an apology for not being able to help. The Patricks would again be slated to die while we were in the wilderness. Prior to the killings, Tonya went to Jeff privately to inquire about whether or not the three of them would die. I seriously doubt that she was given a direct answer, yet I do know she pled for mercy for Molly. She did not discuss this with Dennis, or with the police when they came to the farm the night before we left Ohio. In fact, Tonya pled only for the life of her daughter. She was still willing to die at Jeff's judgment.

They all went back home that night, across the street from the police station, and did nothing to inform authorities. In no way do I record these things in order to demean the Patricks, or the Johnsons. I just want to illustrate how strong Jeff's influence was. It's my sincere prayer that the reader carefully consider the scenario I've described. To go to an outside authority was as unthinkable as to reject the judgment of Jeff as the seer, even if the sentence was death to one's self.

* * *

THE TASK HAD BEEN COMPLETED: the covenant had been fulfilled. The fury of god's wrath now awaited us in the wilderness. It was time to "be approved" by god in order to carry out the purpose he had for us. It was time to be redeemed and to receive the "endowment from on high." But the only real truth about it all was that Jeff now owned each one of us. And he would exercise that ownership in the Wilderness.

In the same way that Chinese handcuffs tighten their grip as the victim pulls away, no matter how much evidence seemed to scream out a particular message or opinion, our ears were trained to hear only the word revealed and relayed through the seer. We were to be servants with ears trained to hear only the words of the seer, God's spokesman (Exodus 4:16). Therefore our thoughts were to be inclined only to Him. "Incline your ear, and come unto me: hear, and your soul shall live; and I will make an everlasting covenant with you, even the sure mercies of David" (Isaiah 55:3). David was a warrior of the covenant and we were to be likewise; first, by training our ears to hear nothing but God's instruction, clear of all supposition from our own thinking, then to carry out this instruction without wavering. To waver would nullify all that we had already endured. Our minds became vacuums that heard only the bits of information provided to us by God's seer. Such mental oppression may be difficult to imagine, but I referred earlier to the fear of thinking a thought lest it be contrary to the thoughts we had been given to think. Self-examination was continuous.

Chapter 11

IN HASTE AND FLIGHT

A family was now dead. But even their deaths were used against us as one more example of our sin and failure. The Averys were good people whose benevolent dreams and passions had become distorted through their belief system. Yet, I believe our heavenly Father sees through the confusion and directly into the intentions of the heart (Hebrews 4:12). They dared express their heartfelt convictions in everyday living. They had a passion for a better world and these passions, though good, victimized them by way of desperation. This fervency dictated the need to give their all; and their *all* they did give. They became economically victimized by their relocation to a region offering less secure employment. After relocating, they relinquished the remainder of their assets to the "cause," thereby suffering more abuse. They relocated away from family and loved ones thinking that by conforming to (Jeff's) god's will they would be protected. As with we who remained, their minds had become subject to a belief and doctrine that ever so slowly and unobtrusively developed contrary to their own heart's desires. The Averys' perception of what God's will was for their lives victimized them further, lured by desires of a possible future fulfillment while ever more greatly eluding the completion of that fulfillment. Earthquakes may tremble, floods may destroy, and winds may utterly sweep away, but the shattering of dreams within the human heart is the most devastating of tragedies. Without them, neither repair nor rebuilding is possible. In this manner they were greatly victimized long before their deaths. Their dreams became a mere plaything within a very evil and surreptitious process that had become reconstructed by the influence of a very evil and cunning man.

* * *

THE NIGHT WAS LONG, but the morning seemed to come quite early. I had the responsibility of caring for the rabbits, which took me into the barn that next day. Though shamed by thoughts of it at the time and then repentant of such thoughts, I could feel the presence of the Avery family as I performed chores in the barn. My conscience would provoke my memory from time to time the next few weeks, as I would find myself thinking that I had seen Dennis. I came to master the art of suppressing these thoughts in the belief that they were evil and that the thoughts were prompted by influences contrary to the will of god. Upon completion of my morning chores, I was sent to the grocery store with Debbie in order to buy more food in preparation for our departure from society. I had recently obtained a credit card for a particular store, so I was sent to maximize the card's five hundred dollar limit. Debbie was the "food sheriff," in charge of food purchasing and preparation. Each of us was labeled as sheriff over some particular area of responsibility.

That morning, agents from the FBI gathered at a location in Kirtland. Unknown to us, it was for the purpose of raiding the farm, ironically, not because of the previous night's activities, but as a result of reports filed with the FBI by Kevin Curry. An old-time Navy friend of Jeff's, he had been living with the Lundgrens when we arrived in Ohio, but left shortly after they moved to the farm. Kevin apparently had informed the FBI of Jeff's leanings toward violence, prompting an ongoing investigation. This raid transpired while Debbie and I were at the store, but was still in process at the time we started back. Greg had been allowed to leave the premises after being questioned, in order to go on an errand. In so doing, he crossed paths with us on the road and flagged us down, telling us that we should not yet return to the farm. I remember thinking that perhaps the world was trying to destroy us before we came into the Lord's presence and received the power of our calling. I drove around for a while, then called the farm in order to see if Debbie and I should return. The phone at the farm was usually not plugged in. Even when it was, Jeff had seriously insisted that no one was to use it nor even answer it without his permission. Nonetheless, when I called, it was Jeff who answered, which was as would be expected, and responded that we could return to the farm. The atmosphere was very hectic as everyone scrambled meet us, each giving accounts of what had happened. Everyone, that is, but Jeff and Alice. With help of the others, we unloaded our stock of groceries from the car.

Jeff would later become very somber, but at that point he was at the fireplace burning his divisions from various class topics along with other papers. An uneasiness began to settle over us as we saw an indecisiveness come over Jeff. Everyone looked to him for direction, but he openly stated the need to be left alone. I had become accustomed to this type of behavior from him since it most always meant that we had done something wrong. When there was sin in the camp, Jeff informed us, it was quite burdensome to him, but blinding as well. He was the seer and, as his people, our sin closed his eyes so he was unable to receive guidance from God. It became apparent to me that whatever this failure, it would cost us. Yet even in these thoughts I was being tempted to supposing, which was sin in itself. I felt pretty useless in that I didn't know how to respond, or what I should say. The day was spent with Jeff conversing with Greg quite a lot, yet mostly with Alice.

Eventually, he began giving instructions to Greg and me how he wanted us to prepare to leave. We were going to leave for the wilderness…*now*. Much preparation had already been made, so leaving a few days early would not be that difficult. Reservations had been made for the rental of a U-Haul, which was ready to be picked up. Jeff had many times coached us of a particular story line (lie) to use, in the event that we were questioned about any of his plans, so the responses the group had given to the FBI that morning were primarily versions of that coaching. Since Debbie and I had not been there, we

Chapter 11 IN HASTE AND FLIGHT

never were questioned; yet the others had responded with the story about leaving on an extended camping trip. This was somewhat true, but hardly for vacation purposes.

I was assigned the task of driving the U-Haul. Jeff stated that (as the seer) it was he they were most interested in, so he would leave ahead of the rest of us. He pulled me aside and said that he wanted to take Susie and our two children with him, Alice, and their four children. He convinced me that despite the fact he was the one they were likely to come back in search of, my family would be safer by leaving early with him. In my mind, the issue was not debatable. If that was what he wanted, then that was what was best.

I was deluded in many ways through my subservience to Jeff but I still perceived him as being much like myself. It would be years later, while in the Lucasville penitentiary, that I would come to learn in a biography of sorts on Jeff, how extremely repulsive he was, even in his sexual relations. The relationship that Susie and I had was not only very precious to me, but also absolutely monogamous. I was under the mistaken perception that Jeff's relationship with Alice, along with his moral preferences in general, were similar to my own. Though topics of sexuality had been a big part of Jeff's teaching, I very stupidly failed to see where such teachings were leading. It still amazes me to find out what type of activity had been going on in Jeff's sex life, even before we met him. Therefore, Jeff kept this particular aspect of his nature quite secret, while reflecting to me the illusion that we were much the same in our marital loyalties and passions.

I must confess I could more easily be induced to warfare than to sexual promiscuity. Warfare is an issue dictated by a perception of authority, yet for me, the marital relationship runs not only deeper into the heart, but from a separate view of moral conduct. I realize, however, that this is not always the case with others. I, therefore, trusted Jeff with my family, despite what had happened to the Averys the night before. Yet trust would not really be the most accurate way of expressing my compliance to Jeff's orders. It was quite possible they would be safer with Jeff, wherein staying behind with me could actually place them at risk. My death had been prophesied, yet Jeff had the promise of a security by which I was not covered. "And thus prophesied Joseph, saying: Behold, that seer will the Lord bless; And they that seek to destroy him, shall be confounded: For this promise, of which I have obtained of the Lord, of the fruit of thy loins, shall be fulfilled" (2 Nephi 2:25–27). If the seer spoke it, then it was the will of god. No debate on the issue was necessary.

It's clear now that Jeff didn't trust me. I didn't know at the time, of course, but he had a large number of things he was keeping secret from me. Therefore, it only stands to reason that he could not reveal his complete agenda to me, and he never did. He took Susie and our children so that he could better control me if he needed to. And to add more weight to this leverage, I was neither informed of where we were going, nor where we were to connect with Jeff, as we had done from time to time. As the "words of Christ" were to tell us "all things" that we should do, this next part of our journey would mimic the account of a *Book of Mormon* character named Lehi.

As a prophet, Lehi set an example for going into the wilderness.

> "And it came to pass that the Lord commanded my father, even in a dream, that he should take his family and depart into the wilderness. And it came to pass that he was obedient unto the word of the Lord, wherefore he did as the Lord commanded him. And it came to pass that he departed into the wilderness. And he left his house, and the land of his inheritance, and his gold, and his silver, and his precious things, and took nothing with him, save it were his family, and provisions, and tents, and he departed into the wilderness." (1 Nephi 1:26–29)

Multitudes had done likewise, and we, as the household of the choice seer, were to draw instruction from all their accounts without repeating their mistakes. In fact, we were to be wiser than they, in that we were to be the last to finish this great task; and by the benefit of everything those before us had endured.

> "Behold, I speak unto you as though I spake from the dead; for I know that ye shall have my words. Condemn me not because of mine imperfections; neither my father, because of his imperfection; neither them who have written before him, but rather give thanks unto God that he hath made manifest unto you our imperfections, that ye may learn to be more wise than we have been." (Mormon 4:96–97)

All these things had been recorded for god's purpose in us for His restoration in the last days. We were to raise up the same mountain which Enoch was to have raised before us.

Much as any cult doctrine, Mormonism takes a reading of the Biblical text, vague in nature, and elaborates on it as though it were revealing a mystery. I wrote of this earlier and mentioned the expansive doctrines built up about Enoch in Section 36 of the *Doctrine and Covenants*. Sections 77 and 101 also speak of Enoch and the people he was to have led into righteousness. It is a commonly accepted RLDS doctrine that these Sections (77 & 101) were not speaking solely of Enoch and his people, but also were dual messages from Joseph Smith, incognito, to others of the early church movement at a time when anti-Mormon residents within the area were less than cooperative as neighbors. Jeff took these teachings of Enoch, already heavily "leavened" with Joseph Smith's teachings, and embellished them even more. The "mountain" was a central theme for Jeff and in actuality was to have been the true interpretation of topics, such as the rapture doctrine where people are lifted up to meet Christ. By way of Jeff's teaching, the lifting up would be due to a great earthquake, which would thrust up a mountain beneath their feet, hence, "How beautiful upon the mountains are the feet of him that bringeth good tidings, that publisheth peace; that bringeth good tidings of good, that publisheth salvation; that saith unto Zion, Thy God reigneth!" (Isaiah 52:7). The "publishing of peace" would be the opening up of the treasury, or library, as mentioned in *D&C* Section 101, verse 11, and "thus shall ye preserve all the avails of the sacred things in the treasury, for sacred and holy purposes; and this shall be called the sacred treasury of the Lord; and a seal shall be kept upon it, that it may be holy and consecrated unto the Lord." Treasuries such as this were part of the Old Testament ritual, but by the blood of Jesus we are to now have a better relationship with God based upon better treasures and eternal promises.

The sections that Joseph Smith disguised as revelations of Enoch were taught by Jeff as actual revelations from Smith for the purpose of illustrating the extremely holy location of Kirtland. He taught that the revelations of Enoch were speaking of Enoch, because he and his people were from this continent before the earth was divided. "The name of one was Peleg; for in his day was the earth divided; and his brother's name was Joktan" (Genesis 10:25, *Inspired Version*). Section 36 speaks of how Enoch built a city of righteousness, which was too holy to remain on earth. Therefore, God translated the City of Enoch up into heaven, which Jeff identified by division to be the raising up of a mountain; by his teaching, our calling in our day. "And Enoch and all his people walked with God, and he dwelt in the midst of Zion: and it came to pass that Zion was not, for God received it up into his own bosom; and from thence went forth the saying, 'Zion is fled' " (D&C 36:14e). With the teachings that the treasury was literally resident within the City of Enoch, it would not be incomprehensible to tie in instruction to Joseph Smith that he should build a print shop in order to "publish" these things.

> "And again, verily I say unto you, the second lot on the south shall be dedicated unto me, for the building of an house unto me, for the work of the printing of the translation of my Scriptures, and all things whatsoever I shall command you...and this house shall be wholly dedicated unto the Lord from the foundation thereof, for the work of the printing, in all things whatsoever I shall command you, to be holy, undefiled, according to the pattern, in all things, as it shall be given unto you." (D&C, 91:3a,c)

Enoch, one of our forefathers, was an example to us for the building of a holy city and the establishment of a holy treasury containing a library of sacred writings so that we might publish these commands of God for the benefit of all people.

> "And it shall come to pass in the last days, that the mountain of the Lord's house shall be established in the top of the mountains, and shall be exalted above the hills; and all nations shall flow unto it. And many people shall go and say, Come ye, and let us go up to the mountain of the Lord, to the house of the God of Jacob; and he will teach us of his ways, and we will walk in his paths: for out of Zion shall go forth the law, and the word of the Lord from Jerusalem." (Isaiah 2:2–3)

Remember that within Mormon teachings, Jerusalem is identified as Zion, which will be established on this continent (North America). The "Centerplace of Zion" is understood by RLDS members as being Independence, Missouri. Church members await the call to gather home to Zion—Independence. Jeff, however, taught that Independence was not the Centerplace, but rather that it was Kirtland, Ohio. He showed how chiasmus revealed this, and also that the church went into apostasy when it left Ohio back in the late 1830's. We were now called and chosen to establish Zion. And as it was to be the last time, it also would be in the same location as the first time, the location of Enoch's city. The example was used of "the first shall be last and the last shall be first," chiastically typified by the pattern. An interesting note in summation of this principle is how it all became a tool of manipulation for Jeff because Joseph Smith, long ago, found the necessity to place revelations from "god" incognito for the purpose of protecting himself and others from the "evil persecutors" who plagued him. Deceptive means seem only to have produced deceptive ends.

* * *

IT WAS ABOUT 7:00 P.M. ON THE 18TH when Jeff left the farm with his family and mine. We were to pick up the rental truck after dark and finish loading the remainder of items Jeff had determined as necessities for our departure. Due to the hurried nature of our exit, we were unable to take our few rabbits and cages, despite the fact that they had been chiastically identified as provisions we were to take with us. Jeff told us to free them as we prepared to leave. In the light of day we did the less conspicuous forms of packing. When the Johnsons moved from Missouri, they brought with them a sixteen-foot horse trailer. We loaded it with the generator, barrels of wheat and other staples, still leaving enough room in the back for the two horses. After nightfall, I drove the rental truck to the farm where everyone helped load it with items from the house, and then from the barn. We had two freezers full of meat and produce. There was also a cooking range and microwave oven, though we had no idea how long it might be before we would be able to use them. Our wilderness venture would clearly differ from that of our forefathers.

We were to take "flocks and herds" with us as provisions, and though the rabbits were to be a part of that, we never took all that had been planned. We were to purchase cattle, which was the purpose for the hay that had been stored in the barn. But Jeff rarely came through with completion of any specific project—except for the killing of innocent people. The truck was loaded quite hurriedly, as we supposed the FBI agents might return, or continue observing us. But with the story that we were leaving, we hoped that our activity and consequent absence might not be an issue of concern to them. The Jaredites took honeybees with them into the wilderness (Ether 1:24). Absent the bees, we took a large amount of honey. They had grain, which we also had, only in the form of wheat-filled barrels. Their livestock was on the hoof, while

Chapter 11 IN HASTE AND FLIGHT

ours was in the freezer, but the end result was meat. This was all collected and accepted by us as being fulfillment of, and obedience to, the will of god from His word. With the packing completed, our journey began.

As mentioned, Jeff and Alice left much earlier in the day driving the blue Nissan pickup, followed by Susie, our children, and his two oldest sons in our '78 Plymouth. The remainder of us formed a caravan led by Greg in his Honda, followed by the Johnson's yellow Suburban pulling a bright red 16-foot horse trailer. I took up the rear in a 24-foot rental truck, all of which made us an observable convoy that stood out like a blasting foghorn in a sea of silence. Though we left in "haste" and by "flight," we clearly fell short in any effort to do so covertly. Richard and Sharon rode with me in the cab of the truck. Merely one day earlier, I could have very well been involved with their deaths if Jeff had spoken the word, yet we now shared the cab of a truck while traveling toward a destination, the whereabouts none of us knew. Only Greg had been given instructions where to rendezvous with Jeff, who carried the money necessary for our travel.

I'm reminded of a time when Alice spoke of holding Jeff's head in her lap one time in order to relax him because of all his stress. She said that as she was massaging his temples it dawned on her that she was holding "all things" in her hands. She described all things as everything revealed with and through Jeff's mind. They managed the illusion of having everything under control at all times. Alice would give testimony at my trial, surprisingly, that she never believed in Jeff the way the rest of us did. Perhaps at an early point, she may have suspected that he could be a prophet, "The Prophet," but by the time the rest of us came on the scene as a "family," she testified that she no longer believed it. Alice, then, was the only person in the group who knew what no one else knew—Jeff was a fraud. I have tried to convey a more succinct view of which of them was in charge and how the influence of leadership was misused. I don't believe Alice was ever in charge but she was most definitely the glue Jeff used for holding all his lies together.

Our first rendezvous with Jeff took place at about 5:00 a.m. on an overpass. Susie and the kids had already been long asleep at a nearby motel, so Jeff suggested that I go on with the others to a motel down the road and share a room with Danny. About noon I awoke to Susie knocking at the door; it was time to get up and on the road again. In the large parking lot area behind the motel we gathered for a short while to get organized and discuss any problems. Keith asked Jeff if he could speak with him at this little gathering and they walked away from the others. Keith had a confession to make: when asked by the FBI what the intentions were for the guns we possessed, he apparently made up a story about believing the Russians were coming and that we needed guns for protecting the temple. This upset Jeff, though it really did nothing toward the detriment our mission. What it might have suggested was that we were fanatically zealous (which we were) and might have prompted the FBI to watch us more closely, and that was what clearly disturbed Jeff.

Therefore, for this great sin Keith divulged to Jeff, we would not be able to raise the mountain, as planned, by the designated date that year. It was already April 19th, and we were to raise the mountain on the 3rd of May. But now there was sin in the camp because Keith had been thinking thoughts that had not been given to him to think. He used a storyline other than that which Jeff had given him to use, and this great sin would cost us. The price would be that we would have to go another year without the mountain for refuge. Of course, this was due to Jeff's great mercy and care for each one of us, because if any of us had gone before the Lord with a sin such as this among us, we would suffer immediate extinction. All would be lost. It was also apparent that this extra year of "tarrying" would be difficult for us because we had already ignited a fire by way of the covenant (the deaths of the Averys). How would we survive another year? Would we endure more losses? I asked Jeff if we could still obtain the records from the library (of Enoch), which was a treasure I seriously hoped for. He said "yes," that we would, but that we would need the sword, in order to make it through. The sword, breastplate, and Urim and Thummim were supposedly all contained within the treasury of Enoch under the watchful care of the Keeper of the library. We had only just started, and already our purpose was delayed again. We stopped at another motel the second night and I was given a map although I never really knew where we were going. I spent that night with my family, but we would continue to travel separately.

From time to time Jeff would drive ahead of us, yet at other times we would all be together. Eventually, we found ourselves in Davis, West Virginia. We couldn't have known it at the time, but this would turn out to be our home for the next seven months. Just as had been required of us as recorded in the words of Christ in the parallel story of Lehi and his family's departure, we had traveled for three days. "And it came to pass that when he had traveled three days in the wilderness, he pitched his tent in a valley by the side of a river of water" (1 Nephi 1:33). Davis is a small town that sits next to the Black Water River. Obviously, a mere river would not be the identifying landmark for setting up camp; we had crossed so many. But in stopping for fuel at a little grocery mart and gas station, we noticed the name of the motel and restaurant that was attached to it, unbelievably, named the Highlander. Believing it authenticated his own life and mission, now at the end of our three days of wandering and at a location directly on a river bank, like a huge X marking the spot on a map was the "sign" Jeff was looking for in his journey—The Highlander.

Whether Jeff knew it was there and had thereby charted a three-day course to it or not, to the rest of us it was more than a mere coincidence. It became to us a god-provided-beacon for the moment we would need it. It was a sign that we had found our stopping point. And because we were extremely desperate for some type of assurance that God was still mindful of us, especially in lieu of the year delay we had just acquired, it was not only believable to us, but strongly embraced. In a sense, we now knew where "home" was, at least for the time. About three more days were spent in the luxury of motel rooms in Davis while Jeff looked for a suitable campsite. Each night we would gather for class, which added a degree of order again to an otherwise fluid instability of emotions within each of us. We were frightened wanderers and now our faith was being tested beyond any ordinary means.

Chapter 12

SETTING UP CAMP

Our arrival in Davis did not go unnoticed, nor were the people unfriendly towards us. Davis is bordered on one side by a state park through which the Black Water River flows. A deep valley region within the park provides a cascading series of waterfalls that are beautiful to behold, yet this was not where we set up camp. Bordering Davis from a different direction is an abandoned strip mine, which has been restored in harmony with nature. The openness of this area enabled us to set up camp without registration through any park authority. Other campers had been known to stay for lengthy periods of time. Jeff felt the need to stay in a room at the Highlander.

About a week or two before leaving Kirtland, Debbie had been given to Greg Winship as his wife and Sharon had been given to Richard Brand. The "marriages" were not legal, but they were accepted as the will of god. The marriages were based upon Jeff's view of all things, thereby knowing which man and woman belonged together. As a child, I recall being curious about who would be my "rib," as portrayed in the account of Adam and Eve. This principle of finding one's rib was taught extensively by Jeff. If the woman you were married to was not "flesh of your flesh" (Genesis 2:23), then the entire relationship was in a state of sin and adultery. And of course, in a world so populous, only a seer could actually see who went with whom.

Richard and Sharon, along with Greg and Debbie, also stayed at the Highlander. The remainder of us stayed at a separate motel. During his outings on the ATV Jeff not only found a location suitable for us to set up camp, but he also discovered another "holy hill." He told me about it after returning to the motel one night. Knowing it was sacred ground, he knelt and prayed. Of course, he knew what words to say, having been ordained, in some way, to say them. He recounted how suddenly the clouds parted and a ray of light shone down on him. The 36th Section of the *Doctrine and Covenants* illustrates this idea. "And it came to pass that I turned and went upon the mount, and, as I stood upon the mount, I beheld the heavens open, and I was clothed upon with glory, and I saw the Lord" (D&C 36:1c). He then proceeded to explain how he had been instructed to say a prayer over the course of seven days, which would begin the process of ending this world that all things might be restored. Jeff taught that this earth was used over and over, and that we were merely entering into a new beginning.

> "And the Lord God spake unto Moses, saying, The heavens, they are many and they cannot be numbered unto man, but they are numbered unto me, for they are mine; and as one earth shall pass away, and the heavens thereof, even so shall another come...And now, Moses, my son, I will speak unto you concerning this earth upon which you stand; and you shall write the things which I shall speak." (D&C 22:23a, 24a)

By way of customary Mormon belief, it would be taking these passages out of context to suggest that this process was speaking of a continual destruction and rebirth of this planet. Most would agree that Joseph Smith, in writing these words, was simply suggesting that the creative process is an ongoing one, and as one planet dies or the sun fades away, the others are being born, as an ever-growing procreation of God. However, though Jeff taught an ever expanding and growing universe, he also applied these passages as a life and death process illustrated within this single planet as well. This was reinforced by the example of Moses as portrayed in Section 22 (above), since he was only shown this earth.

Jeff was convinced he'd received revelation that he was to be "like unto Moses." Therefore, Jeff taught, and we believed, that this 22nd Section spoke of Jeff as much as it spoke of Moses. Jeff had "seen all things," but particular scrutiny of all things was revealed to him in accordance with his particular calling. Despite the position of "god of the earth" that Jeff would later claim for himself, he could never be the infinite God of all things. And to receive an intimate revelation of the infinity of all things would mean the transfiguration of a man (such as the city of Enoch). Transfigured, he (or they) could no longer remain on the earth. A few more passages from Section 22 illustrate the point.

> "And God spake unto Moses, saying, Behold, I am the Lord God Almighty, and Endless is my name, for I am without beginning of days or end of years; and is not this endless? And behold, thou are my son, wherefore look, and I will show thee the workmanship of mine hands, but not all; for my works are without end, and also my words, for they never cease; wherefore no man can behold all my works except he behold all my glory; and no man can behold all my glory, and afterwards remain in the flesh, on the earth."
> (D&C 22:2–3d)

As quoted earlier from verse 24a, Moses was only shown this earth, this one thing. "And now, behold, this one thing I will show unto thee, Moses, my son; for thou art in the world, and now I show it unto thee" (D&C 22:5).

Although I introduce these as additional concepts taught by Jeff, they were principles we were taught early on while in Kirtland. We had wandered three days. We had found the "Highlander" as a sign that we were at the right place. Now Jeff had found his "holy hill." This clinched it for us, in that we were not only in the right place, but much like warriors in the battlefield, we now had communications with "headquarters," even air strike support from

Chapter 12 SETTING UP CAMP

above to be called upon if needed. The Mormon doctrine all seemed to be speaking of Jeff as the choice seer. However, I now see Jeff as merely one of the false teachers that we are warned against as recorded in the Bible. Although we read from the Bible continuously, we were not only steered away from the majority of the New Testament, but had a totally obstructed view of the overall message as well. Jeff truly did manage to fulfill some passages of scripture, but not in the context that he claimed. Luke 12:45–46 is a parallel of what occurred not only earlier on within the group, but also the type of treatment that would be exploited by Jeff now that he had us locked in to his service and obeisance.

> "But if that servant say in his heart, My lord delayeth his coming; and begin to beat the menservants and maidens, and to eat and drink, and to be drunken; The lord of that servant will come in a day when he looketh not for him, and at an hour when he is not aware, and will cut him in sunder, and will appoint him his portion with the unbelievers." (Luke 12:45–46)

Our sin had continually caused the Lord to tarry, so the price for our failure continued to increase.

The day came for us to set up camp, actually, two separate campsites. One was at the top of a plateau area and the other below. The upper camp was where Jeff's family, mine, and the Patricks set up. In the lower camp were the other three families, along with storage and a cooking tent. The lower camp was alongside the smaller Yellow River that emptied into the Black River nearby. There was a spring a few miles away from which we drew our drinking water. While Jeff was staying at the Highlander motel, they allowed him to plug into their electric supply in order to run the freezers that were stored in the rental truck. But within a week or so we moved the freezers into the horse trailer and brought them to the camp. Our campsite was about two miles into the backwoods area over a very rough road, so we didn't take the U-Haul. Once the freezers were in place, my responsibility was to set up the generator. We endured very cold weather and even snow, so our food in the freezers was pretty safe but such weather made our first days in the wilderness a real trial. The weather was inescapable; there was no way of getting away from it. Once the generator was set up, space heaters were placed in the Johnson's tent, mine, and Jeff's. The Johnson's tent was close to the generator in the lower camp, whereas mine and Jeff's shared about 150 yards of extension cord. I was told I could not use the one in my tent because it drew power away from the current that flowed to Jeff's. Quite an endurance. We really were now in the wilderness and all that came our way was in order to test us, to see if we would "murmur."

> "And it came to pass that Laman and Lemuel, and the sons of Ishmael, did begin to murmur exceedingly, because of their sufferings and afflictions in the wilderness; and also my father began to murmur against the Lord his God; yea, and they were all exceeding sorrowful, even that they did murmur against the Lord" (1 Nephi 5:25)

The *Book of Mormon* plagiarizes the biblical account of wilderness living, in that it was a sin against God to murmur at times of trial. We too, had to endure the difficulties, and complaining was not only unacceptable, it created consequences of increased affliction. Dennis Patrick was assigned the job of fire sheriff, which was an ongoing and laborious task. The task of heating water for necessities such as bathing, laundry and washing dishes was endless. Keith was the firewood sheriff, so he provided Dennis with wood ranging from small brush to logs cut with the chainsaw. Keith had been instructed to cut only the dead trees in the area, but after a while at this campsite, as well as the others that we would move to, it would soon become impossible to find deadwood. Tonya was placed in charge of the laundry and Susie was responsible for the dishwashing. Those first few weeks were so cold that we seemed to simply hibernate in the tents as much as possible; yet even then Jeff often insisted on the need to have class (which Alice, by this time, seldom attended). There we were: a cold band of fugitives huddled around picnic tables, listening to the seer "rightly divide." It even snowed lightly, as winter imparted its final gust of cold weather.

We would walk to the lower camp for meals, after which Susie had to take charge of the dishes. Several others would pitch in and help, myself included. But on the colder days I returned to the tent with the kids, in order to keep them warm. I was aware that it would be taken by Jeff as supposing or counseling (the Lord), if I were to stay and do the dishes myself while Susie took the kids back to the tent to keep warm. Dennis would later interfere with the job assigned to his wife, Tonya with devastating results. As Susie came back to the tent after doing the dishes, she was in tears. She was so cold and the hardships that we all were enduring were weighing heavily upon her. Confusion and deep frustration of the recent events was taking its toll. I thought that I was being a good husband and father by ensuring my family was prepared in the sight of God. Yet all I was really doing was subjecting them to continual abuse. We had been part of the greater household, or family, for sometime but had never actually been such an intimate part of the daily functioning, having moved to the farm only days before the deaths of the Averys. Due to our disconnected view of how Jeff's more immediate household was run, I found frustrations of my own to deal with once we found ourselves continually together.

Jeff always presented himself as a very fatherly figure with the children. This included the Avery children as well as any of the others. As I've stated, his strict disciplinary tactics are now a repugnant and shameful memory to me, but at the time, we believed these things had a purpose and were crucial

Chapter 12 SETTING UP CAMP

for our survival and eternal wellbeing. Though strict, Jeff presented himself as being infinitely gentle as well. During the time they lived on the farm, Jeff would often invite children into the class area in order to talk with them, quite tenderly. As he was god's representative, it was important that the children not fear him, nor even respond shyly, lest they do likewise in the presence of Almighty God. Children are the very epitome of innocence and we are truly blessed to have such living examples to cherish and nurture. We thought that at the appearance of Christ, our children might be beckoned by Him to come forward. They were to be prepared to do so with open and trusting hearts. What a shame that people such as Jeff only seem to create the opposite in people.

This meant our children should deal with Jeff likewise, being god's representative and provided for the purpose of our preparation. As incongruous as it may sound, despite killing an entire family, Jeff appeared to us as being loving, tender and very altruistic. Death was justified by Law and Judgment, which we did not have to like, but did have to obey unwaveringly. I recall while in Kirtland, as well as during our travel, how Jeff made it appear as though he and Alice had endured the worst of conditions. For us to complain in any way was immediately marked as sin. Yet with him, it was a continual issue for the purpose of establishing guilt within us while giving the appearance that he suffered greatly with us. A bad mattress at a motel, an improperly prepared meal: no opportunity was missed to introduce guilt and shame within us. We were so busy looking behind at our failures and sin that we completely lost sight of the path ahead and the reality of what Jeff's actions were doing to us.

* * *

JEFF HAD NO PREFERENCE TO ANY PARTICULAR CHILDREN. We were fathers of our own children, but Jeff was father over all. Despite the differences I noticed in the gifts his children received at Christmastime, I continued to think of him as non-preferential. Yet when we found ourselves camping together those thoughts became difficult for me to sustain. I did sustain and saw the issue, though difficult, as one that was clearly beyond any choice or discussion. I could hear laughter coming from the Lundgren tent while they would watch a videotape and I could see the tent aglow from the lamp they had. When I needed to speak with Jeff, my glasses would fog up from the warmth that would come out of the tent opening. Yet my family, my wife and my children, were huddled together for warmth with only a candle for light and a heater we could not use. I, of course, had to repent of the frustrations that these things produced; and I did. But Jeff owned us now. People like Jeff are seduced by desires to obtain for themselves, while altruistic people tend to sacrifice themselves for the common good of the whole. Jeff's shedding of material things gave the reaffirming appearance that he was not a self-serving individual, yet it's clear now that it was the power and the control over the lives, and even deaths, of others that he hungered for all along. The death of the Avery family was not only contrary to the very fiber of everyone's passions and desires, it required continual mental reassurances as to its justification and necessity. Any justification remained crystallized within us, as murmuring or sin of any kind was directly reflected as a statement that their deaths were in vain. This was not only inexcusable, it was impossible. Therefore, whatever the imbalance I saw within the treatment Jeff showed his "naturals" [his immediate family], I had to believe it was for a reason. I had to equally accept by faith that the reason was simply beyond my ability to differentiate. Any frustration over the matter was perceived as counseling or supposing and necessitated immediate repentance.

Three-year old Amy became fussy one day. Jeff told me that any further fussiness would require his personal attention—I had not instilled within her the proper discipline for better behavior. This command was put into place for all the children in the camp with the understanding that Jeff's children were properly disciplined. Shortly thereafter, Amy misbehaved again. This meant that Jeff would have to discipline her. I was sickened as I sat in my tent where I could hear her screaming. Thankfully, she had not been physically hurt as much as she was emotionally that someone other than her parents were disciplining her. She was terrified at being alone with someone other than her parents. I sometimes fear that my consent of this type of discipline may have left a permanent impression on my children, perhaps they feeling as if I had abandoned them. With the number of complications, including the current and continuing Mormon fervor in their lives, and the physical distance between us, we've had no opportunity to heal as a family should, in order to recover from so much confusion, exploitation, and abuse. Going to Jeff and Alice later in the evening, I had tears streaming down my face as I expressed my apologies for Amy's behavior, along with my fear that she might not "make it." If she had sin bound up in her little heart, she could not go before the Lord as we were to do. Tenderly, as a natural mother would, Alice expressed how certain she was that the love I had for my daughter would be sufficient for ensuring that Amy would make it. Remembering now that Alice knew all along it was a fraud, her attempts at consolation sicken me. But at the moment it had a profound affect on me. From that time forward, I ensured that there was no need for either Amy or Matthew to go to Jeff for discipline. I spanked their little bottoms far too hard and now I no longer have the opportunity to show them the tender love that I'd much rather have them remember. That's not to say that I didn't treat them tenderly as well. Chasing "tickle bugs" and games of rubbing noses was always a prized time together. But the fear that any one of my family might not make it through Redemption Day created an ongoing fear that influenced my behavior toward them greatly. Now, there's no other way but this book to explain to them how sorry I am for my utter foolishness.

Mine was not the only family affected by Jeff's stringent disciplinary measures. As noted before, Tonya was the laundry sheriff, which turned out to be an enormous task. Her hands became badly blistered due to constant expo-

Chapter 12 SETTING UP CAMP

sure to the bleach. When the cold weather finally broke, the rainy weather set in. Eventually, the laundry became backed up and Jeff sent Dennis and Tonya (along with their daughter Molly) into town in order to use the laundromat there. This was expensive, but there seemed to be no other choice. When they returned, all the clothing had been washed, but not all of the clothing had been dried. They had run out of money and Dennis decided they should finish all the washing that they could, leaving the remainder to dry out on the lines as weather permitted. His thinking was that at least all of the clothes would be clean. Tonya, however, thought that it would be best to have as much dry as possible, therefore, they should only wash as much as they had sufficient funds to dry. In that Dennis was the husband and that his family had just nearly been killed due to accusations from Jeff that he was not adequately in charge of his household, Dennis' decision on the matter was final. Much like the issue of Richard and the chocolate chips, I doubt that there was actually a right decision that could have been made. However, if there was, the one Dennis made was not it. Jeff charged him with counseling the Lord. Jeff, as god's servant, had placed Tonya in charge of the job of doing the laundry. The fact that Dennis was Tonya's husband had nothing to do with the fact that god through Jeff, had placed the responsibility upon Tonya. Therefore, to question her judgment on the matter was to question god. To overrule her decision on the matter was to at least attempt to overrule god. Due to the fact that god had only recently extended His tender mercies toward Dennis and his family by sparing their lives, it was clear that the lesson had not been fully learned by him. Therefore, a punishment was necessary. Dennis' wife and daughter would be taken from him.

Alice was the queen, and she had no difficulty meeting the requirements of that position until it appeared that another woman was about to share the throne. Tonya and Molly were removed from Dennis' tent and placed in Jeff's. Tonya was considered a handmaiden to the immediate Lundgren household and Molly was viewed merely as the daughter of Alice's handmaiden. Dennis stayed in his tent alone: very much alone. He was being marked for death and he knew it. The job he had been assigned to was that of the fire-pit, essential for our hot water needs and even cooking at the time. He developed quite a talent for this task, as it became the one thing that he was to offer in service and stewardship to god. All else was gone. The turmoil, pain and emotional trauma were overwhelming for him, though each member of the group could well describe his nightmare as viewed from their own experience of it. Tonya and Molly stayed in Jeff's tent about four months before being returned to Dennis. It would be much later, and only shortly before leaving the group, that Susie and I would discover that Tonya performed more than servant's chores within the Lundgren tent. She had performed wifely duties as well. That there had been a degree of sexual involvement between Jeff and Tonya was suspected. Within a week or two prior to Jeff sending her back to Dennis, he taught class on enlarging the place of his tent. "Enlarge the place of thy tent, and let them stretch forth the curtains of thine habitations: spare not, lengthen thy cords, and strengthen thy stakes" (Isaiah 54:2).

* * *

JEFF WOULD ACCRUE FOR HIMSELF many names throughout this time in the wilderness. Being "god of the earth" was a title that he would also later claim. At this point of the wilderness experience polygamy was not yet a reality, but later on it would be as Jeff would teach us that Tonya was to be his wife number two. But this happened much later, as we had become so intoxicated by the whole process that the minor ever-increasing changes were wholly embraced. I recall speaking with Tonya after those four months she spent in Jeff's tent when she suspected she might be sent back to Dennis, her husband. She was very upset and brokenhearted over it, as her convictions toward who and what Jeff was thought to be overflowed into misplaced feelings of love. Tonya thought that she really loved Jeff, which is something I'm sure she finds repugnant now that she and Dennis are so distant from all that transpired those months and years under Jeff's influence.

One day, after completing the dishes, Susie offered to help Tonya hang up some laundry. They worked together for a while until the job was finished. As it was an unusually pleasant day, Alice decided to venture to the lower camp. In doing so, she noticed that the laundry that Susie had hung was not to her satisfaction. I heard nothing about the incident until that night at class, when the issue became introduced as the class topic. As noted before, we had various names: one of mine was Israel, and another was Jeshurun. These names were never really used by us. In fact, their only purpose seemed to be as a way to identify us, individually, with various passages with which Jeff desired to associate us. Sometimes these associations were uplifting, but usually they were dealt in painful or negative ways such as the time Greg and I by use of our spiritual names were associated with the deaths of millions of people. That night, however, Susie's name was associated with a threat of death. She had not been given a name up to this point, but tonight Jeff determined that she was Rachel. This name would not be officially given to her until sometime later, yet this night, it was a name used to refer to her by way of the context of the class. "Thus saith the Lord; a voice was heard in Ramah, lamentation, and bitter weeping; Rahel (or Rachel) weeping for her children refused to be comforted for her children, because they were not" (Jeremiah 31:15). Interpretation of this passage placed serious threat of death over our children and it was determined to be Susie's doing. As with others, her own life had been threatened, but the threats against our children were the most disconcerting. Jeff's charge was that she took it upon herself to help Tonya with a task, without inquiring beforehand about the matter. Perhaps Alice would have wanted her to do something else, or more to the point, Susie "supposed" that she knew how to do the job the way Alice wanted it done, without properly inquiring for instruction.

Chapter 12 SETTING UP CAMP

It's clear these things are outrageous and absurd, but it was all very real to us. It was, in fact, our reality. For me, it prompted continual fear of more deaths, possibly including my wife and children. This constant memory of failure toward my wife and children, as well as toward the Avery family, creates cycles of frustration and struggles that still attempt to destroy me with feelings of futility and depression. As I continue to gain understanding of the indoctrination and controlling processes that were used on us, I find a degree of comfort. But the most beneficial relief I have comes from finally seeing the message of truth as contained in the Bible and through the relationship I now have with God's amazing grace.

It was Jeff's design to find some type of shelter to buy or lease so we could make it through the year. The first month or so Greg was given large sums of money and assigned the job of finding us a more stable place to live. By moving, we would have the necessities that would allow us to hire ourselves out for cash jobs and also have a way to get out of the weather during the next winter. We had seeds and gardening tools, as outlined by the words of Christ. We could raise crops and trade for livestock with the assurance that God would provide for our needs. We had all moved to Ohio on faith, and had maintained a lifestyle of continuing to live by faith. In fact, that faith was a major factor of our existence and the very foundation of our confidence toward survival. Had Greg been able to find housing within the limitations Jeff set, I have to wonder how many of us would still be alive today. Not being blessed with a more secure place to live at that time was truly the greatest blessing the Lord could have given us. Had we been able to establish ourselves in a location with more permanency to make it through the winter, I have little reason to believe that the Avery's deaths would yet have been discovered. I feel just as strongly that the rest of us could be dead as well. Jeff had become completely intoxicated with the power he exerted over us as did we, becoming increasingly certain in our convictions that we were under god's all piercing scrutiny. We were god's chosen servants, not worthy, but set aside for his purpose, all the same. We were willing to endure any hardship or personal loss necessary in order to please him. This willingness gives view not only to what could have been, had we found a suitable dwelling, but also opened the way for the abuse that was soon to follow.

Chapter 13

CONFINED WITHOUT WALLS

With the onset of warmer weather, the location of this first camp soon became a little too bustling with activity. Fishermen passed by on their way to the river about a hundred yards away. Just off the side of the main road bordering the river's edge, we quickly found ourselves in the center of the summer traffic as activities increased. Departures from camp were always cleared through Jeff. If we wanted to take a hike in the woods, permission was required. Voluntary or prolonged interaction with other campers was prohibited. A degree of interaction was necessary in order not to draw attention to ourselves, yet for the same reason, the least exposure necessary to outsiders was also essential.

Ironically, the only thing restricting any of us from simply leaving the camp was our conviction that Jeff was the seer and would know in advance our intentions of doing so. Even after Tonya and Molly were removed from Dennis' tent, and he was marked for death, he remained in the camp; never attempting to leave for help. Sometimes campers would be so close that interaction with them was unavoidable. Our perception of these people is difficult to describe. We saw them as "the world." That meant, to us, that they were spiritually dead. Only those who were on the journey toward Redemption ("feel and see" encounter) had even a spark of life within them; and this too was our fault. If we had been better servants and not hindered Jeff so long by way of our multiple sinful procrastinations, we would have already been able to establish Zion. Then the living "dead" would have a place to look in order to find "life."

We were to establish an ensign so that all nations would have a place to turn for peace. The people around us were perceived by us as not having peace. They were seen as in turmoil. We had the seer, we had the promise: therefore, we had the hope in an otherwise hopeless world. We pitied those around us, yet felt responsible for them as well. The sad reality was that it was we who were spiraling deep into a hopeless state of mental and spiritual bondage. We were not a light on a hill, radiating God's truth and loving hope to those around but were becoming increasingly drawn into a vacuous black hole which sought only to strip us of any trace of God's light within our hearts.

It was essential for us to make trips outside the camp for purposes performed in accordance with Jeff's instruction. We rented a storage locker at Elkins, West Virginia, to store items for which we did not have space at the camp. Initially, items which we weren't ready to use were stored there. Weights and weight training equipment, barrels of wheat, and a grinder were the types of articles which offered no immediate use to us. However, as we became more settled in, trips would be made to retrieve items from the storage area. Greg and Debbie were once sent to Washington, D.C., to mail letters. We had been instructed to write a letter to family members mentioning that we were well and not to worry about our disappearance. All letters were reviewed by Jeff before being mailed. Once the letters were ready, they were taken to Washington to keep from disclosing our location. I heard later that Jeff had instructed the Averys to write a letter prior to their deaths. I don't know if this is true, or if the family members of the Averys ever received such a letter. Jeff's attempt to disguise our location somehow failed. A few months later, Danny's father actually found us after only two weeks of searching. From this encounter we would learn that the letters mailed by Greg and Debbie had actually been postmarked from West Virginia. We interpreted his visit as a friendly one, despite the fact that he was entering a zone of danger for himself. I have no way of knowing exactly his perception of us, but I'm reasonably certain it was a frustrating and bizarre experience for him; bizarre in the aspect of the setting within which he found his son living, and frustrating in that he surely felt powerless to free Danny from it.

When the contract agreement for the rental truck came due, Greg followed me in his car and we made a trip to Washington D.C., for its return. During this trip I stopped, by way of Jeff's instruction, making a phone call to my son's school in Ohio, since we had never informed them we would be taking Matthew out of school. Along with having the storage locker in Elkins, we also did a great deal of shopping there. I made a few trips, but after a while, it became more of a weekly outing for Jeff and his "naturals." He and Alice, with the three younger Lundgrens, would go into town for groceries, and it would be obvious from the empty paper wrappers that it was a junk food run as well. Damon seldom went with them during these runs. It was clearly unfair that the other children of the group were unable to get a treat like that once in a while, and perhaps Damon thought it more fair if he stayed in camp with the others. A chastisement occurred once when Jeff found out that Tonya and Molly were washing their hair at the laundromat because of easy access to hot water. This was determined by Jeff to be unfair to the rest of us, as we did not have equal access to such a luxury. The issue remained as one of the many threats that seemed to ever hang over our heads, but clearly Jeff never considered his own abuses of unequal advantage.

Along with these occasional laundry runs, there were regular trips to town for drinking water and diesel fuel for the generator. At the first campsite I usually made the water runs. At the second location, we would find a spring that gave us more immediate access to fresh water, eliminating our need to go into town for water. This is how we interacted with the world, but were no longer a part of it. Much as in the words of Jesus who said "let the dead bury their dead" (Luke 9:60), we thought those who were not with us were against us (Romans 8:31). Sometimes I would be allowed to take Matthew and Amy with me on the water runs. It now sounds strange to think that any form of permission would be required for taking my own children on a short drive in order to help fill some plastic jugs with water. Although they went with me only a few times, it was gratifying to be able to give them an opportunity to enjoy the warmth of being inside the car.

Once, shortly after our arrival there when it was still quite cold, we had somewhat of a family outing. It turned out to be a disappointment due to the rainy weather, but it was still time together. Although we were with each other every day within the area of the camp it seemed as though we were actually quite distant. When possible, I tried teaching Matthew and Amy. As their father, this was not only my pleasure, but my duty as well. I'm saddened today to reflect on that memory of us being molded into the greater household, thereby diminishing the affection and loyalty of individual family units. So, on our family outing, we were sent to Elkins with a list of items to bring back from storage and also some things to buy at the store. The drive was nice, and just the four of us being together was great, but the rain clouds refused to break up. When we got to the storage locker I dug through to find what we were looking for, the kids remaining in the car to stay dry. Once again, Jeff managed to give us just enough money to buy the items needed at the store, so when we got hungry, we simply had to wait until we got back to camp. By this time we no longer had any discretionary money for ourselves. We pulled into a McDonalds in order to use the restrooms, which was a treat in itself, given the arrangements we had at camp. But being unable to afford anything to eat, returned to camp. Jeff had expressed the need for me to be back by a certain time, so the entire trip turned out to be quite hectic. In looking back, due to the limitations he put on our trip to keep us reminded of his priorities and the need to get back quickly, Jeff surely didn't trust me . Despite his claim of being the seer, with supernatural control over various acts of nature, the rainy weather was just an added disappointment.

* * *

WHILE AT THIS FIRST CAMP JEFF DID QUITE A LOT OF SHOOTING, sometimes at a shooting range. Damon was instructed to teach me how to clean the two guns I had, and in doing so he realized that they had never been sighted in. With this, he asked Jeff if we could go to a quarry area nearby and fire a few shots. Conservation of ammunition was important to Jeff, so less than two dozen rounds were fired between both guns; but on another day, Jeff would have me and the other men expend a thirty-round clip in a sudden burst. So sighting in my two guns with Damon would be the grand total of experience I had firing them. What it amounted to was that Jeff prided himself in being a better shot than the rest of us and he intended to keep it that way. He also enjoyed shooting, but like any other plaything, it was a habit that required money, and we were no longer bringing money in.

Grocery runs would be an ongoing part of our survival, but we also supplemented our food supply with what we found in the wild. This was an area of responsibility for Sharon, as she looked for various herbs and berries for us to eat. Jeff also began poaching deer. I'd never been much of a hunter, so skinning a deer and preparing the meat was a new experience for me. Keith showed how to do it the first time; after that the men in the group became skilled at getting the deer skinned and quartered very quickly. This would usually be done at night, then the next day we would all work on the remainder of the butchering. All but Jeff and Alice, that is. The perception was that we were all quite fortunate to have Jeff the mighty hunter to provide for us. I suppose he considered himself to be a cross between Nimrod of the Bible (Genesis 10:9) and Nephi of the *Book of Mormon* (1 Nephi 5:22–30). Nephi's bow had become broken and as the bows of the other men had lost their spring, he was the sole provider. Nephi's broken bow had been made of steel and was impossible to replace, but he was able to make one out of wood. By contrast, it had always been we who had provided for Jeff and his family. He did nothing to ensure that our needs would be met except by way of his manipulations for us to provide for him. Yet in Jeff's eyes, everything was his; sadly, it was that way in our eyes too. In the *Book of Mormon*, Joseph Smith illustrates the concept of there being two basic types of people: the industrious ones who build, and the predators who exploit. Like the Nephites, our challenge was to be an industrious people. Unfortunately, the description of the Lamanites now seems to be a better portrayal of our group as a whole. "And because of their cursing which was upon them, they did become an idle people, full of mischief and subtlety, and did seek in the wilderness for beasts of prey" (2 Nephi 4:39) Yet in our defense, most of us truly were industrious. We simply found ourselves overtaken by a doctrine that greatly influenced our vision as the object of our labors. By all description of the Lamanite behavior, Jeff was a supreme example, yet we mistakenly perceived his leadership as essential and our labors as scripturally sound.

In that the Nephites are an icon of Mormonism for good and righteous behavior, most Mormons (no matter their faction) are hard working, industrious people. While these are indeed noble attributes, works should never be confused for grace. "For we know that it is by grace that we are saved, *after all we can do*" (2 Nephi 11:44). To think that we only have salvation as a result of this growing process makes the entire doctrine of Christ out to be a coercive necessity for works. The quote above is a misleading notion that *Book of Mormon* believers have believed and trusted for nearly two centuries. We can do nothing to enhance nor diminish the grace of God toward us (Romans 8:38–39). Perhaps young Joseph Smith and his colleagues, in compiling the book, confused grace with fellowship. We can truly hinder our fellowship with God by living a lifestyle in darkness. "If we say that we have fellowship with him, and walk in darkness, we lie, and do not the truth; But if we walk in the light, we have fellowship one with another, and the blood of Jesus Christ his Son cleanseth us from all sin" (1 John 1:6–7). But our salvation is already complete by way of God's grace. We are to grow in that grace, in that we grow "from glory to glory" (2 Corinthians 3:18) in fellowship with Him.

However, "for it is by grace you have been saved, through faith: and this not from yourselves, it is the gift of God: not by works, so that no one can boast" (Ephesians 2:8–9, NIV). It is by faith that the blood of Jesus has truly washed us clean of all sin and we find God's grace. His grace is already there, but we find it by believing in faith that His Son, Jesus, did *already* die for our sins. "while we were yet sinners" (Romans 5:8). Even the faith it takes to discover His grace is a gift from God. Yet Nephi would have us believe that we don't have salvation until after we do all we can do.

To grow in fellowship starts with the assurance of salvation in Him and continues with the desire to increasingly open our hearts to His love. Yet we are taught not only in the following passage, but by the overall view of Mormon doctrine, that no salvation is possible until [after] works are performed.

> "And notwithstanding we believe in Christ, we keep the law of Moses, and look forward with steadfastness unto Christ, until the law shall be fulfilled; for, for this end was the law given: Wherefore, the law hath become dead unto us, and we are made alive in Christ, because of our faith."
> (2 Nephi 11:45–46)

This teaching comes from the proposed time period of 600 B.C., therefore, we are to believe that there was a need to continue on with the performance of Old Covenant law, despite the claim that the Nephites already had a deep understanding of what Jesus would do in the future. I must admit that this only makes sense in a sewer of logic sort of way. But compare it with the 10th chapter of Hebrews. "And their sins and iniquities I will remember no more. Now where remission of these is, there is no more offering for sin. Having therefore, brethren, boldness to enter into the holiest by the blood of Jesus" (Hebrews 10:17–19). If the law was so dead in the Nephites, as mentioned above by way of their faith toward Christ who was yet to come, then why did they keep it so very much alive in their daily performance of it?

This type of contradictory doctrine and behavior is common within cult settings, and so it's also the exact issue that Jeff's doctrines revealed in us. We perceived ourselves as living the Nephite lifestyle, yet we accomplished exactly the opposite. We were "Lamanites" in every way. It is by faith in the blood of Jesus that we no longer need to carry the blood of goats and calves into the Holy of Holies. Yet Mormon, and other cult teachings, suggest that works must continue in order for salvation to be accomplished. After all, if we fail to do all that we can do, it's quite clear that we cannot be saved. Paul, however, introduces the standard by which others must be measured on this issue. "If what a man had built survives, he will receive his reward. If it is burned up, he will suffer loss; he himself will be saved, but only as one escaping through the flames" (1 Corinthians 3:14–15, NIV). This scripture says that our fellowship may fail the refining fire of God's all piercing scrutiny, and our flaws will be revealed, but the heart that embraces the remission of sins as offered through the blood of Jesus shall be saved. Indoctrination by way of contradiction will eventually create an unstable individual who already comes with an altered perception of reality. Reality becomes not only distorted, but fluid and ever-changing. The only thing solid and stable was our rock-hard convictions toward Jeff's authority over us. We had no idea what lay in our future; not by way of Jeff's teachings, nor by any limited view of our own. Our eyes were solely locked onto Jeff, with no view of where we were going, or what God's plan for us, collectively and individually, really was. We lived not only in an ever-changing reality, but one not even visible to us. Our reality was one that only the seer could see—and all we could see was him.

> "But if our gospel be hid, it is hid to them that are lost; In whom the god of this world hath blinded the minds of them which believe not, lest the light of the glorious gospel of Christ, who is the image of God, should shine unto them. For we preach not ourselves, but Christ Jesus the Lord; and ourselves your servants for Jesus' sake." (2 Corinthians 4:3–5)

I can now truthfully say that I was lost, but now am found. Jeff pretended to teach of Jesus, yet to the contrary, taught only exaltation of himself. We became blinded to any vision of truth because all we could see was Jeff.

An ancient myth speaks of the great leviathan (Job 41) as a sea monster so great that its tail could eclipse the light of the sun. Anything that hinders our view of God (through nothing in and of itself) greatly affects the one whose vision is hindered. Any insignificant creature can create a shadow, but to the eyes of the one whom the shadow covers, the shadow is all that they see. No light, just darkness (1 John 1:6–7). The result is a devastating depravity. "Who opposeth and exalteth himself above all that is called God, or that is worshipped; so that as God sitteth in the temple of God, showing himself that he is God" (2 Thessalonians 2:4). People such as Jeff oppose God in that they exalt themselves. The *Book of Mormon* captivates its disciples with the search for the seer, not the messiah, which eclipses the relationship that could and should be established in Jesus; if only He was their focus of scrutiny. I'm not proposing that Mormonism is the only means or doctrine capable of hindering our view of God, but no matter what we believe and where we place our trust, care must always be given that nothing restricts us from seeing clearly. "But if thine eye be evil, thy whole body shall be full of darkness. If therefore the light that is in thee be darkness, how great is that darkness" (Matthew 6:23).

There we were, living in the open wilderness with no ties to the "world." We had cast it all away in search of a better and essential communion with God. "And save they shall cast these things away, and consider themselves fools before God, and come down in the depths of humility, he will not open unto them" (2 Nephi 6:84). Yet He did not open unto us. We became fools, but our efforts only managed to increase and deepen our captivity.

Chapter 14

BREAKING CAMP

TO

BROKEN HEARTS

A precept that had long been taught was the issue of speaking intelligently. "The glory of God is intelligence, or, in other words, light and truth; and light and truth forsaketh that evil one" (*D&C* 90:6a). For some reason, the revelation in D&C 90 seems to focus a bit more narrowly than merely as instruction to the church. It singles out just one man with a stern command that he get things straightened out within his house.

> "But verily I say unto you, my servant Frederick G. Williams, you have continued under this condemnation; you have not taught your children light and truth, according to the commandments, and that wicked one hath power, as yet, over you, and this is the cause of your affliction. And now a commandment I give unto you, if you will be delivered; you shall set in order your own house, for there are many things that are not right in your house."
> (D&C 90:6e–f)

As I go through these doctrines with a new awareness about control and subjugation, I see an intention within passages such as these that I had never before noticed. Joseph Smith, as a prophet of God was acting as a mouthpiece for the presentation of God's holy commands to his people of the one true church. He was the only one able to function in this capacity. Is it possible that this man, Frederick G. Williams, at some point had a conflict with young Joe Smith and that it was not God, but rather Joseph who was calling him on the carpet? For me, the answer to that question is as clear as the multitude of memories that I now have to live with.

My "house" was condemned as needing to be set in order, as was everyone else's in the group. Almighty God was to have scrutinized each of our individual households and instructed Jeff as to which areas needed attention and repentance. Such revelations and instructions concerning the problems in my household were constant. Jeff knew that the best way to control me was by the threat of danger to others, and this control intensified as the target of these dangers focused upon my own wife and children.

The committed relationship that my wife and I once had has since been dashed to pieces as a result of the long-term ramifications of our actions. I will always cherish the memory of the time we had together. Susie was truly a precious lady. She was sometimes teased because her qualities of innocence were confirmed through her vibrantly talkative personality. As sunshine personified, her Pollyanna attributes could brighten the cloudiest day. Unfortunately, I also recall the abuse and deterioration of these qualities. They were considered contrary to "speaking intelligently." Similarities between our chastisement sessions and later passages of that verse cannot go unmentioned.

The precept of speaking intelligently had long been a part of our mindset. One episode came about as the result of a conversation some of the women were having about childbearing. Susie had said something to the effect of how a pair of stretch pants had slimmed her hips after giving birth. Debbie, a registered nurse, said that Susie's claim on the issue was incorrect, therefore the matter was placed before Jeff. To Jeff, the stretch pants issue was a serious matter. As I recall, all that was claimed by Susie was that the pants seemed to have helped tighten her hips after childbirth. But now, Jeff had made it an issue of sin; she had not spoken intelligently and her "chatter-box" personality had allowed her tongue to cause her to sin. Being the precious and innocent person she was, this type of threat and coercion created a strong sense of fear within her, and also within me. As our lives spiraled downward into a figurative pit, similar to the literal one prepared for the Averys, I began losing all perception of self-value, to myself or even to my family. No matter what I did, sin seemed to remain not only within the camp in general, but even within my own household. Feelings of inadequacy set in, because the self-image I had was based upon the measurements given to me by Jeff. I no longer saw myself through a loving, gracious God's eyes, nor even my own, but only through Jeff's. And all that he or his god seemed to see was a lacking—and sin. Jeff would state from time to time that he had no fault with me, but always my family was held over my head as being either under threat or the cause for others to be threatened or to die.

This frame of mind had been slowly constructed even from our first encounters with Jeff. As seer, he was a godly authority, and he increasingly used this perception to his advantage. Recall an earlier statement in which Jeff identified me with the church of Pergamos in the book of Revelation. He identified himself with Philadelphia, which mentions the "key of David" (Revelation 3:7). Through his interpretation of chiasmus, Jeff had laid extensive claim upon them. When Tonya and Molly were taken from Dennis' tent, the manner in which Jeff would handle the issue would be an interpretation of what those keys were. In other words, how he dealt with the issue would define those keys. As I would later find out, the stealing of other men's wives was all it amounted to.

As I lost sight of my own worth by my weakened relationship with the True and Living God, the abusive efforts of Jeff to drive Susie and I apart became all the stronger. He would later link his wife-stealing passions with teachings about David and Bathsheba. I was unable to provide to my family the way in which they needed most. Yet this too, I now see as a lie; we lived

Chapter 14 BREAKING CAMP TO BROKEN HEARTS

throughout the entire venture on what had been amassed by the efforts of all except Jeff. By believing that everything actually belonged to Jeff, each day's survival became a blessed token of Jeff's compassion towards us in seeing to our needs, both spiritual and physical. Later, he taught that even the eternal salvation of my wife and children would come through him. This is clearly a concept against all Christian teaching, yet by the time it was taught, we not only embraced it, but felt guilty for not being personally capable of seeing and providing for the salvation needs of our families.

The entire local area was a gathering point for a number of activities; endurance trail bicycle racing, motorcycle and ATV races, all of which seemed to draw large crowds and lots of campers. Local media sources would sometimes cover a particular event, all of which were things we needed to avoid. Jeff had taken the ATV deeper into the woods quite regularly by this time and had found a new campsite where we would soon move.

But before we could move to the second camp, we would need to build a bridge for getting across the river from one camp to the other. Though the water level in that area of the Yellow river was usually pretty low, with the heavy current from that very rainy spring the little bridge remained quite sturdy. Once it was completed, we made the move to our second camp—and deeper into the "wilderness."

Chapter 15

"My Lord Delayeth His Coming"

From delay to delay our "lord' seemed to ever elude our approach of him (Luke 12:45). We needed to obtain the sword (sword of Laban, *Book of Mormon*) in order to survive the year, as well as other necessary items and records from the library. We were beginning to adjust to the wilderness lifestyle. But no opportunity to humiliate or threaten was ever missed by Jeff. I've experienced acute bouts of self-hatred from the memory of these things, and I can easily understand how difficult it can be for someone who has never experienced such mental entrapment to simply throw their hands up and call it absurd. Tragically, it is absurd. How could I have put up with such abuses, let alone allow such abuses toward others, especially my own wife and children? The frustrating and shameful reality was the power Jeff had over us. It controlled him, and us, in a highly intoxicating manner.

A short distance outside the camp, was a fire pit for burning trash. Danny was usually responsible for this task, one among many that filled the hours of his day. We had been awakened on a few occasions by visiting raccoons that entered camp and knocked over trashcans. Actually, the sound of the trashcans clanging was usually secondary to the barking that would resound from the two canine members of the group. One was a huge white Malamute, the other a half-Collie, half-German Shepherd. The Malamute was brought by the Johnsons when they moved to Ohio. The shepherd mix was Greg's. He got the dog as a pup when he worked as a tour guide at the Temple. Later, when Jeff merged all personal belongings into central ownership, Damon was assigned responsibility for the Malamute, but Greg continued caring for his dog.

One day, we noticed the prints of a bear around the trash pit area, apparently visiting us during the night. This was also the area we used for skinning deer. As a result of this visit, we became more cautious when processing deer. Nevertheless, the bear continued to dig through trash, eventually approaching nearer our camp while it was still daylight. It was a beautiful animal and we all enjoyed watching it. Jeff thought that the bear might become a threat to the horses while they grazed, or even the children and decided to shoot our big visitor. Jeff, as the "mighty hunter," strutted around after killing the bear, as though he'd done something quite brave. We ate bear meat for awhile, but even though Jeff was "like unto Moses," he seemed a bit hesitant to know whether or not it was "kosher." The day Jeff shot the bear, two more were seen running about fifty yards away. Fortunately, we had no more visitations from neighboring bears after that. If it hadn't been for the usual noise of the camp and our mere presence in the area, there would probably have been more wildlife nearby. We had a couple of berry-picking and mushroom-hunting days. Sharon informed us of the types of mushrooms to look for, as well as those to avoid. My daughter, Amy, could spot the tiniest, most nearly invisible, inedible mushrooms that nature provides. But despite the lack of productivity of her mushroom hunting, she showed a definite alertness in finding what she was looking for. The loss of interactions such as these with my children is quite distressing.

Next to the bridge we'd built, there were some boulders that could be used as stepping-stones to cross the river. The children had been told not to run on the bridge or the rocks. However, even in the choice seer's camp, a child at play could still forget a rule. This particular violation probably drew less attention from Jeff because it involved a game of tag initiated by his two youngest children. While Matthew was chasing them across the river, he fell and severely gashed the area above his eye. We had medical supplies for stitching up such a wound, so Debbie lay Matthew down on one of the tables as she closed the cut. A local anesthetic eliminated the pain, but he still had to endure the needle so near his eye.

During this time, Jeff's desire was that we become more militant. A chain of command was established and various levels of rank were assigned. Jeff was a four-star general. "God" was considered to be the only five-star general. Being Jeff's spokesman, I was a three-star general. This was due more to my being the only member, besides Jeff, with previous military experience. I once said something to the effect of not feeling much like a general, in that we had so few among us over which to command any authority. Jeff thought I lacked vision of all the other people who were supposed to be joining us soon. With the loss of the five Averys, we were to gain a number of people who would be "freed" from their "worldly" bondage. "One thousand shall flee at the rebuke of one; at the rebuke of five shall ye flee: till ye be left as beacon at the top of a mountain, and as an ensign on a hill" (Isaiah 30:17). I recall looking out over the valley where we were camped and trying to picture how such a collection of people could be organized. There were seven churches in Revelation, chapters 2 and 3, and I was to lead one of them. It would be a church, yet it would also be an army. Once again, Old Testament practice was replacing New Covenant grace. And warfare became altogether physical.

We practiced military exercises morning and evening. Jeff initiated war games a couple of times, yet this didn't really include any training. We would divide into two groups, one of which defended the camp while the other attacked. He handed out a few books from time to time on battle tactics. Watches were posted at the entrance of the trail leading to camp. To be leaders of churches meant that the men were to be leading generals over armies as well. Jeff had become quite adamant about not wanting anyone to discover the camp. We had a problem with people riding into camp on their motorcycles and ATVs, only to find that the trail didn't go anywhere. Whenever this happened, Jeff would get upset and yell about how he had been "compromised."

Chapter 15 "My Lord Delayeth His Coming"

It's very clear now that Jeff was never the one who was compromised or violated.

WHILE AT THIS CAMPSITE, Jeff declared that we had greatly worn Alice and him out. They made us believe it was a matter of their being so righteous that being surrounded by rebellion day in and day out became an exhausting burden for them to bear. For this reason, they needed a vacation, which would be a trip to Gettysburg. We were told it was an opportunity for Jeff to experience the days of battle that were fought there. To Jeff, any place where blood had been shed, particularly in battle, was considered sacred.

Whatever may be the truth about the matter and the purpose it provided for Jeff, at the end of their short trip to Gettysburg, Alice seemed much happier. She had a history of headaches, and the point in taking the trip in the first place was to give her some relief from them that our sin was supposed to have caused. However, Alice spoke of how she could feel the painful atmosphere all coming back again as they drew closer to the camp on their return. While living in Kirtland, it was insinuated that we were a burden to them and that the pressure was painful and exhaustive to Alice. But even Alice was not exempt from being singled out by Jeff as rebellious. Because I was his designated workout partner with weights, he often spoke to me about the burden of rebellion she was. It never occurred to me that he might not be the perfect head of household; nevertheless, he vehemently declared that the rest of us were to be. I now know there was much more to his statements about Alice than we were ever aware of. Jeff often stated to me how he feared he might lose her by way of death, but this never seemed to affect the slightest change in Alice's behavior. It created sympathy towards him in having to endure such an ongoing burden. Alice went through obvious abuses of her own. Yet, whatever she endured behind closed doors, was far less than that which she knowingly and willingly participated in. It was Alice who was the most vocal of the two when it came to a session. She had a healthy set of vocal cords and expressed no hesitation in using them. However, from the testimony she gave at my trial, it became clear that she had no difficulty using people in the same manner that Jeff had done. It's my belief that the day comes for each of us when our hearts reveal the results of our actions. Until that day comes, we are to seek truth with honest and contrite appraisal.

Upon their return to camp, Jeff mentioned that he wanted to make another trip to Gettysburg. He felt that his "three witnesses," (Greg, Damon and I) needed to experience the atmosphere it offered and also learn of the battle strategies that were used there. When he and Alice went, they were gone two or three days. This undoubtedly gave anyone with notions of leaving the group an opportunity to do so. I was left in charge of the group then, but on the second trip, Danny was in charge. I was clearly Jeff's second in command during this later part of the wilderness experience, but only in the military "chain of command" sense. I was not the second in command while we were in Kirtland and I was never, at any time, in complete possession of Jeff's confidence. He often stated that I was, but as I began discovering things others already knew, I began to see that, despite his proclaimed confidence in me, this was not the case. He claimed that I was acceptable to him and that he trusted me, yet continually lied.

So plans were made for a second trip, but this time Jeff took all of his immediate household, including Tonya and Molly. Greg and I also went, since we were two of his three witnesses.

> "And behold, ye may be privileged that ye may shew the plates unto those who shall assist to bring forth this work; and unto three shall they be shewn by the power of God: wherefore they shall know of a surety that these things are true. And in the mouth of three witnesses shall these things be established; and the testimony of three, and this work, in the which shall be shewn forth the power of God, and also his words of which the Father, and the Son, and the Holy Ghost beareth record; and all this shall stand as a testimony against the world, at the last day." (Ether 2:2–3)

These passages are traditionally understood in church history to be speaking of the three witnesses mentioned in the introduction of the *Book of Mormon* (e.g., Oliver Cowdery, David Whitmer, and Martin Harris). It is clear that this portrayal, while correct, is nonetheless based upon fiction. But as it was taught by Jeff through chiastic division, he too, should have "three witnesses" for the purpose of teaching of the "sealed portion." Look again at the words of Ether.

> "And now I, Moroni, have written the words which were commanded me, according to my memory; and I have told you the things which I have sealed; therefore touch them not, in order that ye may translate; for that thing is forbidden you, except by and by it shall be wisdom in God." (Ether 2:1)

What "Moroni" is recording concerns the issue of how the "sealed portion" is included within the golden plates (from which the *Book of Mormon* was later to be translated by Joseph Smith). This instruction from Moroni to Smith on the matter was to inform him that he was not to translate the sealed portion—but that "by and by" it shall occur by the "wisdom" (plan) of god. As I hope to have conveyed in previous chapters, the temple in Kirtland was identified as being the standing example of god's holy "pattern," or chiasmus. It was to be a physical representation of the language of god. "For, See, saith he, that thou make all things according to the plan showed to thee in the mount" (Hebrews 8:5).

> "And so great was the faith of Enoch that he led the people of God, and their enemies came to battle against them, and he spake the word of the lord, and the earth trembled and the mountains fled, even according to his command; and the rivers of water were turned out of their course, and the roar of the lions was heard out of the wilderness, and all nations feared greatly, so awful was the word of Enoch, and so great was the power of language which God had given him." (D&C 36:2b–c)

Chapter 15 "My Lord Delayeth His Coming"

The House (Kirtland Temple) was to have been built after god's pattern, just as the tabernacle was in Moses' day. By rightly dividing the word of truth according to this pattern, we were to be mighty in language and servants by god's wisdom. By using this pattern, it was taught that we were actually given the sealed portion and that the interpretations of god's message became unsealed through the dividing of the words. This process created a new language by way of the redefinition of terms. As his three witnesses, we were to witness the library of sacred records and thereby behold all things. These principles were taught while we were still living in Kirtland, though Jeff's "witnesses" had not yet been identified. I understand how bizarre these things must sound to the reader, especially those with no previous exposure to Mormon doctrines. But the purpose in writing this book is to offer how perceptions, as held by others, are not always close to that of our own. Concerning what I've just written on the issue of language, consider this quote from a member of the group in Waco, Texas, as printed in a local paper. "We were just people who were studying the Bible. We just had a different language than they did."[9] This ex-member from Mt. Carmel was probably yet to discover exactly what they had been involved in. They were not "just people who were studying the Bible," yet the statement made about having a "different language" speaks volumes.

Those of us who were taken on this second trip to Gettysburg left early in the morning and returned late in the evening. No time was wasted as we toured the area of the three-day battle. Much as in Enoch's day (Joseph Smith's version of history), Jeff was to lead "god's people," while our enemies would attempt battle against us. Therefore, he, as well as the modern-day "three witnesses," had to prepare for the purpose in our lives. We were passionate people with unyielding desires and belief toward God. I know that our behavior in no way represented that of true Christian example, but I hope at least for the moment, that the reader might consider us as the sincere and hard working people that we were, and that somewhere in the region of the heart where compassion allows understanding to illumine even the most hideous of actions, we might be seen as people who truly loved God. We gave our all, not for ourselves but in a passion to serve God and our fellow man. Yet our view of how to do that had become tragically distorted. As for doctrine, the potential for distortion was there even before meeting "the seer."

Laundry was undoubtedly the most pressing of chores that needed attention. The job was basically ongoing and never ending. Despite the chore, it became a time of sharing and camaraderie. One of my jobs was to grind the wheat for our baked goods, which I often did while others worked on laundry. As we worked in the campsite, whether heating water or washing laundry, grinding wheat or processing a deer, our minds would reflect upon those heartfelt passions by way of the view we had acquired toward them—rather than a view that was true. The purpose of this book is that these situations

---

[9] *The Vindicator*; Waco, Texas; April 20, 1994.

might be understood more thoroughly, and therefore more clearly so that we might find ways to deal with disturbing doctrines and mind control without the loss of life. I loved the people in the group. We shared, as well as endured, a great deal together by way of our common desires to serve God. The Averys were the finest of people and not at all deserving of the often disrespectful portrayal they sometimes received from those looking to produce a story. All of this creates a loss of friendships, which I miss. Work was a major part of our lives in the wilderness, yet not all of it. Classes were, of course, a continual part of our activities but several times there were events planned for us to have fun. Yet even at these times, hidden agendas were involved, but I see now that "hiding" was a basic principle within all of which Jeff did.

At one point we had a dance. For me, it was more a matter of having to be there than wanting to. It was much like an invitation to the King's Ball. Not only your attendance, but also your appreciation for and participation in the activity, were expected. Another activity requiring attendance was a "wrestle-mania." Jeff and his son, Jason, were both enthusiasts of the WWF (World Wrestling Federation). They loved to watch the "Wrestle-mania" competitions each year and even videotaped them. So when Jason asked Jeff if we could have a wrestle-mania of our own, plans began in preparation for it. An arena was made, complete with posts and ropes fastened around. The matches were all to be choreographed, yet Jeff made a few last minute changes for the purpose of humiliation.

It may sound odd, but there were many things about Jeff's behavior that I never liked, yet these characteristics he explained merely as his humanness. Though definitely weaknesses on his part, they did not hinder his position with god, or with god's work through him. This position with god, which he held as the choice seer, had by this time, grown to encompass a large area of scripture. The main character within the *Book of Mormon* is that of the choice seer, and the main theme is the establishment of Zion, which is to take place through him. More references speak of the coming seer than of the Messiah, Jesus Christ. Smith's translation of the bible also speaks of the choice seer— "another who should come and restore all things" (Matthew 17:14, *Inspired Version*). Eventually, our view of the Bible became not that which foretold of Christ and recorded His fulfillment, but rather a prophetic text speaking of Jeff as the seer and restorer of all things. Actually, this displaced emphasis for the Bible was present before meeting Jeff, merely by my own exposure to Mormon doctrines. In my own studies, the cross referencing of biblical passages with their Mormon counterparts gave false association to their intention.

* * *

MUCH AS ANY ANTICHRIST WOULD DO, Jeff began taking upon himself any name or reference that spoke of God, "so that he as God sitteth in the Temple of God, showing himself that he is God" (2 Thessalonians 2:4). Jeff boldly gave us each the assignment of searching out all his names, as referred to in

Chapter 15 "My Lord Delayeth His Coming"   127

scripture. The lists were quite long, and included references like Isaiah 9:6. "For unto us a child is born unto us a son is given: and the government shall be upon his shoulder: and his name shall be called Wonderful, Counselor, The Mighty God, The Everlasting Father, The Prince of Peace." A "son" was any man who had been redeemed (re-deemed: to feel and see). Terms like "mighty God" would be identified as not being the Almighty God, but rather it was a term used in association for various "seers" throughout time. In that we did not believe in a multiplicity of gods, Jeff was only a god of a physical type. It would have been correct "language" to state that the seers were all examples of the infinite god. Each of us had to exhibit a "strong faith and a firm mind, in every form of godliness" (Moroni 7:31). One of those "forms" was to be called "the god of the earth" for these final days.

We read in the first few verses of the book of John that Jesus was the Word made flesh. Jeff's teachings were the same, in that Jesus was the only perfect representation of the Father (John 12:45). However, though this precept is true, in that Jesus is the tangible, physical manifestation of the infinite and eternal Father, Jeff's teachings nullified the very thing that Jesus is a fulfillment of—the law and ordinances against us. "Blotting out the handwriting of ordinances that was against us, which was contrary to us, and took it out of the way, nailing it to his cross" (Colossians 2:14). We have a mediator for our petitions to the Father by way of that which Jesus nailed upon the cross and by His Victorious resurrection (1 Timothy 2:5).

Even untainted verses of the New Testament frame one's call according to gender. "Let the women learn in silence with all subjection. But I suffer not a woman to teach, nor to usurp authority over the man, but to be in silence" (1 Timothy 2:11–12). However, our view of God's word had been turned away from a grace-oriented view of Christ and toward an Old Testament view of the quaking law of God, rigidly defined. According to the RLDS bible, mankind became "carnal, sensual and devilish" from the transgression of Adam while in the garden.

> "And he said unto them, because that Adam fell, we are; and by his fall came death, and we are made partakers of misery and woe. Behold, Satan hath come among the children of men, and tempteth them to worship him; and men have become carnal, sensual, and devilish, and are shut out from the presence of God." (Genesis 6:49–50, *Inspired Version*)

Hence, the need to come back into his presence. This is clearly plagiarism on the part of Joseph Smith in order to apply a principle mentioned in the New Testament book of James with the philosophy of his newly created religion. Notice above the similarity with the third chapter of James, "This wisdom descendeth not from above, but is earthly, sensual and devilish" (James 3:15).

To connect the expulsion of Adam and Eve from the Garden of Eden with that of leaving or being cut off from the presence of the Father is commonly accepted in Christianity. However, Jeff associated this teaching from James with principles of gender, a subtle deflection away from the truth of God's word as introduced by Joseph Smith. In this case, the teaching was an Old Testament view of church authority, wherein women under the New Covenant were still perceived by the principles associated with the fall. This places the woman in subjugation to the man, with the ministry of childbearing as defined in the remainder of 1 Timothy chapter 2, quoted previously. Consider the remaining verses.

> "For Adam was first formed, then Eve. And Adam was not deceived, but the woman being deceived was in the transgression. Notwithstanding she shall be saved in childbearing, if they continue in faith and charity and holiness with sobriety." (1 Timothy 2:13–15)

There is a purpose in male and female, and that purpose was formed according to the image of God (Genesis 1:27), in that the two, as one, bear His "likeness." Therefore, we have the statement in verse 26 to "let Adam have dominion," because "in that day that God created man, in the likeness of God made he him; male and female created he them; and blessed them, and called Their name Adam, in the day when they were created" (Genesis 5:1–2). By placing James 3:15 in connection with the fall, it keeps our eyes (in the application of the passage) looking backward, toward Old Testament roles of gender, instead of forward toward the Messiah. This end result was that woman became responsible for the earthy, sensual and devilish spirit of wickedness as described by James. Although Joseph Smith plagiarized this principle, with Jeff's ability to distort scriptures even further, "carnal, sensual and devilish" behavior was taught to be the correct position of women; in complete harmony with God's "creative plan." Joseph Smith's intention in doing this was most likely to make the bible message collaborate with what he was teaching in the *Book of Mormon* (Alma 19:91). But as falsehood only produces more falsehood, Jeff took it a step further. I have hesitantly entered into this issue, because even in the most well-balanced settings of Christian church structure, when the topic of operational authority from God arises, lines between genders often become lines of battle. However, despite variations of scriptural interpretation as applied in the most healthy of settings, we had quite a variation of our own.

As women were vessels for physical procreation, men were considered vessels for the spiritual. This meant that women and children (as offspring through them) were the anchoring element that kept men spiritually fastened to the earth. This wasn't intended to be negative toward women; we were taught it must be understood in order to grasp the purpose God has for His creation. The following passage could well be used for representing this principle.

Chapter 15 "My Lord Delayeth His Coming"

"But if I tarry long, that thou mayest know how thou oughtest to behave thyself in the house of God, which is the church of the living God, the pillar and the ground of the truth. And without controversy great is the mystery of godliness: God was manifest in the flesh, justified in the Spirit, seen of angels, preached unto the Gentiles, believed on in the world, received up into glory." (1 Timothy 3:15–16)

The pillar and the ground of God's purpose in creation is a mystery that bridges the gap between the tangible world and that which is not. How does that which is mortal become immortal? How does that which is corruptible put on incorruption? Jeff, as the seer, was a "god of the earth" by title. This meant that he was to act out the spiritual principles of god in a physical way.

One day a fight erupted between Jeff's two younger children and my son Matthew. Anyone familiar with Matthew's personality is aware that he is not an overbearing child, yet Jeff's daughter came to him with the complaint that Matthew had been too bossy at play; therefore, the issue was introduced at class time. I noticed situations where Jeff's youngest, Chrissy, considered it her responsibility to govern the play of the other children. I also heard her speak on occasion about how her dream in life was to be a queen, with lots of servants to do things for her. Children's playtime fantasies involve acting out imaginary roles ranging from everyday people to superheroes, and variations between. In that Chrissy's mother was a queen within the scope of our group environment, it's no wonder that her expressed desires were so similar. She was a sweet little girl, but the accusation she made about Matthew was false. Matthew told me previous to this, that Chrissy and Caleb kept trying to tell him what to do. What a shame that I failed to have the perception of my son. When Jeff introduced the issue at class, I made a very short rebuttal of how all the children had been a little bossy toward each other lately. Jeff immediately became angry and accused me of having "anger against god." He dropped the matter by stating that we all needed to keep a closer watch on the behavior of our children, then proceeded with class. However, the matter was not closed, and he managed to work it into his agenda at a later time.

* * *

WE WERE INDOCTRINATED. We were seeing whatever Jeff produced from the words as being true. By way of his chiastic manipulations of what we believed to be God's word, he produced yet another necessary ritual. Since women were vessels for physical procreation and our children are the result of that process, Jeff, as the "god of the earth," was soon teaching that he alone was the salvation for women and children. The men had to endure the fire and scrutiny of the everlasting god, but women were to endure the scrutiny of Jeff. Much as recorded about Esther and her encounter with King Ahasuerus (Esther 1 and 2), four women were to come before the "god of the earth" in order to become "acceptable" as part of his household. But, with this encounter, Jeff would take the "sin" of them and the children upon himself—then he would go before the Lord with their sin. As seer, there could be no question that he rendered himself in the Messiah's stead. The men of the group, as heads of households, were to go before the Lord ourselves carrying our own sin. This increased the already existing inferiorities resident within all of us. We were of very little value to our families, yet Jeff was the mediator for them all. In recording these things, I reflect from within my heart just how vile and decadent our view of salvation had become. We kept striving to perform "all we can do," under the illusion that only after such accomplishment can we obtain grace—grace which has been freely given all along.

The ritual just outlined had also been approached from another direction. Four women who had been set aside for this purpose were identified as the "four corners of the earth." What they performed would represent the carnal aspect of mankind. By reading various passages on the "gathering" process into Zion, Jeff created a basis for this performance. And by this performance, the process of gathering could then begin. "And he shall set up an ensign for the nations; and shall assemble the outcasts of Israel, and gather together the dispersed of Judah from the four comers of the earth" (Isaiah 11:12). The ritual would be that of a dance and the women were to dance naked before Jeff. Such passages as in Hebrews 4 were used as expressions of spiritual things that Jeff was to make manifest in the physical. "Neither is there any creature that is not manifest in his sight: but all things are naked and opened unto the eyes of him with whom we have to do" (Hebrews 4:13). Also passages such as,

> "Again I will build thee, and thou shall be built, O virgin of Israel: thou shalt again be adorned with thy tabrets, and shall go forth in the dances of them that make merry...Then shall the virgin rejoice in the dance, both young men and old together: for I will turn their mourning into joy, and will comfort them, and make them rejoice from their sorrow." (Jeremiah 31:4, 13)

Women, the fallen or carnal side of mankind were identified with Babylon. It was time for "Babylon" to be humbled before god. Yet as the process was portrayed through the words of Jeremiah (quoted above), it was also to be a rejoicing time of rebirth and new life. Zion would be established through the labors of the choice seer, another Elijah who would restore all things. As Elijah, Jeff identified himself as the angel that ministered to Jesus at the garden of Gethsemane, "Saying, Father, if thou be willing, remove this cup from me: nevertheless not my will, but thine, be done. And there appeared an angel unto him from heaven, strengthening him" (Luke 22:42–43).

It was in this area of his teaching that his accusation of my becoming angry against god comes back into the scenario. His three witnesses (Greg, Damon and myself), were made synonymous with Peter, James and John. Unable to stay awake at Gethsemane, Jeff determined that this was a form of rebellion, or more specifically, anger. So, when I made the statement a few days prior to this night's class about all the children having been acting a little bossy, it was construed by Jeff as having caused a "rippling effect" throughout time. This caused Jesus to be without comfort from his companions of that day, in that they were unable to stay awake for one hour (Matthew 26:40–41). In speaking out about the children, I had given way to temptation and allowed place in my heart for anger, even though just for a moment. This anger was the torment endured by Jesus that night at Gethsemane. Jeff identified himself as the angel who was able to be the sole source of comfort through His pain, therefore, Jeff had endured the one hour with Him already. We had not. And as restorer of all things, we had to set that one hour in order. Therefore, the dance was the one-hour price to be paid which I and my household owed. For Susie, it was a one-hour ritual of humiliation and degradation. For me, it was the process of keeping my mind on the word of God during that one hour. The spirit had been willing, but the flesh had been weak, so now it was time for the spirit to subdue the weakness of the flesh and keep my fleshly concerns in subjection. The scenario would be the same for the other spouses of the women who were identified as corners of the earth. After its accomplishment, each husband had to swear an oath to Jeff. As servants, our households were thereby bonded to Jeff in that he was the seer and the only one who could stand before God in atonement for the sins of our wives and children. This abominable act was also labeled god's "strange act."

> "For the Lord shall rise up as in mount Pergamos he shall be wroth as in the valley of Giboan, that he may do his work, his strange work; and bring to pass his act, his strange act. Now therefore be ye not mockers, lest your bands be made strong: for I have heard from the Lord God of hosts a consumption, even determined upon the whole earth." (Isaiah 28:21–22)

This sacred act was not to be mocked, and the women involved were to be highly respected. A topic which had long been taught was that a man's true wife was flesh of his flesh.

> "And Adam said, This is now bone of my bone, and flesh of my flesh: she shall be called Woman, because she was taken out of Man. Therefore shall a man leave his father and his mother, and shall cleave unto his wife: and they shall be one flesh." (Genesis 2:23–24)

The earlier stages of Jeff's teachings had been quite chaste in that they seemed to magnify a monogamous marriage relationship. However, the madness of this wilderness timeframe seemed to have opened the door to a new dimension of depravation. A man's true wife was given to him from God (Genesis 2:18, 22). But it was becoming increasingly accepted that in a fleshly sort of way, Jeff was god. By this time, the issue of polygamy was appearing to be something which "god" may have required at some time. I recall Jeff's earlier statements that Alice was all he wanted in a wife and that he had no inclination toward others. He spoke of how even though polygamy had been practiced long ago, it would not be needed this time. But when he remarked about Alice being all he wanted, I asked, "May the spokesman be like unto the seer?" Verbal structuring of such inquiries was very important. He gave me no answer, but equally, no reason to be concerned. I wanted no other wife than Susie and considering any fearful preoccupation with the issue to be sin, I therefore dismissed it. As Paul teaches in his letter to the Ephesians, the church is Christ's bride. "For the husband is the head of the wife, even as Christ is the head of the church: and he is the saviour of the body...For we are members of his body, of his flesh, and of his bones" (Ephesians 5:23, 30). So, by way of the dance as an ordinance, the women were all to become Jeff's bride. Though this would not cancel out the marriages that we already had, it still appeared that Jeff would be able to make somewhat of an ongoing claim upon them.

Keith and I inquired what these things meant and Jeff responded that all women were to be his wives and he was the only man upon earth who could carry their sin before god. "Man" was another term identified that basically meant "redeemed." However, his assurance to us was that he would make no such claim. He emphasized that Kathy was Keith's true wife and that Susie was mine. He also explained that though David had claim upon the women of Israel for a bride, he did not make physical claim of them all (2 Samuel 12:8). This eased the trauma to some extent, but it still seemed as though god was becoming more and more of a test and less of a promise. I had shed the world for this god. I had moved out on faith alone against many odds. I had even participated in the deaths of a family for this god and accepted threats on my own life as well. I was ready to go to war for this god. But none of it ever seemed to be enough.

"There are three things that are never satisfied, four that never say enough! the grave; the barren womb; land which is never satisfied with water; and fire, which never says, 'enough!' " (Proverbs 30:15–16, NIV). As the proverb indicates, we could never give "enough." As death itself, Jeff's god would never be satisfied. Like a barren womb, his teaching could never bear fruit and give birth to life. We had been led into the wilderness, but not by any Moses. Jeff was merely a cloud without rain (2 Peter 2:17; Jude 12), which promised water that never came to quench our desert souls. And though we were to have started the fire by way of the covenant performed in Kirtland, the god he had ignited was known only to him. To this day, the destruction still fails to cease, but at least I can now say that I know the True God, who is able to say: "It is Enough" (2 Samuel 24:16).

***

ALICE SPENT FIVE CONTINUOUS HOURS OF PREPARATION with the women on one day. During this period of indoctrination, threats were made and deeply engraved upon their thinking. There were details of instruction that we as husbands were not to know. Jeff had begun the annihilation of our moral codes

Chapter 15 "MY LORD DELAYETH HIS COMING"

long before this time, with all the subtlety of slow and continual redefinition. Use of tobacco is considered a fairly major issue within fundamental Mormon belief and doctrine, yet this too had been redefined and he had begun buying cigars; even his smaller children were introduced to this habit. The time eventually came for the dance. During the one hour Susie and I had to separately endure, I cloaked my mind with "god's" word while smoking a cigar, alone in my tent. Upon completion of the act, I went to Jeff's tent and swore my oath of service to him. Susie had been targeted over and over as being a big part of the hindrance in my life, which kept me from fulfilling God's purpose for me. The dance was a way to improve that hindrance, thus opening the way for our continuation with what we had started. Susie saw herself as being the one thing that stopped me from fulfilling God's purpose in my life.

As the servant over the church of Pergamos, the place of my dwelling was also where Satan resided.

> "I know thy works, and where thou dwellest, even where Satan's seat is: and thou holdest fast my name, and hast not denied my faith, even in those days wherein Antipas was my faithful martyr, who was slain among you, where Satan dwelleth." (Revelation 2:13)

Susie had been singled out as that presence of Satan in my household. By not "speaking intelligently," she was labeled as the snare in my path that kept me from moving forward. This continued the suffering of thousands who endured the affliction caused by my "sinful procrastination." But with her dance finished, we were free to move on with the mission we had been "chosen" to establish all along—at least that was our belief. We had become highly intoxicated by the mental process that used what we believed to be God's word. Though Jeff claimed to have fulfilled many things, our extreme "drunkenness," by way of a doctrine, was his only real accomplishment. "Woe unto him that giveth his neighbor drink, that puttest thy bottle to him, and makest him drunken also, that thou mayest look on their nakedness" (Habakkuk 2:15). Jeff quoted Isaiah 5:20 quite often as a statement that tradition had distorted. "Woe unto them that call evil good, and good evil; that put darkness for light, and light for darkness; that put bitter for sweet, and sweet for bitter!" Once again, his ability to employ the process of contradictions was well developed. While saying and teaching one thing, he was truly accomplishing quite the opposite. Like a magician, he kept us distracted while creating an illusionary view of reality. Eventually, everything took on totally different meanings, and the god of our viewpoint grew demanding and all-encompassing. However, with that all behind us now we were finally moving forward again and would soon be able to go before the Lord. Or would we?

Chapter 16

HIS KINGDOM BEGINS TO TOPPLE

With the dance process completed, the way was now open. Any day now we would be able to travel back to Kirtland and enter the library. We would be able to get the sword for Jeff's great purpose and we would be able to obtain the records of our forefathers for the restoration of all things. We were finally pleasing and acceptable before God. Jeff had taken upon him the name Jesus, but not "the Christ." He was the physical messiah, of sorts, but not the Messiah of spiritual salvation. Only the Eternal God could fill that position. Yet, Jeff was to take upon him "every form of godliness," therefore, he was to be like Christ, in taking upon himself the sins of flesh.

> "Behold, I say unto you, Nay; neither have angels ceased to minister unto the children of men. For behold, they are subject unto him, to minister according to the word of his command, shewing themselves unto them of strong faith and a firm mind, in every form of godliness. And the office of their ministry is, to call men unto repentance, and to fulfill and to do the work of the covenants of the Father which he hath made known unto the children of men, to prepare the way among the children of men, by declaring the word of Christ unto the chosen vessels of the Lord, that they may bear testimony of him." (Moroni 7:30–32)

Angels were to appear to us at the day of our redemption and also when we received the library records. It had been determined through division that angels were really the prophets throughout time and Keepers of the records. As the seer, Jeff would be able to identify exactly who was to be present (angel/prophets) so that we would be prepared.

> "And the veil was taken from off the eyes of the Brother of Jared and he saw the finger of the Lord; and it was as the finger of a man, like unto flesh and blood; and the Brother of Jared fell down before the Lord, for he was struck with fear. And the Lord saw that the Brother of Jared had fallen to the earth; and the Lord said unto him, why hast thou fallen? And he said unto the Lord, I saw the finger of the lord, and I feared lest he should smite me; for I knew not that the Lord had flesh and blood." (Ether 1:69–71)

The Brother of Jared did not know that Christ would take upon Himself flesh and blood, along with revelations of other things he needed to know (this was to have been around 2200 B.C.). Therefore, he was not completely prepared to enter god's presence. For this reason, he "fell" (associated with the "fall of mankind"), and god told him to arise.

The term "arise" became a common cliché among us and it was always associated with redemption from the great fall.

> "And in that day, the Holy Ghost fell upon Adam, which beareth record of the Father and the Son, saying, I am the Only Begotten of the Father from the beginning, henceforth and forever; that, as thou hast fallen, thou mayest be redeemed, and all mankind, even as many as will." (Genesis 4:9, *Inspired Version*)

The next verse explains a little more about the fruit of Adam's redemption—the opening of one's eyes to see God.

> "And in that day Adam blessed God, and was filled, and began to prophecy concerning all the families of the earth; saying, Blessed be the name of God, for, because of my transgression my eyes are opened and in this life I shall have joy, and again, in the flesh I shall see God." (Genesis 4:10, *Inspired Version*)

Through this process, Adam was to have received a language "pure and undefiled."

> "And then began these men to call upon the Lord; and the Lord blessed them; and a book of remembrance was kept in the which was recorded in the language of Adam, for it was given to as many as called upon God, to write by the spirit of inspiration; And by them their children were taught to read and write, having a language which was pure and undefiled." (Genesis 6:5–6, *Inspired Version*)

This language, as noted before, was identified as the pattern, and the pattern was to be seen within the house of god. "Thou son of man, show the house to the house of Israel, that they may be ashamed of their iniquities: and let them measure the pattern" (Ezekiel 43: 10). "Who serve unto the example and shadow of heavenly things, as Moses was admonished of God when he was about to made the tabernacle; for, See, saith he, that thou make all things according to the pattern shown to thee in the mount" (Hebrews 8:5). The RLDS temple in Kirtland bears no resemblance to any Israelite temple, or to the tabernacle of Moses. It's just a nice building that became confused as the pattern of God. With all these things done, God's people gathered, taught the language which was to be pure and undefiled, followed the seer's instruction even to the rebuke of five and by the placement of sin upon him by way of the strange act (dance). We were now ready to establish Zion.

Woman was flesh of man's flesh, bone of man's bone (Genesis 2:23). Jeff, as the seer, was provided as a flesh and bone representation of the eternal salvation through Christ. Like John the Baptist, he was to be another Elias—a

Chapter 16 HIS KINGDOM BEGINS TO TOPPLE

wild man from the wilderness. The lesson was learned, in part, from Joseph Smith's account of Enoch.

> "And it came to pass, that Enoch went forth in the land, among the people, standing upon the hills, and the high places, and cried with a loud voice, teaching against their works. And all men were offended because of him; and they came forth to hear him upon the high places, saying unto the tent-keepers, Tarry ye here and keep the tents while we go yonder to behold the seer for he prophesieth; and there is a strange thing in the land, a wild man hath come among us." (Genesis 6:39–40, *Inspired Version*)

As the TV newsman would later say, it all became real to us in a sewer of logic sort of way. Like a form of mental, emotional and/or spiritual osmosis, we had long been bathed in a sewer of logic and saturated with warped and deceptive imitations. Our senses had become altered, moral values and even conscience had become redefined. Jeff had performed all these things, thereby fulfilling the command to be of "strong faith and a firm mind in every form of godliness" (Moroni 7:31).

It was done, culminating with a class stating that none of us would be "lost." Up to this point, any of us were scared to die without being "redeemed." But now, we were finally moving forward with an open door before us. Jeff actually seemed relaxed among us, as though we were no longer so much of a burden to bear. Tension in the group seemed to decline, but with fall weather just around the corner, temperatures were soon to decline as well.

One day I went to the quarry area in order to do some exercising. This was not a common practice, as our activities were generally more group oriented and supervised. But continual individual preparation had been urged by Jeff so on this particular day, Susie had been able to come with me. As I ran, she sat down on the grass to enjoy the solitude and calmness. Later on, while I was running, I noticed that I could no longer see her. I became panic-stricken. I had heard the sound of motorbikes in the area earlier, and my mind began racing with thoughts of her being abducted or harmed. I guess we had simply been through so very much and my view of the outside world was so alien, that in my mind, we were quite literally at war. The entire world was a dangerous enemy. I didn't really fear this enemy, but with Jeff's continual threats, feared losing Susie or our children. My mind had become full of such scenarios by way of the sessions that had long been a part of our learning process. Eventually, I found Susie sitting on the ground of a sloping hillside and surrounded by high grass. I had been calling for her, but she couldn't hear me. She had felt the desire to sit there and sing. And she sang songs about God that we had once known and enjoyed a "lifetime" ago. Today our relationship has been severely crushed, if not permanently destroyed, primarily due to our inability to heal together as a family, from all that we have been through. The problem evolved from poor communication, to miscommunication, and finally to no communication at all. But I know there was a time when Susie possessed a childlike innocence and her heart was full of prayer toward God.

Perhaps it still is, but not all that now comes from her heart is true. However, on this particular day, I think perhaps our True and Living Heavenly Father had His ear inclined to her voice and the heartfelt praises she sang. It was too late for the Avery family, and for the abuses we had endured and long term effects of all that had occurred. It was too late for the rest of us, but Jeff's kingdom was beginning to topple. Many loving friends and family members had been praying for us, and the destructive nature of Jeff's doctrine was bound to destroy itself in the end.

* * *

WHEN WE WERE LIVING IN KIRTLAND, Jeff and Alice had taken Greg and I to a park in southern Ohio. I don't recall exactly where it was, but it had a canyon running through it with several huge sinkholes. Despite the covert planning employed by Jeff, behavior such as this makes me think that he actually believed his lies. We, in turn, by being his disciples, undoubtedly served to strengthen his self-delusion.

Our baptismal font would be one that Jeff determined to be at one of the very locations where the flood waters of Noah's day had receded.

> "For behold, they rejected all the words of Ether; for he truly told them of all things, from the beginning of man; and that after the waters had receded from off of this land, it became a choice land above all other lands, a chosen land of the Lord." (Ether 6:2)

This prophet named Ether would speak of the unique blessedness of this land and how a New Jerusalem would be established here in the last days, no doubt as a result of the choice seer.

> "And that a New Jerusalem should be built up on this land, unto the remnant of the seed of Joseph, for which things there had been a type…Wherefore the remnant of the house of Joseph shall be built up on this land; and it shall be a land of their inheritance." (Ether 6:6,8)

And when the end comes, when earth and heaven pass away.

> "Then cometh the New Jerusalem; and blessed are they who dwell therein, for it is they whose garments are white through the blood of the lamb; and they are they who are numbered among the remnant of the seed of Joseph, who were of the house of Israel." (Ether 6:10)

There is a great deal of emphasis in Mormonism upon the "spiritual" lineage of the Old Testament Joseph who was sold into Egypt. But for us, the coming newness was the time when all things would be restored. Therefore, even the place of our baptism would need to be identified. While not an immediate concern to us, with cold weather coming, it soon would be. When would the day come for Jeff to take us to the library? It never would. As David had gone

Chapter 16 HIS KINGDOM BEGINS TO TOPPLE

into the wilderness in hiding from Saul, we, too, were to find refuge in the rocky areas of our current abode, and where we would be baptized. Ether had done the same. "And as he dwelt in the cavity of a rock he made the remainder of this record...Wherefore it came to pass that in the first year that Ether dwelt in the cavity of a rock" (Ether 6:15,19). But though our minds were full of the numerous types of our distorted reality, things were beginning to crumble.

Both the Johnson's Suburban and our Plymouth had broken down. The Suburban engine was completely shot, but the only thing that needed repair on the Plymouth was the distributor. But since Jeff wanted them both sold for scrap, that's what we did. This left us considerably lacking in transportation, but this was not an issue to us. The horses had been more of a burden than a benefit and since we needed more money, Jeff decided to sell them, too. Kathy was more experienced with horses than anyone else in the group, so she was always involved with plans where they were concerned. Contact was made with the owner of a trail ride operation in the area. Though he wasn't in the market for them, he said he would check around. With no Suburban, we had nothing powerful enough to pull the horse trailer. Jeff's little pickup could manage it through the hills, but only while empty and it was difficult even then. So, Jeff had also sold the horse trailer. The trail ride owner came to transport the horses to his ranch with his own truck. He had apparently promised not to ride the horses, or use them on his trail rides. But when Kathy checked on them over the days that followed, she noticed that they had, indeed, been ridden. Jeff got upset about the horses being used, but there was no way to get them back to camp so he decided to take Kathy and a few of the rest of us with him and walk them back. This turned into a fiasco, with the seer getting lost. It was quite a long distance. Some of us stayed with the horses overnight, but when we thought we were at the final stretch, Jeff and Kathy didn't show up—and Alice was furious. In retrospect, Alice's behavior was quite inconsistent with her own acceptance of Jeff's teachings.

Only a few weeks prior to this episode with the horses, a class was taught concerning the "enlarging of Jeff's tent." Tonya was to have been Jeff's second wife and Alice expressed no problem with this. The morning that Jeff and Tonya were supposed to consummate their marriage, Alice sat at the table quietly. Like Sarah sending Hagar to Abraham, she was in conformity with the wifely position (which is not to suggest that Hagar's going in to Abraham was ever proper conduct before God). We were told that nothing ever actually happened and within weeks, Jeff gave Tonya back to Dennis. But where Kathy was concerned, Alice was not in conformity. She did not hesitate to express her disapproval.

When Jeff and Kathy finally returned in late afternoon of the following day, Alice was enraged. These outbursts of rebellion caused Alice a great deal of grief during the months to follow. As I see it, she helped to create a monster, and the monster was out of control. However, this was not the only situation that would heighten Alice's concerns about Jeff and Kathy. Following the "dance," Kathy apparently expressed concern regarding Tonya's husband, Dennis. Tonya was living in Jeff's tent at the point of the dance although clearly identified as being Dennis' wife. Yet Kathy's concern was that Dennis had no wife to dance on his behalf at that point. Since the women were to dance for the benefit of their children and themselves, and not their husbands, it seems odd that Kathy would have that as a concern in the first place. Besides, neither Damon nor Danny had wives to dance, so that was clearly not the issue. Jeff had been working on Kathy for a long time and what I'm about to explain was merely a part of Jeff's plot to take Kathy from Keith. By her expression of this unnecessary concern for Dennis and offering to dance a second time for his benefit, Kathy was in essence offering to "intercede" for him. This topic of "intercession" had already been taught, in preparation for the dance. Everyone knew what the term meant. It was when a woman would go to the seer to have sex with him, as a sacrifice of herself in order to appease God's wrath toward some other person. This is how women were used in ways that tore them away from their husbands. This is clearly a disgusting topic, but everything had become redefined in accordance with Jeff's tastes of sexual preference. Kathy's concern for Dennis and offer to dance, was interpreted as an offer to intercede. But there was no need for intercession. Jeff had not expressed that Dennis needed to be interceded for. Nevertheless, the words had been spoken so it was "sealed" as having to be done.

A strong sense of legalistic process was our lifestyle. Jeff made claim of how he searched the scriptures for an avenue of which to annul the offer that had been made. But of course, none could be found. The day came for the dance to take place. Alice was visibly upset, so Jeff told Greg and me to go with her while she walked outside the camp, which we did. Much as two sons comforting their mother, we tried to keep her calm until Jeff came out from the tent. By that time, Alice was actually quite calm. This forgiving, or accepting attitude, despite all that Alice truly knew about Jeff's plans and abuses, makes me think that he did have some type of control over Alice. Yet by all the other evidence it appears that her love for him was the only source of that control. I don't understand how she could have known what she knew and still loved him so much. Having searched out the matter, I do know exactly how the rest of us became so hypnotized by his leadership. There were no limits of our subjugation to Jeff.

* * *

SOON AFTER THIS, the geographic boundaries of Jeff's small dominion would greatly expand, by way of a helicopter visit. It didn't land, nor even really try to communicate, but circled around the camp several times just above the treetops. Later, we would be told it was an investigator hired by family members of Dennis and Tonya. But at this immediate time, we thought we could be under attack. As with the assault on Mt. Carmel in Waco, some form of helicopter reconnaissance is often the prelude to a ground assault. Greg was sent out to the road where the cars were parked, in order to look for signs of any activity there. The helicopter made a few wide sweeps in order to keep track of where Greg had gone, but he soon returned with news that no one was in the lot. However, Jeff seemed pretty certain that we were under threat, so the women and children were sent to a predetermined area of safety. I was to escort them there without being seen, but this was impossible to do and the attempt only made us appear peculiar. I had changed to camouflage gear by this time, presumably not visible by the helicopter. We dashed from one group of trees to the next, none of which offered much cover. We finally made it to our hiding area and soon the other men joined us with whatever ammunition they could carry. Of course, the fifty-caliber had been brought. The ATV trailer, pre-loaded with ammunition stood ready for just such an encounter. However, it didn't work well, in that no trail was prepared. An earlier day, Jeff had decided to take the fifty-caliber to the quarry and shoot it. As it turned out, the gun was quite well made and gave very little recoil. I was allowed one shot with it that day, and even as a novice, I had no difficulty. I throw that in here to illustrate how Jeff was not well prepared. At least not in the testing of his own "armor" (1 Samuel 17:39).

So there we were—waiting for the world to come against us. I'm thankful today that no one did. By this experience, I feel that I can understand the unyielding dedication of those who were in the compound at Waco. To me, the issue of Waco has more than one facet of concern. There is the issue of constitutional freedoms and the protection of one's home. But what occurred prior to that? What created the scenario in the first place and formed the actions that would be assumed by the compound members that first morning of the assault? We were on "holy ground" with the choice seer, who was, in our reality the god of the earth. Had anyone come against us that day, I'm convinced that there would have been bloodshed. That is, of course, unless Jeff was to surrender, and I find that an absurd possibility. But as before and many times over, our minds were locked into the command. If the command had been to stand our ground, we would have done so. As it was, there was no necessity to do so. The helicopter finally left and we took precautions to ensure that no one was in the camp, and to change where the vehicles were parked. Eventually, the area was determined to be safe and we moved everything back into camp.

While still in the safety area, Jeff began talking about finding a way to send Alice and their three younger children to her parents in Missouri. He cited the occasion where Moses had done similarly (Exodus 18:2). Therefore, plans were made for their departure. Alice was not pleased with this episode, as she saw it as a ploy to get her out of the way so he could make further advances on Kathy, and she was right. I was frustrated that, after so much failure and so much sacrifice, she continued to fight against the command of god, through His seer. Yet what I didn't know was the very thing she most definitely did know; that Jeff was nothing more than a fraud, working his way through each of the wives and in fact, lives, of the entire group. As the plans were made, he told me he wanted to send Susie and our two children with Alice. At first he wanted me to escort them on the trip, but later decided that I would not. The small pickup was loaded with whatever items they were to take with them. I kissed Susie and our children good-by, and they were on their way. It was a very emotional scene from Jeff. In times past, he would shed tears while recounting an experience or revelation of some sort to us. However, this night he wept bitterly and continually at their departure. He also promised me that I would be back with my family in no more than two weeks, although more than twice that time would elapse before I would see them again. We had been through so much, and even though integrated into the group as a whole, we were always together. As each day passed, I missed them more.

With the loss of the Suburban and the Plymouth, our sources of travel were greatly decreased. And now that the pickup was gone too, the only vehicle we had left was the two-seated Honda, but a hatchback area allowed for cramped travel of two more. By this time, we had long been told that our money situation was worsening. I never knew how much money we actually had, nor really even saw any, other than small sums given to me for errands from time to time. Jeff had apparently been selling off personal effects, due to our sin. So Jeff was sacrificing his things (bought with our money) in order to care for and feed us. Jeff and Alice had taken items to a flea market in Elkins a couple of times. I recall spending a few hours there myself one day, as I was taken along to run some other errands. It was at this flea market that the gun that Jeff used to kill the Avery family was sold. Jeff may have deluded himself to the point of thinking otherwise, but I believe he took these precautions for the purpose of concealing forensic evidence. It also clearly demonstrates his innate lack of confidence toward divine intervention. Losing weapons was a major offense to Jeff. Therefore, the selling of this one and others had to be due to our sin. During this process of selling things, Jeff met a man who offered cash payment for some work he needed done. Only a few days after Alice left with Susie and the kids, Jeff made the arrangements and four of us were able to work a few days removing some large trees that had already been cut down. The man was a caretaker for a number of summer homes by a manmade lake. The level of the lake would be reduced through the winter season, and a number of floating docks extending from the lakeshore property needed to be brought ashore and stored. Jeff had already instructed us to accept additional work, so, when approached to do more, we said we would. After a day or two, Jeff went to town and called Alice to ensure they had made it safely to her parent's house. She and Susie, along with the all the children, stayed in Mack's Creek, Missouri, until other plans could be made.

It was here that Alice reported back to us of intercepting a call where the caller thought he was speaking to Alice's mother, and so Alice found out who had been in the helicopter that day. She also filled Jeff in on what some of our family members around the area had been saying and the concerns they had. They had made it back to Missouri, but only barely, as they had very little

Chapter 16 HIS KINGDOM BEGINS TO TOPPLE

money and only overdrawn credit cards with which to make the trip. Susie and I were allowed to talk for about two or three minutes once, when Jeff called Alice (which was daily). Over the four or five week period apart, this was all the communication we had. As an attempt to drive Susie and I further apart, it would fail, but it wasn't due to a lack of effort on Jeff's part. Despite our extremely deluded thinking and sheer wickedness of our actions, Susie and I never diverted our eyes from one another by way of our affections. This seemed to be the approach through which Jeff managed to sway some of the other women. He would use his position of authority along with the humiliation of husbands to exert power with affection. Some of the women confused these emotions. Jeff promised my family and I we would be together again within two weeks, but when the time came, I was told I would have to stay at the camp. Nevertheless, Jeff told me that I could write a letter that he would deliver when he returned. Imagine needing permission to write a letter to one's spouse. My letter never made it to Susie, nor did I ever receive the one she had written to me. Apparently, the seer wasn't capable as a mailman. I have little doubt that the letters were read—just not by Susie or me.

* * *

DURING THE FIRST WEEK AFTER ALICE AND SUSIE LEFT, Jeff took Greg and Kathy into town with him to buy groceries and search for a buyer for the horses which had still not been sold. While they were gone, the same helicopter came back that had previously hovered around the camp. As Alice had the truck with her in Missouri and Jeff was gone with the Honda, they probably wondered where all the vehicles were. The women who were in the camp went about their chores as usual, but most of the men stayed hidden as they were in battle gear and had been told to remain unseen. When Jeff returned and received a report of what had happened, he decided that we needed to split up the camp. I think Jeff wanted to put a little distance between himself and the most likely place for authorities to appear—but the reason he gave was to intensify the preparation of his three witnesses. His plan was that he would take me, Damon, Greg, and Greg's wife Debbie, deeper into the woods in order to expedite our readiness to get the records. Time was running out and we needed to be ready. But Jeff also had another plan in mind which involved bringing along one other person—Kathy. He said he wanted to talk to me, so I walked with him and Greg back to the car. It was clear Greg already knew what he was about to tell me, as he explained how he had done a lot of soul searching. That statement was a new one to me. Up to now, if it wasn't strictly by division, it didn't exist. However, he also went on to tell me of how he had divided a number of passages concerning David and Bathsheba, and had discovered that Kathy was his Bathsheba. Apparently, he had framed most of this at quite an earlier point. Later Tonya would speak of how he had approached the same topic with her, but then used the "enlarge his tent" issue to confront the group with it. Most of what he said had been covered in previous classes, and continued to work under the guise of the "key of David" (Revelation 3:7). As he explained, Kathy really wasn't Keith's wife but in fact, was really Jeff's wife. If he'd forgotten the earlier incident when he assured Keith and me that our wives were truly our wives, we hadn't. Would I accept or reject this new plan? I had noticed that Kathy was spending more time with Jeff than with Keith, even before Alice left. Therefore, this revelation did not come altogether as a shock to me. Apparently, Alice was aware of Jeff's plans for Kathy, which explains why Alice was so jealous of her. Why this jealousy didn't seem to be as strong where Tonya was concerned is something only Alice could answer.

Keith and Kathy had over twelve years of marriage together and four sons. Yet, by the time Jeff was finished defining the situation Keith had been living in, the four boys were illegitimate. Jeff destroyed what had once been a happy family, living together on a Missouri farm until they got the call to go to "the Ohio." If I rejected the precept of Kathy as Jeff's wife, I would be rejecting its source (Jeff, as seer) and to reject its source was to reject all that he had ever taught. So much had happened and five people had been killed. How could I reject his teachings now? Keith was faced with the issue at gunpoint. The plans to split camp were carried out in such a way as to pile all the weapons each of us had onto the table. With the other men surrounding the table, Keith was unarmed in the event he decided to retaliate. Whether or not he would have, if able, is not the point I wish to make here. The point is more to the effect that Keith very nearly died that night, just as Dennis Patrick's life had long been under threat before that. Yet Keith did not leave. Whatever gear Jeff planned to take deeper into the woods to a new campsite was gathered onto the ATV and trailer and the remainder had to be hand carried. I don't recall any sort of watch being posted on Keith as we left for the new campsite. Though he had his four boys with him, he never left camp. He reminded Jeff how assured he was that Kathy really was his (Keith's) wife and asked Jeff how he was ever supposed to continue to believe him. At this, Jeff told him that he simply was going to have to. Though every fiber of Keith's being was surely screaming out that this was all a lie, I'm just as certain that his mind was saying it was true. Jeff moved us to an area up river that he had spoken of before where he knew of a hunting cabin.

* * *

THE MOVE TO THE NEW LOCATION WAS MISERABLE. It had been raining earlier that evening and continued through most of the night. Like a king with his new queen, Jeff rode off in the ATV with Kathy nestled closely behind him. The rest of us followed along carrying what we could, while keeping the overloaded trailer intact. We were instructed that no artillery should be found at the main camp, so what we didn't take with us to the cabin area was to be wrapped and hidden per instruction from Jeff to Danny. The camp was to appear completely passive in the event authorities came to question or search.

Chapter 16 HIS KINGDOM BEGINS TO TOPPLE

The cabin was in need of cleaning and as we had no idea whether the hunters who owned it would show up, we slept in our tents as usual—well, not quite as usual. We only brought two tents to this location. Jeff and Kathy slept in one tent while four of us slept in the second. However, we did use the cabin for storing food supplies and a few guns which we had brought with us. The next morning finally arrived after a long rainy night. After breakfast, Jeff received a report from the other camp. I recall it was Dennis who brought the message that Keith had spent the night dividing the word and had concluded that Jeff was in error. He also concluded that Jeff needed to repent of what he had done in taking Kathy. What adds to the pathos is that even then, it never occurred to Keith that Jeff was really not a seer, and that the "pattern" was merely a word game. Any confrontation on the matter, based upon those terms alone was a lost battle from the start. Jeff set a time to meet with Keith at a location between the two camps. This was done and Keith explained what he had divided. Jeff wasn't the least bit interested, but rather told Keith that he was in violation of "counseling" and that he had a choice of either repenting or dying. Keith repented. I know that most of the men present, myself included, would have killed, if so commanded. Death is a hideous and repulsive thing to me and the last thing I wanted was to perform it again that day. All I seemed to know evolved around whatever Jeff taught. Having repented, Keith was re-accepted by each of us as one of the brethren. But complete trust did not exist within Jeff, so he had Keith and his boys moved to the previous campsite. This raised a lot of tough questions from Keith's sons about why their mother wasn't staying in their tent anymore. Keith was instructed to tell them just what Jeff had told him—that their mother was really Jeff's wife. Another tough question, which I hope Kathy will someday face, is why she had no problem with the serious possibility that the husband and the father of her four boys could have been killed. I've faced many similar questions as to my own involvement and have found some answers. With the exception of Tonya, Kathy is the only woman of the group that was never incarcerated, yet she's the only one that still believes in Jeff as the seer. If she finally breaks free, the reality of her deception and abuse may be overwhelming. Some people remain as casualties in various ways, for the rest of their lives. Therefore, although she's "free," she is yet more of a slave than any of us.

As with the previous night, we left a few of the guns in the cabin. This gave us more room in the tent and the guns were kept drier. But in the pre-dawn hours, we awoke to the sound of a truck pulling in and Jeff yelling to us. The hunters who owned the cabin had come to clean it and check out the area for the approaching fall hunting season. Our guns were in the back room, so while they were loading their supplies through the front door, Damon and I were passing the guns out the back window to Greg. They didn't seem to mind that we had stored our food supplies in the cabin, but Jeff didn't feel it would be wise to let them see the guns. However, the quantity of ammunition we had might have been more alarming than the few guns we had. It was only a weekend venture for them, so they weren't there long, but by the next weekend, we had moved once more to avoid contact with them a second time.

This was supposed to have been a time for expediting the readiness of Jeff's witnesses. But even the standards of preparation that had been typical of us were not met. There was always class, and usually sessions for chastisement of sin. But Jeff didn't appear as involved as in the past. Actually, he was quite involved, but only with his new "wife," Kathy. They seldom left the tent. During this time, Jeff told me to prepare a class. I prepared a division and then went through it with the others. Jeff was present to ensure I taught nothing varying from that which he had taught, but by this time he no longer really seemed to care. As he had taken Kathy as a second wife, the topic of a duality of wives had to be taught again at this time, and was. I taught a class on this myself, though it was outlined by Jeff. Actually, I guess everything was outlined by Jeff in our thinking, anyway.

It's easy to sit in judgment, but I never had any desire for another wife. No matter what it is, if temperance is not applied, it soon loses its value and ceases to be precious. What was precious to me, in the form of the relationship Susie and I had, was now being labeled as sin. All men of God were to have two wives. This was the great "mystery" that Jeff was revealing to us. This meant that the relationship I had with Susie would eventually have to be shared. This all worked as a means to drive a wedge between Susie and me, in that she was quite likely his next target if time would have allowed. The destruction of these types of relationships is the power that people like Jeff feed on. He had already retracted his assurance to Keith that Kathy was truly Keith's "flesh of his flesh." It would have been "supposing" to consider that he might do the same to me. My mind no longer seemed capable of individual thought.

* * *

DURING THIS WEEK AND INTO THE NEXT, we worked for the caretaker I mentioned earlier. Jeff had promised me that I would be back with my family at the end of two weeks, but his promises were no more truthful that his prophesies. Kathy called her brother in Missouri and he was very happy to hear from her. She called to see if he would be interested in buying the horses, or knew of anyone else who would. He was interested in the horses, but was also very interested in us. Due to our disappearance, all our various families had become deeply concerned. His church congregation had pooled a little money to help us out in the event any contact was made. He had gone on to say that there were people willing to open up their homes to us and perhaps even offer us some employment. Jeff perceived this information as an open door invitation and made plans to go to Missouri.

He decided to take Damon with him to help deal with Alice. He was planning to tell her that he had another wife. He knew things would get worse, but he didn't tell her that this new wife was Kathy, although she must cer-

Chapter 16 HIS KINGDOM BEGINS TO TOPPLE

tainly have suspected it. When he told her about it, he made it sound like a new revelation and that he didn't know yet who this woman was. Since the three of them, Jeff, Kathy and Damon, were traveling in the Honda, there was no room for me. Jeff told me he needed me to stay back at the camp anyway. We moved the two camps together prior to their departure. Jeff told me what time to expect his call at a certain pay phone in town each day. He also gave me "permission" to write the letter to Susie, mentioned earlier. Jeff never gave the letter to her, nor did he give me the one she wrote. In fact, I never even had her address, much less a stamp with which to mail a letter myself. But then, the thought to do so never entered my mind.

The trip took them a few days. Plans had been made to work for the caretaker one last day, but as I had been given instructions to stay at camp, Dennis went in my place. We had no money, so that day's earnings would have to supply us. I was going to shoot a deer so we'd have some meat, but I never saw one. I also spent time with Keith, trying to help him understand how Kathy was no longer his wife. But since I didn't really understand it myself, I wasn't of much help to him. The anguish wore heavily upon him. Damon stayed in Missouri with Alice upon Jeff's return. Kathy stayed with her brother on this trip, so Alice never knew that she had accompanied Jeff and Damon to Missouri. Because Jeff had to tell Alice about this new "dual wife" principle, Susie became aware of it, too. Her anxiety over it was no different than mine had been over the claim of "wife" that Jeff had on her due to the dance. It was all such a sickening "reality." The "god of Israel" was beginning to appear ferociously demanding. Yet, this gave a whole new dimension to the increasingly repugnant view that we were being shown. I felt myself to be far beyond the point of no return.

Upon Jeff and Kathy's return to camp, we received the bad news. Jeff had met with Kathy's brother and a number of people from his church. Whether Jeff shared his "doctrine" too freely with them, or due to his having been "god" for so long that his demeanor expressed blatant evil, I don't know, but they rejected him and his teachings. As an addict becomes accustomed to a specific drug, needing continually larger doses, in much the same way, Jeff had become "accustomed" to the power he had exercised over us in this isolated wilderness setting. Perhaps the signs of his "addiction" were what helped in the rejection of him. He had been entrapping the minds of followers for at least five years before the church in Kirtland relieved him of his duties of running the Visitor's Center and teaching Sunday School. It's too bad we are not equipped with some type of false teacher alarm that responds in the presence of people such as Jeff. The Holy Spirit directs us to all truth (John 16:13). But only then, to the extent that our view of God's Word is not based upon the precepts of man (Isaiah 29:13). Unfortunately, we all tend to believe that our own view of the truth *is* truth. Yet this is seldom the case, and only sincere humility can reveal any fallacy of our view to God's throne. For me, the view has admittedly been densely obscured.

I HANDED OVER TO JEFF the remainder of the last day's wages that the other men had earned. But it wasn't enough to last very long, and I'm fairly confident Jeff had more money hidden somewhere. Eventually, the time would come when we would have to break camp and move all our supplies out to the main road. Everything we moved to the camp had been taken the long way around, in order not to create a trail to the camp that others might follow from the main road. When we first made the move there I doubt any of us but Jeff knew how close to the main road we really were; as it was, only about a quarter of a mile. Then again, the "road" was not much more than a dirt trail itself. In preparation to leave, Jeff had us make a trail out to the area where we had parked the cars. Once this was done, one of the tents was set up near the parking area and we began moving things into it.

Alice was not handling the duality principle well. Jeff called Alice every day in order to maintain some degree of control, yet it wasn't working. Susie, on the other hand, had no communication from or to me. Even though she was equally disturbed by this latest doctrine, her greater fear was rebellion. The point here is that both women were dealing with the same issue, yet Alice was uncontrollable because she knew Jeff was a fraud. Susie held up through it all without any help or assurances because she was still subject to the ongoing behavior control and abuse. About two weeks after Jeff's return, he said another trip to Missouri was necessary. This time he took me with him. His kingdom had begun to topple. Like ripples upon a still surface of water, his lies, as well as his people, had begun to spread beyond his control.

Chapter 17

ALMOST HOME

It was early September when Jeff and I made our trip back to Missouri. I had been through the Ozark mountain area many times before, but this time I felt as if I were a foreigner. Susie and I had been separated many times throughout my tour in the Navy, sometimes as long as six and a half months. But no matter how long we were apart, whether six months or six days, being reunited as a family was always beautiful. Our time apart had been for a "call to duty" from an authority structure far greater than ourselves. I recall hurricane warnings while living in Florida. We were to leave our spouse and children and take the ship out to sea. I understand the necessity behind such action, but this separation had been under far different circumstances, although the call to duty felt much the same. I would return to troubling issues. Being back in Missouri, Susie and I were very near to home, geographically. Yet, in other ways, we were as far distant as we had been the last two years. Alice's father was in poor health and was confined to the house, while her mother had a job working in town. To have their daughter, three grandchildren, and a friend with two children suddenly appear needing food and shelter was undoubtedly a burden, yet not completely monetary. I'm certain our beliefs were confusing for them, as well. Even though the numbers increased, they dealt with us quite generously. Originally, it wasn't intended that I would stay with them on this second trip, but with Jeff's latest doctrine of wife duality, Alice was highly upset most of the time, therefore, I was needed in order to help keep her calm.

Susie and I had known periods of separation before, but this time our reunion involved a doctrine that would affect the very core of our family. Alice dealt with the issue through fits of rage, but Susie was simply devastated. She was so scared that any rebellion might cause more calamity to thousands, as had been charged to us so many times in the past. An accumulation of doctrine had long since destroyed our future. We were destroyed by what we had that made life so precious. But if we did not go forward and fulfill the commands of god, millions would die by our failure. We still, however, seemed to have the audacity to be concerned about our own happiness. Something that appeared quite "normal" at the time was that Susie was pretty much involved with various domestic chores while Alice did basically nothing. The role-playing of different positions appears more vivid in my memory now, where at the time, it was simply "the way things were." No contact was made with any of our family members to let them know that we were back in the region. As most of the family of the members of the group had been in some sort of contact, it's surprising that no one knew we were there. Before heading back to West Virginia, Jeff told us to sign up for government food stamps. Dennis had been in charge of things there until Jeff's return, and had been given similar instructions.

So after a few days, Jeff returned to camp while I stayed in Missouri. We applied for and got the food stamps, which eased the burden of expenses for Alice's parents. Finding employment would be too much like settling in, and we were told not to do that. During the few weeks that Jeff was gone, one night Alice had a mental break-down. Apparently her use of alcohol had long been heavy. I knew that she drank occasionally to ease the pain of her headaches. She also used a strong over-the-counter medication quite regularly in order to relax. But one night she became very depressed. Without revealing detailed events of their marriage to us, she clearly stated that it had not been a good one. At one point, she even said that he had messed up their lives while recommending that Susie and I get away before he messed ours up, too. Again, she gave no details as to what she meant, but I interpreted it as rebellious speaking, and therefore, not truth. I was not capable of putting this together at that time, but what she failed to comprehend was that the "game" she had played had taken the lives of five people. Neither could my conscience comprehend that their deaths were wrong. To leave the group would mean that I had begun to doubt that the act of taking those lives was right— still a long way from identifying it as wrong. I cared very much for Alice, and on that night I listened to her quite tenderly. It's taken years and even the stirring of these painful memories to wake me up to just how little she must have cared about not only me and my family, but the entire group.

Eventually, Dennis and Tonya, with their daughter Molly, joined us in Missouri. While it was good to see them again, we were concerned for everyone back at the camp. It had begun getting cold when I left, and I knew the weather would be threatening, where a large part of the day would be spent around a fire. We were all talented people. Susie and Tonya were both licensed schoolteachers. Richard was a civil engineer and Debbie was a surgical nurse. I was probably the least educated among us, yet even so, I had marketable skills with boilers and turbines. Danny had about two years of college and was a gifted art student. Yet we had become reduced to the point of sitting around a fire in the "wilderness," when any one of us was highly capable of finding employment that would have met our needs. Awaiting the seer's instruction dominated, even suppressed, nearly every facet of our decision-making faculties. The few decisions we were left to make were to be done "like-mindedly" (with the thinking of Jeff). When we finally did leave the group, making even simple decisions was the hardest thing to do.

Keith had done some work for a man who owned a couple of farms in the southeast area of Kansas City. On one of these properties he had a good-sized barn, which would become our next camp. When the really frigid weather hit, it was time to move. Keith also had a friend who owned a large flatbed truck. I can only guess that a trailer was borrowed in order to bring the horses back.

Chapter 17 ALMOST HOME

With Dennis and myself in Missouri, it was now the responsibility of the few men in the camp to load the truck alone. This, too, was done in accordance with instructions from Jeff, and in the event that anything had to be left behind, a list of essentials was prepared. Danny was in charge of the camp at this point, and subsequently, in charge of the move. Because the truck had only the cab for passenger space, the remainder of the group made the trip in a huge wooden crate, or box, which had been turned upside down on the bed of the truck to block the wind. It could hardly have been a more unpleasant trip.

Once everyone was back in Missouri, the man's barn was transformed into another campsite with our individual tents set up like small rooms in the large barn loft. The horses had been offloaded at a separate location. We ran the generator until the owner of the barn allowed us to run electric cables from another building. A young man and his family who lived and worked on the property were quite friendly and welcomed us there. This arrangement at first sounded promising; necessary things for our very survival, like insulating the barn for heat, and the possibility of some employment, but eventually both fell through. We had been given the care of a milk cow, which met our needs for milk. But because Jeff wouldn't spend the money necessary for the appropriate food, the cow lost weight and the owner took her back. Damon and I were to remain at the barn to be available for ongoing chores like mending fence line, helping with cattle, any general labor. The other men were to apply for employment at a company in the city, which they did, and were hired. We had an income once again, but that was the least of our problems.

Jeff's self-image had become as large as the position he claimed himself to hold. He had not made a good impression on the local church people at the time of his first visit with Kathy's brother. Now that we were together as a group and living in a barn, matters only got worse. Hoping to ease some of this justifiable tension, some of us went to the area RLDS congregation one evening, knowing a service was being held and that a number of people would be there. But as one of the men quite appropriately put it, we had "laid a lot of seed bed for rumors" and indeed, we had. If things were not bad enough, Jeff took Kathy with him everywhere he went. This was the same area where Keith and Kathy had lived, and people began to notice. Keith received invitations for Kathy and himself to visit for supper, yet they could not go. Kathy was no longer Keith's wife, even though they were still claiming to the world to be married, and it was well known that Jeff was already married. There were questions about the Avery family during this time, too. We responded as we had been instructed. To us, telling a lie was in reality, the preservation of a sacred honor. In other words, if we were asked a question to which Jeff had given us words to respond, then our response was as an answer from god. The example often used in order to justify this principle was the tool we still use today. What spy walks into the foreign land divulging to all whom they see, that they are a spy? What a spy does, is lie. This isn't to say that these spies are just plain "liars." It's because they believe they have to hold the sacred truth in the noblest way. At one time, I had an impeccably trustworthy reputation. Among the other issues I deal with now is that loss of trust of which I was once held worthy, an attribute not easily reclaimed.

About a month after moving into the barn my brother, Rick, found us. Family members of others in the group began finding them as well. Contact with family members began weakening the hold that Jeff had on us. Sometimes I think I must have been the most deluded of all. The whole experience seemed to work as a pair of Chinese handcuffs; as the contact with family began to pull me away, the gripping hold upon me grew tighter. My family recognized our move to Ohio as a notable step of faith to begin with—no job and no housing. They had been dealing with the same vexation I had been regarding church doctrine. Then the doors opened and we had been blest; at least it appeared that way. But soon, changes in our behavior occurred and eventually all contact ceased. Having placed a call to where I'd worked in Ohio, they were told I'd quit. Now, seven months later, here we were, living in a barn in the dead of winter, not far from my own brother's farm. Hard questions were inevitable.

My parents came to see us several times while we were living in the barn. I'm sure it was peculiar to them on the first visit, as we had to ask Jeff for permission in order to leave the area just to get some ice cream. Such a treat was an unusual event, and the kids really enjoyed it. Naturally, we couldn't be gone long since a time limit had been imposed on our absence. They may not have noticed that these restrictions even existed, but Jeff was very firm about any outside influence. I recall Dennis and Tonya receiving a dinner invitation from their family. I don't remember whether or not they went, or the conditions, but the invitation was met with heavy resistance by Jeff; the occasion would require too much time away. And as a ploy to stimulate guilt, Jeff reminded them of how the rest of us would be back at the barn enduring our "wilderness" experience. My brother began visiting us at the barn fairly regularly. As he, too, was searching for theological answers to questions of his own, he was sincerely interested in what we had to say. This interest was a good thing, because it enabled him to learn things about us that would later serve to heighten his concern for us. In fact, his concern would be essential toward our eventual exit from the group. He had an appreciation for what we had been through and expressed this appreciation without the usual bias about our unorthodox methods of service toward God. The more he dropped by, the more well-acquainted he became with the others, quickly developing friendships.

Jeff was seldom around as he was constantly on the move from the barn to Mack's Creek. This was good, in that classes basically ceased. Jeff was spreading himself too thin. His presence was needed at both locations. Perhaps he'd hoped that I, or one of the others in the group, could fill the gap at times when he was away. But if he thought it, it never was conveyed to us. Anyway, his power in the group was so fabricated as to prevent any such a shared power base. Jeff's philosophy was much like that of the movie *Highlander,* which had so strongly inspired him. The essential theme entails the principle that "there can be only one." This was the essence, along with perhaps the most serious flaw, of Jeff's autocracy: Living, intelligent humans become useless when robbed of their mind's ability to think. Jeff's misuse and misinterpretation of the scripture that we are to have the mind of Christ (1 Corinthians 2:16) and therefore, to strive together in one mind (Philippians 1:27) did nothing but isolate its interpretive application and remold the thinking of all members into the likeness of the One, the leader, whose essence is an antichrist. The mind of Christ should stimulate freedom of thought and creativity through virtuous intentions. It should, therefore, bear fruit of life, with prosperity in peace and happiness. Hardships may occur and material prosperity may never be acquired, but the rejoicing of life and understanding of righteousness can be received in abundance. This happens by way of our individual relationship with the Father, through Jesus Christ. Therefore, as the Father works within us, through Jesus, we individually manifest his presence and kingdom on earth by way of his spiritual house and holy priesthood (1 Peter 2:5). By doing so, he fulfills in us the very thing we pray for, "Thy kingdom come. Thy will be done on earth, as it is in heaven" (Matthew 6:10). But in these controlled settings, all thought becomes molded into the One, rather than the Father. Freedom becomes unknown, creativity ceases to exist and in such captivity, there's no flow, nor rejoicing of life.

I wrote no poetry during my association with Jeff, because that wasn't a characteristic or gift that Jeff had. Danny's creative gifts were not allowed if they did not benefit Jeff and his needs at the time. We became of one mind, but that mind was without life, without growth or expression. As the influence of Jeff began to weaken, the first to be freed from its hold were Greg and Richard. One night after doing some chores, I returned to the barn and noticed that something seemed wrong. Actually, it wasn't wrong at all, but very right, because Greg and Richard were telling Jeff that they wanted to leave. Jeff was furious, yet after seeing how adamant they were, he told them to go. They had planned their departure ahead of time so with bags already packed, they left. Jeff called for an immediate session time. I could say "class," but in essence it was really a session, the only oddity being that the main recipients weren't present for his scathing wrath. He asked if anyone else wanted to leave, and of course we each said "no." Then he went on to promise that they would be back, just as he did when Shar left, even though he'd already betrothed her to Danny. Jeff had already prophesied that none of us would be lost, so, barring any unforeseen change in this purportedly immutable god, it was impossible for them not to return.

* * *

THE COLD WEATHER WAS AGAIN DEMANDING A CHANGE in our living conditions. The man who owned the barn became less interested in giving us work, and Jeff never seemed to want to meet with him. He invited us to his house one evening to discuss Jeff's teachings. Jeff would not go, and made an excuse, sending instead, myself and others. Then, there were the local people who were threatening to contact social services if we didn't move the children into a warmer environment. It began to be troubling to me that Jeff's children were in Mack's Creek during the majority of this time in the warm home environment of Alice's parents. Yet despite the offers from my brother and other family members of those in the group, Jeff insisted that we stay where we were. Rick noticed more peculiarities, asking questions like, if Alice stayed with her parents, why we couldn't move in with family, and then, where did Greg and Richard go? Rick is very good at asking direct questions, so quite often it had become necessary to answer with a direct lie. At one point, he asked if Jeff and Kathy were having some kind of an affair, which was easy to respond to. Since they were "husband and wife" they could not be having an affair. But when he asked me if polygamy was being practiced within the group, there was no recourse but to respond as I had been instructed. I lied. Not long after Richard and Greg left, Debbie left. Her departure was quite secret as she left sometime in the night with a note in her tent.

Prior to Richard and Greg's departure, Alice became frighteningly unstable. There's no doubt in my mind that Alice was an abused woman. One night, Kathy and Damon came to the barn in the early hours of the morning. After waking everyone, they told us very hurriedly there was a problem with Alice. Kathy had moved to Mack's Creek to be with Jeff, but under the guise that she and Keith, having marital problems, were needing some time apart. Alice was to be counseling her. But the real point in Kathy's being there was for Jeff to have both of his "wives" under one roof. Somewhere in the venture, Alice exploded emotionally. She swallowed a large number of pain-killers with an equally large amount of alcohol. Some time after doing so, she attacked Jeff. Something terrible transpired within Alice that night, yet clearly it was a result of the pollution of abuses that had begun long before.

A few of us went to Mack's Creek with Damon. Alice was asleep, and Jeff met us at the door with instructions of what personal belongings we were to take back to the barn. Alice's parents were not aware of why Kathy was really there, nevertheless, Jeff felt it was necessary to leave. I never saw her parents, but apparently they were told that Alice had developed a drinking problem, for which they felt sorry that they had not known.

We headed back with the truck loaded, and later in the day Jeff arrived with Alice and the other Lundgren children. Alice was very nearly comatose. Damon and I helped her out of the car and up into the loft of the barn. We then took her to Jeff's tent where she remained for a day or two. We didn't know how she might respond to being there. Alice had been "mother," and she had been that vibrant character within the structure of Jeff's domain. Yet now she was a woman who had, by all appearances, lost her mind. Her arms were badly bruised, which Jeff said was from him having to hold her back to restrain her that night. I have no way of knowing whether she had injuries anywhere else on her body. Jeff's face was scratched, as well as the rest of his head, with patches of hair missing. "Rejoice not when thine enemy falleth, and let not thine heart be glad when he stumbleth" (Proverbs 24:17). Things were falling apart, and though I'm very thankful they did, I still find no pleasure in the destructive process that took place along the way. Unless there's a notable contradiction within the scripture, God alone reserves the right to laugh at the destruction of fools. "I also will laugh at your calamity; I will mock when your fear cometh" (Proverbs 1: 26). Perhaps it's not fools, but rather foolishness itself that is scoffed at here. It is not the Father speaking, but rather a feminine connotation called Wisdom (verse 20). Whatever the case, I've seen and experienced enough destruction to know that I can find no pleasure in it. But when fools become wise by humility and repentant change, it's a joy to see the foolishness fall away. Alice was a prisoner in that tent, but after several days Jeff took her back to Mack's Creek. Damon may have stayed with us in the barn, but the three younger Lundgren children returned with their mother.

* * *

IT BEGAN TO GET DECISIVELY COLDER. There was no longer any choice about getting indoors for warm shelter. Therefore, Jeff finally allowed us to get out of the cold by going to my brother's house. It's said that some creatures are too stupid to get out of the rain, and in much the same way we needed permission to escape the cold. Jeff only agreed to Rick's home as an area of refuge because he appeared sympathetic to Jeff's teachings. Yet far more importantly, Rick was able to shelter all of us, thereby not forcing us to split up. As a hindsight observation of the decision, and definitely not one that was obvious at the time, Jeff was the one in need of a place that allowed the group to remain unified. Otherwise, the surroundings we might be exposed to would disarm his control over us. Actually, by this move, Jeff became almost completely cut off from the entire group.

My parents owned a fifth-wheel camping trailer at the time, which was equipped with a propane gas furnace. They offered to move it to Rick's house in order to increase warm sleeping space. The offer was accepted. When moving day arrived, a major problem erupted. Instead of using the fifth-wheel in a way to best suite its sleeping capacity, Jeff decided that the seer needed the space and privacy for himself. Of course, this also included Kathy. Rick and his wife, also named Kathy, were in shock as they watched the belongings of Keith and his four boys being taken inside the house, while Kathy's (Keith's wife) belongings were placed in the trailer with Jeff's things. Rick confronted Jeff with the issue and asked him if he and Kathy intended to stay in the trailer together. With this, Jeff told him yes, that they would sleep in the trailer, and asked if that was a problem. Rick was pretty upset and equally confused, yet responded that he would need a scriptural explanation. Jeff said that he would prepare a class on the topic—but he never did. However, this really didn't matter because Rick was merely buying time. He stopped by our parent's house on the way home from work the next day. He had a real problem on his hands and also knew that our parents would want to know what was happening. They were heartbroken with disappointment. My dad, a licensed minister, had married Susie and I, yet our family now had become entangled in something quite contrary to their core beliefs. They'd all noticed changes in our behavior throughout the time we were living in the barn, but during times spent with them while we were living in the barn, they had come to care deeply for the group as a whole. My brother sat in on one of the few classes that Jeff taught and our parents had also attended one. I was told I could prepare a couple of divisions for them and they were quite impressed with the apparent chiastic flow of the words. They loved us and wanted to understand the basis of our beliefs. Much of what we said seemed to make sense to them, but aside from any agreement or disagreement over various doctrinal issues, they came to appreciate the unity we had. The camaraderie and devotion we exhibited was refreshing and even stimulating to see.

As a result of how things worked out, the group stayed at Rick's for about a week. Except for Jeff, I think Rick and my sister-in-law Kathy, found the experience of having us all there a very pleasant one. Unfortunately, Jeff was power drunk, which resulted in his often-obnoxious behavior. How could Rick have known at the time he made the generous offer to us that it would create such a problem? Here was a man with a wife and two small boys who'd just opened his home to twenty people, and upon doing so, discovered that their lifestyle involved practices to which he could not consent. With Jeff's polygamous stance revealed, Rick surely felt cautious that other aspects of our beliefs might yet be unknown, and perhaps more threatening. He delayed making any open statement to us for a couple of days, until he could arrange to be away from work for a while. I noticed and was saddened by Rick's sudden and apparent lack of interest in attending a couple of classes. Then one night, while Jeff was holding class in the trailer, Rick came to the door and stated that he needed to speak to everyone. His ultimatum was that he wanted Jeff and Kathy off the property immediately. He went on to say that anyone who was willing to leave the group was welcome to stay at his place as long as they needed, until getting established again. But anyone who was not willing to leave the group would have to be off the property by the following Saturday, only a few days away.

At that point he asked to talk to me, and as I stepped out of the trailer I saw my dad standing outside. We walked over to the cars in the driveway and a very peculiar sensation came over me. As my dad and brother began firing questions at me, it was as though I was in a metal drum; I could hear their voices, but they sounded muffled. Rick became quite vocal, yet despite the fact that he was standing directly in front of me, I could barely hear him. All the time they were both speaking, my mind was ablaze with scriptures. I saw myself in the place of Amulek, as recorded in the book of Alma (*Book of Mormon*).

> "And it came to pass that Alma and Amulek, Amulek having forsaken all his gold, and silver, and his precious things, which were in the land of Ammonihah, for the word of God, he being rejected by those who were once his friends, and also by his father and his kindred." (Alma 10: 107)

As the story goes, God's church was being restored in the region. Yet the price of this precious event was the forsaking of all material wealth and the rejection of those held most dear. I interpreted my own forsaken wealth, and now the rejection of my brother and dad, with that of Amulek's.

Forsaking material things, along with the rejection of family and friends, is a common principle within Christianity.

> "If the world hate you, ye know that it hated me before it hated you. If ye were of the world, the world would love his own: but because ye are not of the world, but I have chosen you out of the world, therefore the world hateth you" (John 15:18–19)

> "And everyone that hath forsaken houses, or brethren, or sisters, or father, or mother, or wife, or children, or lands, for my name's sake,shall receive an hundred fold, and shall inherit everlasting life." (Matthew 19:29)

But these principles, full of spiritual meaning and application, had become quite legalistically mapped out within my mind. The words of Christ were to tell us all things what we should do. Therefore, this very literal manifestation was occurring within my life, as well. Perhaps my mind was simply overloaded with activity. Jeff, the mighty man of God, wasn't responding like the prophetic image he'd portrayed himself to be. Surely there would be a warning to repent, a proclamation, a revelation, something. Yet all he did was pack his bags and load his pickup as quickly as possible. Even that didn't trouble me. But when Rick brought up the issue, I had no response.

The image Jeff had drawn of the God of Israel had already become increasingly distasteful to me. I hated the things that this "god" had demanded of us. Yet this view of God that dictated to my mind and conscience, had completely eclipsed any I had previously known. The intensity that my brother and dad were expressing began to abate as they saw it was having little effect with me. We continued our conversation in the house where their tone became more tender, and continued late into the night. Since it was late and a long drive from home, my dad stayed there for the night. In the morning, his demeanor was more silent, yet still quite loving.

* * *

THE WAY JEFF HAD OUTLINED THE SLEEPING ARRANGEMENTS those few days prior to being run off Rick's property was continued, as some were still sleeping outside in a tent. As the seer, his living conditions were crucial to our well being—he just couldn't function as well without the appropriate atmosphere. It was therefore necessary for some of his people to sleep out in the cold rather than allow them the warmth of the trailer. Sharon was one of those that slept outside, which was primarily due to her not having children to care for in the night, or so it was thought. She had been heavily chastised for a few months by this time, as she had been putting on weight. What the seer didn't know was that the weight she was putting on was due to a baby. Jeff had earlier prophesied Sharon would give birth to a son by her "husband" Richard. But apparently this foreknowledge slipped his mind when she actually began to show. Then again, perhaps Jeff's lack of divine insight was also due to this little baby not being a boy. In late December, Sharon gave birth to a precious little girl. The group would soon disband, but before it did, the news of Sharon's pregnancy became known.

The knowledge of her pregnancy came by way of a medical examination, not by way of the seer. When Jeff was told about it, Sharon asked if this would be the son that she had previously been told she would bear. Jeff said that he'd look in the word to find out, but that he would wager it was the son he had mentioned before. Once again, Jeff didn't give prophecies by traditional methods, but rather gave prophetic information through division of the word. I guess that in this case he figured he stood a good 50/50 chance of being right. But the real revelation in all of this was that the seer was being instructed by God, through the division of his word, to chastise Sharon for gaining weight, yet he failed to perceive that she was pregnant. Prior to Jeff's eviction from the farm he received a call from Debbie stating that she wanted to come back to the group. I don't remember the details of her return, but she was portrayed as one of God's "lost sheep" returning to the fold. It also seemed to add momentum to the promise that Greg and Richard would return too, but like the promise of Shar's return long before, it never happened.

Rick had no objection to our removal of property from the farm, as long as Jeff didn't enter the premises. Jeff told us to find a storage place for our things, which we did. Unknown to us at the time, all would be lost soon enough. Jeff told us what items he wanted to take with him and we brought them to the road each day where he waited in his truck then returned back to Mack's Creek where he was staying. Kathy moved in with family of her own. When we moved to Rick's the horses were put into his pasture, so now also had to be relocated. Rick had taken time off from work for this adjustment, so he was usually around to work on me. He was diligent in trying to break me free from the maze-like thinking that always led back to Jeff as the seer.

There were many indications that Jeff was a fraud, yet my mind seemed to be full of detours around such conclusions. Alice put it very clearly once, while we were still in West Virginia. It was at the time when Kathy was going to "intercede" for Dennis. Alice, highly upset, said "This is your god, people. Look at your god!" I had no idea what she meant, sadly, at the time, interpreting it to be only her rebellion. What she was actually saying was that Jeff, by way of his plotting imagination, thought he was our god—and we, in turn, had allowed him to become so. It was all just a game, and this was the result of what he had created. Yet even in that very decadent truth, what he claimed to

Chapter 17 ALMOST HOME

be all along—a seer fulfilling "every form of godliness"—he had become a creator.

At a much earlier time in West Virginia, we received an assignment from Jeff. The assignment was to memorize Isaiah 64:8. "But now, O Lord, thou art our father; we are the clay, and thou our potter; and we all are the work of thy hand." Once the words were memorized, they were to be spoken back to Jeff. The highly unpleasant truth about it is that we were reflecting back to him what he had done to our minds. As with the Brother of Jared account, we were the vessels that would not be complete until it was determined that there was no light within us. Then he, as seer, would provide that light, through the pattern written by God's own finger, just as Jesus was to have touched the stones in Jared's day, giving them light for their vessels. Jeff had become our only source of light, in that he had become our only source of thought. So, in that sense, he had become the potter, and we had become the clay. Therefore, does the clay ask, "What makest thou?" (Isaiah 45:9)? Surely not. But, because Jeff was not God, nor any fulfillment of godliness, his creation was flawed and void of life-giving perseverance. The foundation of all that he had built within our thinking was the Pattern, the "language" from the finger of God. It was this foundation that finally cracked and provided the long needed view that Jeff was nothing but a liar.

* * *

PRIOR TO LEAVING THE GROUP, I knew nothing of the poetic structure within the Bible. But back in Missouri again, I began to write poetry as an expression of my heart's passion and thoughts. Referring to this in an earlier chapter, on the second trip to Kirtland, I gave a copy of one of my poems to Jeff and asked if the "pattern" resided within it, since I'd been told by people who appreciated them far more than Jeff, that the poems I'd written had to be inspired. Exactly what that means in relation to God's direct intervention is different, perhaps, with each believer. But in this case a very legalistic belief was being imposed, and words written about God—yet not from God (by the pattern)—were determined to be blasphemy. I had eventually come to repent of this "sacrilege," and never wrote another poem while in the group. Yet now, while living at Rick's, my poems would serve as past testimony that would crack my convictions. My poetry had long been disposed of and forgotten by this time. Rick, however, kept the copies I'd given him. Visiting us in Ohio, and several times now in Missouri, he was gaining familiarity with the pattern himself.

One day, after many failed attempts to shake my established faith, I found him in his bedroom in a moment of frustrated laughter. When I asked him what he was reading, he shunned me off and said that it wouldn't matter to me anyway. When it came to the poems I'd written, it really didn't. In fact, he had asked me before if I had written any more while I was in the group and, of course, I explained to him how they had been sin and I had repented of them. I didn't know what he was reading to provoke such a response, but I told him that we could still be friends despite the situation we were in, and he softened up. Rick was familiar only with the pattern, whereas for me, it was the language of godly thought. In matters of righteousness, there was no other way to read and I had become quite proficient at measuring the words in these parallel comparisons. He then went on to say that he wasn't all that good with the pattern, but that since it appeared very chiastic to him, he couldn't find anything wrong in what he was reading.

In handing it to me, I saw then, that it was one of my poems. Whether coincidence or providence, our Savior only knows, it happened to be the last poem I had written, and the one which Jeff had rejected. As I read those words which had once flooded from my heart and out of my pen, something happened. Much like an old and forgotten friend, the words seemed to awaken old passions along with a memory of the view I once had of God, an image I had once loved. But these passions had lain dormant for a very long time, finding no place to reside in the structure which had been built within my mind. However, even with the scrutiny of chiasmus applied to measure the words, they flowed harmoniously together, division after division. I applied the first verse opposite the last verse and divided toward the middle. I randomly chose various center points and divided outwardly toward the ends of the poem, yet in each division, each statement melodiously blended into whatever was placed opposite.

I now hold a quite different appreciation for chiasmus as a structure of poetic writing. However, at the time, all this worked only to reveal that Jeff was out to do me harm. In fact, it almost immediately became personalized. Jeff surely knew that the structure of that poem was chiastic; so why didn't he want me to know that? Why did he want me to throw away the poems which I did in accordance with his desires? Much like Rick at this point, I had no experience with this style of reading upon meeting Jeff. Therefore, when he had explained that they were actually not of God, I eventually came to accept that as the truth; not immediately, but I did become convinced of it within time. Rick went on to explain that Jeff had mentioned something to him about how the poems ought to be burned, and again, in my mind I asked, "Why?" None of this worked to convince me that Jeff was not who he claimed to be, yet in a very mild way, it did establish doubt. Perhaps the strongest reason I can give, was that of an increase of the already repugnant feelings I had toward this present view of God.

My decision to leave the group was a gradual one. When it was finally made, it was more with impending feelings of doom that I might be committing the unpardonable sin than having discovered that Jeff's god was not God. It finally came to the point, for me, where that god had become too ugly. I just couldn't go on any further. I cannot overemphasize that this was not a decision of Jeff's false teachings but rather a beginning of doubt, and the decision that I could simply no longer serve "Baal." Rick continued talking to me and eventually persuaded me to leave the group.

Chapter 17 ALMOST HOME

Up until that point the plan had been that, along with Jeff, we would eventually just disappear again. Rick said many times over that he wished we would decide not to leave again. It probably seemed a far simpler decision to him and the rest of our family than it was to me. The slightest hint of doubt was immediately met with conscience about the Averys, and that seemed to work as a door that slammed shut at any consideration to get out. We were almost home, in that we were back in our homeland of Missouri and among family. We were also nearer the passions and dreams and lives we had once known. Yet we were only *nearly* there. A tragic line had been crossed during the course of this journey that would block our ever returning. In sensitive ways, other lines were crossed as well.

The day finally came when I knew I could go no further. When I told Susie that I could not continue on whenever Jeff might leave again, she was initially shocked. Slowly, eventually, she formed the thought, and the words came out, "But what about the dance?" I didn't know how to respond. Fear and threats had been part of the process used by Jeff to guarantee her participation. But in a far deeper sense, she had become convinced that the dance was truly a sacred event. To leave the group would mean a denial of her participation in the "atonement" which had occurred that day; not necessarily a denial that an atonement had actually been secured, but the denial of the benefit of it, now that it was done. I can't say how long it took for Susie to completely discard the conviction she had of the dance being a truly sacred event, but much like my own re-familiarization with the conscience I had once known, I can only assume it was not done easily nor quickly.

* * *

I HAD BEEN TO MY PARENTS HOUSE ONLY ONCE since they'd discovered we were back in the area, and that had been to borrow money. Even then, Jeff did not allow me to take Susie or the kids and I could be absent only briefly. Along with his limited number of choices, probably the main reason Jeff returned to Missouri was due to our families being there. Seeing only the potential for draining money from as many as he could, yet still cautious about such a move, he totally underestimated the influence a supportive family would have on us. With the decision to forsake the god we had come to serve, we decided to spend some time with my parents. Susie's parents lived about three hours drive from Rick, and we eventually visited them, too. But this night we left to be with my parents. The only members still staying at Rick's were Keith and his boys.

Since the ultimatum Rick had given was that members were to either leave the group or leave the farm, everyone found places to move. By the time I decided to leave, all of the others except Keith and his boys were living with family or friends in separate homes. As we left to visit my parents, Rick asked if I wanted him to tell Keith I was leaving the group, to which I responded "No." I couldn't trust anyone in the group with information like that, and when I left I wanted to tell Jeff myself. Yet, I felt equally certain I never wanted to see him again.

As it worked out, Rick called in a few days at our parent's house to tell me that Keith wanted out too. I didn't know it, but Rick had been working on Keith. Upon hearing this, I agreed to let Keith know what I'd decided. Returning to Rick's, we settled on the timing to tell Jeff of our decision. There remained a few items at Rick's farm that were being moved either to Mack's Creek or into storage. Jeff had been making trips back and forth from Mack's Creek in order to move items that he wanted, while Keith and I had been putting other things into storage.

Rick was there the day that Jeff would make his final pickup. I didn't understand what had happened to us, and I was still far from convinced that Jeff was not who he claimed to be. Yet I had come to see that Jeff had power over me, so I asked Rick to come to the road with me, which he did. Keith was there too, but somewhat believing the lies only on a different level, neither of us could rely on the other for support. It turned out to be a very simple event—aside from the issue that I was committing the "unpardonable sin." I told Jeff that I couldn't go any further and he responded by asking me if I was out. To this I said, "Yes, I am out." He then asked Keith if he was out, too, at which time Keith also said yes. Jeff didn't act altogether surprised, or even angry. That said, he left.

A day or so later I received a phone call from Jeff who was still trying to sell the horses and wanted to know if someone would be allowed to come and get them. It amazes me now, how this man basically stole, or otherwise emptied us of everything. However, I wanted nothing associated with the group. It all still seemed to belong to him. Before ending the conversation, he apologized for having failed me. Even this brief interaction I feel was used as a ploy to stimulate pity for him, while yet maintaining the assurance that he was who he claimed to be. This began to change after a couple of weeks, along with changes of many types that were inevitable.

* * *

NOT LONG AFTER GETTING OUT OF THE GROUP, I received a call from Dennis Patrick. When he asked if it was true that I had left the group, I immediately felt anxious. I wasn't at all sure as to my decision to get out of the group, and I didn't want to be subjected to any conversation with Dennis in which he might try to persuade me to come back. Yet I also did not want to be in a position to influence him to leave. Again, I left because I simply could go no further and in no way wanted to influence others to do likewise. But Dennis explained that he had just gotten out, too. He said that there were a number of things that just didn't make sense and that Tonya had been told things that created a lot of questions. He went on to say that Debbie had decided to leave (again) and that it looked like Sharon was also planning to leave. I still felt a little anxious in that I didn't want to be instrumental in pulling people away

Chapter 17 ALMOST HOME

from "God's work." However, just hearing the frustrations and questions that others had, mixed with our own, seemed to offer a sense of comfort.

Susie and I made plans to meet with Dennis and Tonya in order to talk. We'd spent many hours together over the past few years and, in fact, all our time over the past nine months. So, our getting together was perhaps as much of a social event as it was an opportunity for pooling our common frustrations. Yet, as we did so, a number of things began to surface that we had suppressed. They weren't necessarily common things, in that they varied between us. Yet, like separate letters within a single word, they seemed to come together in the spelling of a unified message, and that message spelled DECEPTION. Amazingly, we were still not truly convinced. Understanding how these circumstances establish control, and then maintain it, is what best aids in a more complete escape of the mental entanglement. That sort of understanding was yet far beyond our grasp.

I began to express denials of Jeff, but from time to time things happened which would reveal the hold that was still there. Six months after my arrest, when I was incarcerated in the Lake County Jail, I received a letter from Jeff. It was a letter of warning to repent which included an "Everlasting Farewell" in the event I did not. I was sobered that the letter actually had an effect on me. Several days passed before I shook the feeling it revealed, yet in the exposure of the hold that was still resident within me, I found growth through the opportunity to deal with it.

We next made contact with Greg and Richard, and arranged to meet with them. They had left the group about a month prior to our own departure and did so in such a way as to avoid any contact. When they heard that we, too, had left they were happy to meet with us. As they had already been out of the group for several weeks, they had encountered their own difficulties in interaction with "outsiders." Greg stated that we would notice difficulties in normal communication with others. This was quite true. We began to see that something had happened, but Susie and I had no real comprehension of what it was.

A man by the name of Ted Patrick (no relation to Dennis Patrick) came to see me while I was in jail after my arrest. (We got out of the group on December 4, 1989 and were arrested one month later on January 4, 1990.) We had been in jail about three or four weeks when my attorney brought Ted in to see me. The things he told me that day, having never met me and knowing nothing about what had transpired over the two years prior, opened my mind for the first time to the fact that this was not an isolated incident. The sad reality is that there are people who have a very good understanding of how these controlling settings work, along with the effectiveness of the processes used. A few weeks after speaking with Ted Patrick, I was visited by Margaret Singer and Richard Ofshe. Their experience and research in cults was a tremendous help toward a more comprehensive recovery from the deeply rooted effects of the abuses.

As I occasionally jump forward to things that occurred after our arrest, I hope to convey that this was in no way a simple departure. In our efforts to regain our footing, we were constantly faced with the abstract ideologies that had dominated our thinking. It's a very well known fact that no one ever seeks to "join" a cult. I hope to convey here that in somewhat the same manner, neither does one simply "leave" a cult. Therefore, during this period between leaving the group and being arrested, we were venturing away from the setting that had come to so rigidly dictate every facet of our lives. In fact, we had very little idea of exactly what it was that we left.

* * *

KATHY WANTED TO SEE HER FOUR SONS while Keith was still living at Rick's. Rick allowed her to come on the property, as long as she came alone. He was again working daily, and Keith had a job, too. Since I was still unemployed, I agreed with both Rick and Keith to observe her visit. She dug the toe of her shoe in the gravel driveway as I mentioned things that Jeff had lied to her about. But unfortunately, I wasn't able to offer any understanding as to what we had been through. I could expose a few lies, but I couldn't really affirm any sure convictions. Therefore, the conversation was a failure in terms of helping her get away from Jeff's entrapment. By this time she had an "entrapment" of another sort—she was pregnant with Jeff's baby. I feel that if the day finally comes where she realizes what Jeff is, or more importantly, what he is not, the awakening of her involvement will be quite a heavy burden to bear.

Dennis and I had a meeting scheduled with Danny at one point, in order to tell him ourselves that we had left the group. But he cancelled at the last minute and by the time I attempted to contact him again, Jeff and he had left Missouri.

This was, in some ways, an even more confusing time period than when we were still in the group. Making decisions was very difficult, yet comments from friends and professionals bore heavily on what we did. Those of us who left the group met together a few times as sort of an ex-member support group. Greg got some legal advice, since we were not only fugitives from God in some lingering ways, but we were fugitives from the Ohio justice system, as well. Any view of the future, for us, had been completely dissolved. Even now, the memories of feeling like a rudderless ship are oppressive. Everything we knew and believed in had become unstable. I searched the scriptures to see what answers could be found, but this only led to more confusion. Since Jeff had redefined everything to us, everything I read only seemed to lead me in different directions, none of which seemed possible of fulfillment. I had relied on the seer for so much for so long that when I realized the extent of his control I found my relinquishment of it unimaginable.

My biggest problem came from my view of words. As if trying to read through mud-covered glasses, at first all I could see was the mud. At times some things seemed to show that Jeff and his doctrines had been wrong. Yet I also continued to see things that seemed to prove him right. Eventually I had to start completely over. I had to erase all my memories in order to re-enter new information. Even though I had forsaken God, I didn't seem to feel forsaken by Him. I did not, however, have either the tools or background to comprehend any basis for such a belief. Every facet of my life before meeting Jeff had been intertwined with my relationship with God. Now that relationship was without texture, and every facet of my life was unstable. I had a family to care and provide for, so I began looking for employment. At this time, having a stable home environment seemed unattainable, yet the effort to provide one seemed like the natural thing to do. Eventually, I found employment. But none of this could last. Something terrible had happened in Kirtland, Ohio, and even if it was never discovered or made known, my heart would forever cry out for the need for its disclosure.

Susie and I had once shared a beautiful home life. With the sheer enjoyment we found in just being together, even a trip to the market was an exciting family affair. Every moment together was precious and this carried over to our brief lives together outside the Navy, too. It's clear to me that I've failed my children as a parent. To watch them grow and to nurture their footsteps in life was a passion within me long before they were ever born. The absence of this cherished responsibility and privilege is one of the greatest sources of motivation I have for placing these words on paper. Yet, another precious family was also destroyed—in a far more tragic kind of destruction. The first time I met the Chief of Police in Kirtland was in the Lake County courtroom after my arrest. A brief conversation ensued at which time I asked him the question, "How can we keep this from ever happening again?" I feel that this is still an appropriate question today.

* * *

EVENTUALLY, KEITH WENT TO THE AUTHORITIES in Kansas City and made a statement about his knowledge of a family who had been killed in Kirtland. Whether stimulated by conscience, fear for his life, or merely spite for losing Kathy to Jeff, only he can say. Perhaps it was a combination of the three, combined with his access to a friend who works in law enforcement. Whatever his reason, the matter was now out in the open.

Being acquainted from earlier church associations, the Patricks just happened to be in the Kirtland Police Chief's office to retrieve property still in the barn when the call arrived from the ATF office in Kansas City. Debbie was with them. Since the farm was vacant, they requested permission from the Chief to enter the property. He was delighted to hear that they had left the group and that the group had eventually disbanded. With the allegations about Jeff that came from members who had earlier left the group, the call from Kansas City appeared to be just one more rumor, yet one which still needed to be checked out. Nevertheless, because Debbie and the Patricks heard the call come through, they may have panicked as they scrapped any plans to search the barn for their property, returning immediately to Missouri. Upon arriving, they called Greg, who in turn contacted the rest of us. The news only seemed to state the inevitable. In some ways it was a relief. I didn't know when or how the police would arrest me, but I kissed Matthew and Amy goodbye as they lay asleep that night. Susie was terrified and unable to accept that life as we knew it would soon end. However, that night was uneventful.

The following day, Susie and I took the children with us into Kansas City. We rode with Rick on his way to work, but at this point he was suspecting that something was wrong. Greg had been advised to speak with legal counsel and he urged us to do the same as soon as possible. I spoke with an attorney that night who advised me to do nothing until I was arrested. He also suggested making a trip to Ohio in the event I wished to turn myself in and seek a plea agreement, which I did not do. That night was spent at my parent's house. The next morning I had an errand to run and upon returning to the house, Susie appeared at the door saying that we needed to hurry. I was gone when the call came through from Keith who'd left Susie the number of the ATF office in Kansas City. He said that the ATF told him to call each of us; that they'd begun searching the barn and once they found the bodies of the Avery family it would be too late. Apparently really interested in only Jeff, they nonetheless needed us to come in and make statements. I called the attorney I had spoken with the night before in order to see if he could go with us, but he was unable to leave on such short notice and advised me not to go—but I went anyway. Keith had asked me a couple of weeks earlier if I thought we should go to the police. At that time I answered that I really didn't know because the decision to do so involved so many other people.

Naïvely, I still wasn't convinced all we had been through had been wrong. It seemed as if we had gone wrong somewhere, but I really couldn't put my finger on just where. Yet now the matter seemed as if predestined. Susie and I, with our children, went to the ATF office. Still not certain even that was the right thing to do, once in their office, I stated that I didn't care what they did to me, I just didn't want anything to happen to Susie and the kids. I'm hesitant to write anything more concerning the specific events of their questioning, other than to say that both Susie and I gave statements that day. Certainly, I'm in no position to point out the wrongdoing of government authorities, but we were taken advantage of and lied to that day in ways not that different from the ways we'd been subjected to in our exposure to Jeff and the group. Not being one to hold grudges, I have to admit that it's all in the past now. Five people had been murdered—as the judge in my trial said, two generations of a family were killed. Some believe that punishment is the end-all answer to justice. But I feel in my heart that the question remains to be asked, "How can we keep this from ever happening again?"

Chapter 18

WHY?

When circumstances such as I've written about saturate the lives of people, the universal question always asked is "Why?," or "How could that have happened?" There's an answer to this question, but unfortunately it's not easily grasped. I believe to this day, that all who were in the group did nothing for their own personal gratification. We gave our all for what we believed was God's will and inescapable command.

Human behavior is one of the most beautiful, yet sometimes tragic, of life's mysteries. Like skipping rocks across the water, I've only briefly touched upon the elements of this story. Much like prison confinement, I find myself lacking language to adequately describe the experience. Day-in, day-out, moment-by-moment experiences are simply impossible to share; there's too much detail that is outside the realm of normal human experience. Cult settings are quite similar. The controlled experiences of each day affect the members. It's mistakenly assumed that people who find themselves involved in such a setting are merely weak, or in some way flawed. This would be true only to the degree that we, as human creatures, are all weak in some way or at some time. But should such weaknesses be considered flaws? We all have weaknesses, and we all have weak times. Consider these times much like the formation of a storm. With the right mixture of various meteorological influences, clouds and strong winds appear at the onset of the storm, but it still comes down to the matter of effects mixed with timing.

Jesus spoke of how man watches the sky, in order to forecast the weather (Matthew 16:2–3), yet he also expressed how similar are the influences that work upon man. So, when searching for the answer of how these settings and activities occur, we must recognize in all the humility of human fallibility that when faced with the appropriate circumstances, cultic settings will be the natural result. When human behavior goes astray from what is established as normal, we hesitate to consider the equal possibility of natural influences producing natural results. One of my greatest hesitations in writing this book is that various biases will affect the reading of it. Christians will determine that it is merely Mormonism—and RLDS Mormons will determine that it is merely "Lundgren-ism."

The deficiency I hope will be revealed is not lack of accountability, but rather vulnerability. These deficiencies occur at any of the numerous crossroads of life. We all face times of struggle and weakness in our lives, and the propensity toward these settings are born at those times. The phenomenon does not often affect a large percentage of the people because seldom does the appropriate setting cross the path of the individual's life at the appropriate time. Nor will every setting influence every person the same way.

I recall hurricane Andrew—a mixture of influences and timing. Had the timing been different, the effect of the influence would have come together differently, and the area (and persons) impacted by its devastation would have been different as well. But with all the conditions right for the formation of a hurricane that would hit south Florida, so it did. In like manner, when the right setting crosses the path of the individual's life at the right time the individual will be vulnerable to it. We are not, however, left without an "escape" (1Corinthians 10:11–13). The more we come to understand these stormy settings, the better prepared we are to defend ourselves against them. Sometimes this defense means the ability to forecast, thereby avoiding the point of contact.

Five people are now dead who had every promise of a happy life by way of their benevolent and loving attitude toward others. People in similar groups have also died. Therefore, it's my hope and prayer that we not judge these people more harshly than we would ourselves. In the book of Job we read that there was an unforeseen enemy that came and stole away his prosperity; then there suddenly came a great wind that killed Job's children. The book of Job is a story of human disaster and loss, yet at the end of the book we read that Job's knowledge of God came from his understanding that God is beyond all comprehension (Job 42:1–5). We can come to understand that these settings occur, by way of the influences that create them. But why those influences have the effect they do is something that, as yet, must be attributed to God's omniscience by confession of our own human limitations.

* * *

A SERMON WAS PREACHED IN BRANSON, MISSOURI, one day in May of 1987, which resulted in a change in plans Susie and I had made for our vacation. The speaker was a guest at our congregation and made an abrupt change to his sermon midway through. This was the same day that we would have left on vacation to a different location. Why did he come to preach on that day? Why did he suddenly change the context of his sermon to speak on an issue that I was, at that moment, struggling with? Why, at that particular time, did he suggest Jeff Lundgren, of all people, as a tour guide for showing us the Temple? Upon meeting Jeff and Alice, why did I find that my sister (who had no association with this guest speaker) knew them too, and spoke of what fine people they were? Were this preacher to have spoke just five months later, Jeff would no longer have been working at the Temple. Why such timing? Are these just coincidences that have no answer? How can we make such examples of timing of less effect, and make our belief of God's direction within our life of greater effect?

We are taught to be circumspect as watchmen of ourselves, our households and our church family. Prayer is an essential part of our stewardship in

Chapter 18 WHY?

faith. Even in our natural frame we see only a 180-degree view of our surroundings. This is, perhaps, why we pray for a hedge of protection, so that if and when a destructive influence comes our way, our omniscient Savior will draw our senses toward His protection, rather than toward distractions that serve to pull us to where we ought not look.

Journalism, from the social psychology viewpoint teaches that the media cannot only forecast what public opinion will be, but can actually create it. This is why freedom of the press was so very essential to our nation's founding fathers. To control and centralize the information relayed through the media to a society is to control and centralize the view that that society will have of their world. This heavily influences our view of "reality." Social isolation is a common component of cult settings. Distraction of the individual(s) by stimulating the senses may elicit feelings of guilt, humiliation and fear or, conversely, positive sensations such as love, or sacred duty. But isolation also limits what might be viewed as possible choices of a given issue. The book of Proverbs gives splendid insight. Consider the following. "The first to present his case seems right, till another comes forward and questions him" (Proverbs 18:17, NIV). From another chapter, we find that a balanced view in our dealings is quite important to God. Therefore, our sources of information must be balanced in order to obtain a view of Truth. "Differing weights and differing measures, the Lord detests them both" (Proverbs 20:10, NIV).

Our judicial process has been set up to present two opposing views of a given issue. If only one side were allowed to speak, then it would be impossible to gain a fuller view of the issue. As mankind, we are a step above that of the animal kingdom. Therefore, we have the ability to process information. However, in order to process it correctly, we must be allowed an appropriate, or balanced, view. Otherwise, our only choice will be bias.

Robert J. Lifton has composed a list of eight basic principles, commonly found within cults. They are:

- Control of communication.
- Emotional and behavioral manipulation.
- Demands for absolute conformity to behavior prescriptions derived from the ideology.
- Obsessive demands for confession. (Promotes guilt over minor issues and used as a source of control).
- Agreement that the ideology is faultless.
- Manipulation of language in which clichés substitute for analytic thought.
- Reinterpretation of human experience and emotion in terms of doctrine.

- Classification of those not sharing the ideology as inferior and not worthy of respect. (Lifton, pp. 419–437, 1987).[10]

Each of these principles was not only present, but heavily embraced within all that was taught and lived within the group at Kirtland. When these principles are employed, the effect is quite real and very powerful. As individual and corporate behavior begins to change, even conscience becomes a tool for entrapment. It's a slow process, each step moving in a direction contrary to one's previous actions of conscience. At certain points, one becomes locked into a continuation of that contrary direction by the mere fact that previous conscience values have difficulty processing the steps taken thus far. Therefore, any turning back would be invisible by one's changing view of reality, but also prohibited by the response that would be received by the previous conscience values. This is why, for the Christian, grace is so important. It allows the sinner to become renewed, Jesus becoming our sin of past failure (2 Corinthians 5:21).

* * *

MUCH LIKE HEARING AN OLD SONG CAN STIMULATE MEMORIES, other senses can stimulate memories as well. There was an odd mixture of odors that hung in our nostrils the night the Averys were killed. This lasted about a week or so for me. But after leaving the group, and as time began to separate me from the influence within the group environment, I began smelling those odors of hay, trash, books, gunpowder and even blood all over again. It began about a month after my incarceration, two months from the time I left the group. Even at this time, those odors are frequently revived in my nostrils. We have a Lord that forgives. Even a dead and dormant conscience can be made whole and restored to life through him. But we still must face the pain and the anguish (penalty) that destroyed our sense of conscience to begin with. This can be a very difficult thing to do.

The first two years or so of my incarceration, I was tormented by bad dreams. Eventually, these dreams began to lessen and eventually ceased. Initially, I would find myself back in a group again, Jeff leading and teaching a group of people. Then the dream changed, and I was no longer sitting at the table learning, but rather I was walking around it, challenging Jeff's doctrine. Finally, I would be helping people get away from Jeff's influence and, in a sense, running him off. In the context of my thoughts and the control of my mind he truly was run off—and the dreams ceased. But the mind doesn't function in a vacuum. Whether the vacuum is created by involvement within a cult or leaving one, it is essential to replenish the mind with a process of thought. I'm a spiritual man and always will be. But whether spiritual or not, we all have the same human vulnerabilities, and need, for a belief system. Mao Tse-

---

[10] Edgar F. Borgatta and Marie L. Borgatta, ed., *Encyclopedia of Sociology*, vol.1, (New York: MacMillan, 1992), p. 215.

tung was not at all a religious fanatic, but the power he obtained by way of a political belief system affects the thinking of millions today.

I had to "rebuild" a system of belief. I'd been betrayed by all I had ever known and believed as true. And as to any specific denomination my experience was quite lacking. I picked up the King James Bible and began reading. We'd been so wrapped up by "law." The whole reason I moved to Ohio was to "receive the law," but through all that happened, I failed to see how that Christ had fulfilled all of it. The sad truth was, I really didn't know what the law was, so how could I see its fulfillment? Yet as I read the biblical message, untainted by denomination or traditional belief, I found that "white stone" with a new name written on it (Revelation 2:17). I found a personal Savior. Not that I chose Him, because it doesn't work that way (John 15:16). I didn't have an elaborate supernatural experience. In fact, I've learned that though such experiential encounters may be quite beautiful, they can also be misleading. My heart was shattered. I felt reduced to complete nothingness. It was like floating in space, with no solid ground upon which to set my foot and nowhere to stand. There was no security within which to be rooted. But just as Jesus told the sister of Lazarus, that He is the resurrection (Luke 11:25), I, too, came to know this resurrection power of life within the deadness of my soul. As this resurrection happened within my own heart, I felt like those who were witnesses of His vicarious rise from the tomb.

> "And he said unto them, These are the words which I spake unto you, while I was yet with you, that all things must be fulfilled, which were written in the law of Moses, and in the prophets, and in the psalms, concerning me. Then opened he their understanding, that they might understand the scriptures." (Luke 24:44–45)

Today there are many spiritual beliefs in the world accessible to us. Most of these teachings have beauty as a component within their principles. Following the example of Jesus who did not come to condemn (John 3:17), as a Christian and clearly a transgressor, I feel that neither is it my place to do so. I find joy in what Jesus has done for me and find peace by way of His merits. But, I do wish to expose how Mormonism's teachings differ from Christianity and therefore should not be entwined with biblical text. I've found that the "temple" is not a building that sits in Kirtland, Ohio. Instead, it is under construction within my very own heart. "For we know that if our earthly house of this tabernacle were dissolved, we have a building of God, an house not made with hands, eternal in the heavens" (2 Corinthians 5:1). While my life now is not "roses," I did find what I was searching for. Unfortunately, it was something I had freely within my reach all along. Settings of the type I've exposed will flourish due to the mere timing of our day—a new century and a new millennium. It is a time of vulnerability and a crossroads upon the path of mankind.

This book contains the portrait of a cult follower. But the "why" is hidden within common characteristics of all. While my portrait may vary greatly from that of the individual reader, the real essence is quite common among us all. These groups do not produce fruit of the individuals; they produce the fruit of the leader. Although the activities of David Koresh in Waco, Texas were not brought to public attention until two years after the Avery's bodies were discovered, I've been able to document the Branch Davidians' sincere efforts to serve their God due to the publicity they've received while I've been in prison. (see Appendix A.)

Nevertheless, we can learn to recognize warning signs. Some understand why things like this happen without personally experiencing the tragedy of a cult experience. We don't have to repeat history in order to understand it. Ignorance creates a powerful vulnerability.

* * *

OUR CREED
by Ron Luff

It dominates the way we think, and that which we believe.

It regulates the way we hear, the thoughts which we perceive.

It shows throughout our actions, by the choices which we make.

It separates integrity from motives, which we fake.

Despite the way it's manifest in everything we do,

It's something quite intangible, an active part of you.

It's called the creed we live by, and it shapes what we can be.

By image in our mind as in a mirror—what we see.

A creed can be destructive, or a creed can heighten life.

A creed can cry for peace, or it can pang for fervent strife.

It forms within our mind, the right and wrong in what we do,

By what becomes Authority to act—despite what's true.

So by the forming of the creed by which we choose and live,

We find the view by seeking truth, has choice through love, to give.

The creed by which we live will guide our path in all we do.

For life with love and happiness our creed must seek what's true.

May the creed by which we live be dominated by a view through love; otherwise, bias will always influence, and truth will never be found.

* * *

Appendix

PARALLELS TO WACO

The Lundgren cult functioned, in some form, from 1984 through 1990 when they voluntarily disbanded. They had sought to secure their Utopia in a small Ohio town, whose main claim to fame was that one hundred-fifty years prior, Joseph Smith, the founder of Mormonism, built there, his first temple. The discovery of Lundgren's (himself, a self-proclaimed prophet and god) 1989 murders of the Avery family became headline news throughout the first half of 1990. The multiple criminal trials of the men and women in the cult as accomplices in the murders were essentially over by mid-1991. The Branch Davidians sought to build their Utopia in an isolated area of Waco, Texas, also in the 1980s. In 1993, U.S. Bureau of Alcohol, Tobacco and Firearms (ATF) officials raided, surrounded, then raided again the compound in a final assault, which actions would span 51 days. At the end of the stand-off, the world watched in horror as the Davidian-set fire swept over and destroyed the lives of men, women, and children who had been unwilling to compromise cherished beliefs. By that time, the world also knew the background and motivations of that cult, led by another self-proclaimed prophet, Vernon Howell. For those who cared—and dared—to compare these two cults, enough of a similarity would be seen that there could be no doubt they had been birthed by the same spirit of deception.

The events of the Waco, Texas Branch Davidians have come and gone in the time I've had to collect these thoughts. The outcome of Waco, as directed by the nation's attorney general, could only be considered an acceptable success if the loss of life was in no way the issue. The entire scope of events was particularly painful to me, not only because of the number of deaths that occurred among federal agents and the compound members, but also in the destruction of the dreams the Davidians shared, which I understand all too well. Followers in such cultic settings have a totally alien and extremely narrow sense of reality and cannot be depended upon to react rationally in response to actions from outsiders.

I had no comprehension of the mental isolation I had been subjected to both prior to and after meeting Jeff and Alice Lundgren. *Ironically, it was in jail that I began to experience the freedom to think for the first time in a long time, and in some ways, the first time ever.* So, watching the events that transpired at Waco, I was identifying with the confusion and frustration they were experiencing; the illusion of a noble cause mingled with fear, and in the center of it all, the annihilation of their hopes and dreams.

Let me emphasize how similar the Waco group was to the Kirtland group. I saw no difference between Vernon Howell (David Koresh) and Jeff Lundgren. Howell chose that name for himself because of the interpreted meaning within it. David was another name for Jesus or Son of David, by way of a physical and spiritual lineage and Koresh is the Hebrew/Aramaic version of the name Cyrus, a Persian king who allowed the building of Jerusalem in Ezra's day. Lundgren, as did Koresh, also assumed the name of Cyrus for himself.

Assuming new names in religious cult activity is common, not only by the leaders, but also assigning them to the followers as well. It's unfortunate that the media and law enforcement were forced to refer to Vernon Howell as David Koresh, because of his having legally changed his name. In terms of what was real in the minds of Vernon's followers, each time the world referred to him as David Koresh he was being called Lord God, Lord King, or more expressly, Messiah.

This narrow view of reality makes members of cults much like Japanese kamikaze pilots of World War II. They are willing, with a sense of predestination, to embark upon that mission of no return. Once airborne, there is no choice but to self-destroy. Once the battle in Waco had begun, their destiny was sealed. Bear in mind that these people were living on their "Mt. Carmel." To them, this was not unlike that of Elijah the prophet (1 Kings 18), in which the evil prophets of Baal were overthrown. How did they perceive themselves as standing invincibly and righteously upon God's holy ground? To come against them was not only interpreted as defiance against God, but equally, as a testing of or, rather, proving their obedience. Not to defend this holy ground with their very lives would place them in a position of disobedience. But even more than disobedience, not to defend God's sacred ground would be an act of spiritual suicide.

The question has been asked, "Why were the minor children not released?" The answer is quite simple once we fully grasp the way the "world" is perceived by the cult follower. Imagine your family under siege by a pack of hungry wolves. How quickly would you send your children out to the superior numbers? In my experience, I perceived "people from the outside," or the world, as spiritually "dead." I pitied them, yet rejoiced in faith, toward the day when we would be able to take the truth to them. Undoubtedly, the people in the compound at Waco saw the forces against them in very much the same way. The forces outside the compound were superior in numbers and firepower—but the followers were on Holy Ground, under God's protection. The forces outside offered safety to any who were willing to leave the compound, yet to the follower, leaving the spiritual security of the compound meant death (at least spiritually, if not immediately physically). To leave would be to deny God's protection. The children were perceived as being infinitely safer under the protection they believed was promised by God. Why would anyone send his or her children out into the arms of death, in defiance to God's all-saving arm?

It does not matter that what I'm suggesting is not rational in retrospect. We are not talking about rational behavior. It is my sincere hope that we can learn from that tragedy in order to find ways to diffuse such situations rather than allowing them to evolve into an issue of "superior firepower." Superior firepower means nothing when it's result is the loss of innocent life. What I can offer about how this aspect of Waco mirrors that of the cult in Kirtland is that, thankfully, we never needed to test our firepower against any governmental agency; although that possibility appeared imminent several times. At this time, I've come to believe that Jeff is too much of a coward to have gone through with combat, but this is also due to my equal conviction that he never actually believed anything he taught. Even from death row, he has struggled to continue to promote his proclaimed, albeit polluted, beliefs on followers of his devious and perverted forms of spiritualism. While there was once a time when I was ready to do whatever he ordered—as though ordered by God Himself, I'm no longer captivated like those swayed by his darkened hold.

Drawing similar parallels are essential in portraying with clarity, the vulnerabilities and realities of this type of activity. Aspirin doesn't actually deal with what's wrong, it only deals with the symptoms. Hopefully, the day will come when we desire to learn what's wrong in a situation rather than to simply settle for dealing with the results.